BASIC ECONOMIC PRINCIPLES

BASIC ECONOMIC PRINCIPLES

A Guide for Students

David E. O'Connor
and
Christopher Faille

GREENWOOD PRESS
Westport, Connecticut • London

Library of Congress Cataloging-in-Publication Data

O'Connor, David E. (David Edward)
  Basic economic principles : a guide for students / David E. O'Connor and
  Christopher Faille.
    p. cm.
  Includes bibliographical references and index.
  ISBN 0–313–31005–X (alk. paper)
    1. Economics. I. Faille, Christopher C., 1958– II. Title.
  HB71.O26 2000
  330—dc21   00–021050

British Library Cataloguing in Publication Data is available.

Library of Congress Catalog Card Number: 00–021050
ISBN: 0–313–31005–X

First published in 2000

Greenwood Press, 88 Post Road West, Westport, CT 06881
An imprint of Greenwood Publishing Group, Inc.
www.greenwood.com

Printed in the United States of America

The paper used in this book complies with the
Permanent Paper Standard issued by the National
Information Standards Organization (Z39.48–1984).

10 9 8 7 6 5 4 3 2 1

CONTENTS

Contents

PREFACE

Have you ever wondered why some people will spend thousands of dollars for a certain baseball card, but will not pay more than $1 for a gallon of bottled water at the local supermarket? Have you wondered how goods and services that you consume every day are produced, or how they get from the producer to your favorite stores? And why do we use money to purchase these goods? Why do we save and invest some of our money? And why does the government tax us?

These are just a few of the questions that are examined in *Basic Economic Principles: A Guide for Students*. This guide explores how economic concepts and principles relate to our own lives as consumers, savers or investors, workers, and citizens. It outlines and applies a process for making reasoned economic decisions. It encourages critical thinking by investigating controversial issues related to topics as varied as the minimum wage, the decay of our natural environment, poverty, and business ethics of multinational corporations.

Basic Economic Principles is a comprehensive reference guide. It is organized around 15 essential questions that deal with economics and economic systems, prices, behavior of consumers and producers, money and credit, saving and investing, taxation and government spending, government stabilization policies, income distribution and poverty, workers and management, and international trade. These focus questions invite students, teachers, and other readers to explore the subject, to locate pertinent information, and to devise additional questions. The guide is also comprehensive in that it introduces and applies the 21 basic economic concepts outlined in *A Framework for Teaching Basic Economic Concepts* (Economics America, 1995).

Basic Economic Principles is a convenient guide to the economy and how it works. The 15 essential questions provide a content focus for each chapter. Each chapter is also subdivided into sections and subsections to help pinpoint information. For the reader's convenience an extensive Glossary of Economic Terms appears at the end of the guide. In addition, as key terms are woven into each chapter, they appear in **boldfaced print**. Thus, the design of *Basic Economic Principles* motivates students, teachers, and other citizens to consider key economic questions, and then provides a "user-friendly" format to locate timely, relevant information needed for their responses.

Economics sometimes has been called a "dismal science." But nothing could be further from the truth. Economics is an essential part of our everyday lives. It deals with every production and consumption decision that we make—how to produce goods, how to spend our limited incomes, how to invest our money, and how to meet our personal, business, and national economic goals. And while there will inevitably be debate and disagreement about the decisions people make, there is one certainty—that the decisions we make today will shape our standard of living in the future.

1

WHAT IS ECONOMICS?

Chapter 1 examines economics as a field of study. Because economics is a social science, it deals with human relations and the behaviors of people in the economy. Scarcity is identified as the universal economic problem, a problem that requires people to make choices. This chapter stresses the importance of economics to the decisions that you make every day. It explains the need for a scientific approach to problem solving and the value of reading and thinking critically. It also highlights the fact that economic decisions involve trade-offs, and that there are costs to the choices people make.

ECONOMICS DEFINED

Economics is the study of how people choose to use their scarce resources in order to satisfy their nearly unlimited economic wants. **Scarcity** exists whenever there are insufficient resources to satisfy these wants.

The definition of economics begins with the idea that because resources are scarce people must make economic choices that involve trade-offs. **Trade-offs** occur when individuals, firms, or governments use resources one way rather than another. For example, consider your last trip to the shopping mall. There were many stores and countless items to choose from. You may have wanted to buy a CD, then join friends for dinner at the pizza parlor, and then go to the movies. With all of these economic wants, and just $15 in your pocket, your financial resources were limited. The trade-off in this case involved how you would choose to use your money. You could afford to buy the CD or the pizza or the evening at the movies, but not all three goods.

It may surprise you but the choice that you had to make between a CD, pizza, or evening at the movies is similar to the choices that governments are obliged to make. Your state and local governments, for example, collect taxes from people to raise revenues for needed public programs. Common taxes include state income taxes, local property taxes, and state sales taxes. Like the $15 in your pocket, tax revenues represent scarce financial resources for the government. Public officials choose how to spend these scarce resources. Instead of spending government revenues on CDs or movie tickets, governments choose among a wide variety of worthwhile public goods or services. Should the government build a new elementary school or a new firehouse? Should it hire additional police or spend more money on road construction and repair? These decisions also involve trade-offs. Making reasoned personal and social decisions is an important feature in our study of economics.

Economic Thinkers: Thorstein Veblen's View of Scarcity

Thorstein Veblen (1857–1929), the son of Norwegian-American farmers, made a splash in the world of economics by questioning one of its most fundamental principles—scarcity.

Veblen claimed that engineers and the modern techniques of production of which they were the masters could effectively eliminate scarcity. In Veblen's time, engineers had already given the world such marvels as the generation of electricity, the internal combustion engine, interchangeable parts, and the assembly line. So why couldn't everyone in the world have enough of everything? Because, Veblen hypothesized, engineers were not allowed to run the economic system their way. Instead, engineers always ended up working for the great financiers and businessmen—the "captains of industry" as they were called. These captains, Veblen argued, were concerned mostly with production for profit, not with ending world scarcities.

What Veblen advocated as a substitute for capitalism was a "technocracy"—a system of central planning by benevolent experts who possessed scientific and industrial expertise. While Veblen's central thesis about the end of scarcity has been rejected by economists today, his books such as *The Theory of the Leisure Class* (1899) are still widely read for their sociological insights.

WHY STUDY ECONOMICS?

Not surprisingly, economists consider scarcity to be the universal economic problem. It is at the heart of many of the decisions that individuals, firms, and governments make. Odd as it might sound, if we had no scarcities we would have no need to make reasoned economic choices—and there would be no need to study economics.

Personal Decision Making

Economics, naturally, deals with more than choosing between a CD and a night at the movies. Instead, you will be expected to make a number of important economic decisions in your lifetime. Undoubtedly you are starting to make some of these decisions now. For example, if you have a part-time job you must choose how many hours to work. This is important not only because your decision has an immediate impact on your wages, but also because your decision has an impact on your schoolwork, the amount of leisure time you can enjoy, the number of hours you can sleep at night, and so on. Remember, your time is also a scarce resource, and every economic choice has a cost.

Another decision that you will likely be making soon is what you will do after you graduate from high school. Will you enroll as a full-time college student? Enroll as a part-time college student? Enter the military? Enter the labor force? Receive specialized vocational training? Just hang out? How do you decide?

The process for making decisions regarding your future is similar to the process for making reasonable economic decisions. The first step is to identify the problem. In this case, the problem is deciding what you should do after you graduate from high school. The second step is to identify the alternatives. These alternatives include attending college, entering the military, and so on. The third step is to identify specific criteria or goals that you have for yourself now and for your future. Criteria might include financial security, potential for advancement, self-esteem and status, leisure time, immediate needs for an income, job-related stress levels, and challenging work environment. The fourth step is to determine how well each of the alternatives you identified satisfies each of the criterion you listed. The fifth and final step is to make your decision.

Upon reflection you might conclude that one alternative, attending college, would not satisfy your immediate need for an income. But the college degree *would* help you achieve long-term financial security. For example, households headed by wage-earners with a college degree have a median income about two-and-one-half times that of workers with just a high school diploma. This alternative might also get a favorable response in most of the other categories because the college experience creates opportunities that might not be otherwise available. If you want to become a teacher, engineer, doctor, or stockbroker, a college degree is required.

Another alternative, to enter the military, might also satisfy many of your goals. A career in the military could provide a great deal of financial security, including attractive medical and pension benefits. It could also provide for some immediate income and, depending on the training that you qualify for, could pave the way for significant possibilities for advancement, high self-esteem, and challenging tasks. A career in the military, however, may not totally satisfy your needs for leisure, and the stress levels during any military actions by the government, we might assume, would be high.

What's the "right" decision? Your decision will be influenced by all of the criteria that you named and by the weight—the degree of importance—that you assign to each criterion. While different people will make different decisions, all people can benefit from this reasoned approach to decision making.

Social Decision Making

Social decision making asks people to make responsible decisions that affect the community, state, nation, or even the world. Social decision making involves the same five steps as personal decision making: define the problem, identify the alternative solutions, list criteria, determine how well the alternatives satisfy each criterion, and make the decision.

Most social decisions involve spending public money for a public good or service. It's not uncommon, for example, for communities to identify the lack of recreational facilities for the youth as a problem. You might say that the obvious solution to this problem is to increase the number of recreational facilities for young people to use. But young people have many different interests. Assume that three alternatives are proposed. One proposal is to build an arts center, which would cater to young people interested in the visual and performing arts—painting, sculpting, dance, music, and so on. A second proposal is to build a sports complex, which would cater to those interested in swimming, weight training, and sports played on an indoor court—basketball, volleyball, and so on. The third proposal is to build an arcade, which would benefit those interested in video games, pool and billiards, fast food, and movies.

The community has just $10 million to spend on the recreational facility and, as luck would have it, each of the three proposals—arts center, sports complex, and arcade—would cost approximately $10 million to build and equip. How do you choose the best proposal? You must now identify the criteria or goals that you will consider when making your decision. Some likely criteria would include the number of young people who would use each type of facility, whether similar facilities already exist in the community or nearby, any spillover benefits that might result from the facility, and any related costs associated with each facility. The cost of the facility is often a major criterion, but for our example all have the same price tag.

Assume you have collected data through community surveys and through contacts with other communities, and have discovered the following:

1. Number of youths served: The arts center would attract 1,000 youths per month, compared to 1,250 for the sports complex, and 1,500 for the arcade. Thus, the first criterion favors the arcade.

2. Similar facilities elsewhere: Your community has a number of public museums, art and dance studios, and school music programs. Your community also sponsors an active year-round recreational sports program that uses the courts and sports fields of the town's two high schools. But the town has only one movie theater, which has an attached poolroom that typically attracts townspeople of all ages. Thus, the second criterion also seems to favor the arcade.

3. Spillover benefits: The arts center and the sports complex would likely be able to offer many services to the schools and to community groups. The arts center could host performances, art exhibits, and other cultural affairs. The sports complex could host regional competitions, charitable events, and the like. Except for those who enjoyed the activities of the arcade itself, there would be likely few additional benefits to the community. Thus, the third criterion favors the arts center or the sports complex.

4. Related costs to the community: The arts center would require a large staff of highly skilled professional people, including artists, dance instructors, voice teachers, and others. These costs would be high. The sports complex and arcade would require the services, at a lower cost, of a number of employees from the town's Recreation Department and, perhaps, a few security guards. Thus, the fourth criterion favors the sports complex or the arcade.

What is the "right" decision? Even after applying a reasoned decision-making process to this problem, people will still come up with different answers. This is because people tend to place different emphasis, or weight, on different criterion. For example, a person who sees no value in athletics is not likely to support the sports complex even if it offers spillover benefits to the community. But while disagreements inevitably arise when society makes choices about the use of scarce resources, such differences of opinion are valued in a democratic society. Further, the economic concepts and decision-making skills connected to the study of economics encourage more informed participation in the democratic process.

ECONOMICS AND THE SCIENTIFIC METHOD

Economics is considered a social science. The **social sciences** represent the branch of science that deals with human relationships and the behaviors of individuals and groups. Other social sciences include psychology, sociology, anthropology, and human geography. Economics deals with the behaviors of consumers, producers, and governments.

The social sciences are not exact sciences. That is, human behaviors are predictable but we cannot assume that all people will react in exactly the same way to a situation. Consider ticket prices for Woodstock 99. The price of admission to this three-day rock concert was $150 per ticket, plus tax, and the entire 250,000 tickets were sold prior to the event in the summer of 1999. Suppose that one of your friends had placed an advertisement in your local newspaper offering to sell his four tickets to Woodstock 99 for $75 each. What behaviors would you predict from some people reading the newspaper that night? Most likely your friend's phone would be ringing off the hook. Why? Because people respond to incentives. **Incentives** are the financial factors that motivate laborers to work, firms to produce, consumers to buy certain goods, and so on. In this case the incentive was a reduced price for a good that was in high demand. The study of economics tries to explain why people behave as they do in the economy.

The Scientific Method

The social sciences and the natural sciences—such as physics and chemistry—share a common approach to organizing, studying, and explaining information. This approach is often called the scientific method. The **scientific method** is a five-step process that enables scientists to analyze topics systematically. By using the scientific method, economists and other scientists can more closely evaluate not only the conclusions of the study, but also the process. Figure 1.1 illustrates the steps of the scientific method.

There are no shortages of economic problems or questions for economists to study. One problem that intrigued a famous 19th-century English economist, Alfred Marshall, was how to explain the impact of prices on the quantity of a good that was demanded by consumers (step 1). Marshall collected data on the prices of goods and the quantity sold (step 2). From this data, Marshall was able to propose a hypothesis, or an educated guess, about the relationship between the price and quantity demanded of a good. His hypothesis was that there was an indirect relationship between the price of a good and the quantity demanded of the good. That is, as the price of a good increased the quantity demanded would decrease. Conversely, as the price of a good decreased the quantity demanded would increase (step 3). Marshall continued to test his hypothesis, and organized his supporting data into demand schedules and demand curves (step 4). In his classic *Principles of Economics*, which was published in 1890, Marshall explained his research, and introduced one of the most famous economic theories in the entire study of economics—the law of demand (step 5).

Figure 1.1
Steps in the Scientific Method

Step 1: Identify the Problem

Step 2: Collect Relevant Data

Step 3: Propose a Hypothesis (an educated guess)

Step 4: Test the Hypothesis (using existing and new data)

Step 5: Assess the Validity of the Hypothesis (accept or reject the hypothesis)

ECONOMISTS: WHAT DO THEY DO?

Economists study the economy. The jobs of economists are varied, but all economists study the choices that individuals, firms, or governments make in an economy. The term **economy** refers to all of the production and consumption decisions, and all activities that relate to the use of resources in a society. Economists work in many specialized fields including labor economics, business, marketing, accounting, banking, investing, and international finance and trade. Economists work for private firms, governments, and as teachers at colleges and universities.

Factors of Production

Economists call the resources that are used in production—the **factors of production**. In addition, economists have organized these factors of production into four categories: natural resources, human resources, capital goods, and entrepreneurship. Natural resources, also called land, are gifts of nature. They appear naturally in the oceans, on or under the ground, and in the air. Oil, trees, salt, fish, sunlight, and wind are all natural resources when they are used to produce goods or services. Human resources, also called labor, represent the human element in production. Human resources include doctors, assembly line workers, teachers, custodians, and economists! Capital goods, also called capital, are tangible items that are made for the purpose of producing other goods or services. Factories, tractors, highways, business computers, and office buildings are all capital goods. Finally, entrepreneurship represents the actions of innovators in the economy. Entrepreneurs create new products, new ways to produce products, or new firms (see chapter 5 for more about the factors of production).

Thinking Like an Economist

Perhaps without realizing it, you already think like an economist in many ways. For example, your decision to come to school today reflects a choice that you made about the use of a scarce resource—your time! Every day you make decisions about the use of your time, your money, your talents, and so on. And every time you pause to consider alternative uses of your personal resources, policies that affect your school or community, and so on, you are thinking like an economist.

Economic Thinkers: Adam Smith and Modern Economics

Adam Smith (1732–1790), a Scottish economist, was one of the most influential economic thinkers of the modern age. In his famous book, *An Inquiry into the Nature and Causes of the Wealth of Nations* (1776), Smith explained the operation and benefits of a **free market economy**—an economic system in which individuals and firms, rather than governments, make the great majority of economic decisions.

Smith believed that when "self-interest" was allowed to guide the everyday decisions in an economy, everyone would benefit. Smith reasoned that each individual and each firm in an economy was guided by an "invisible hand" to do what was in their own best interests. It followed that society would also benefit from these numerous personal successes because the economy is the sum total of all economic activity in a nation. Smith also championed the idea of **laissez-faire capitalism**—an economy in which the government does not regulate business activity, or otherwise direct the use of the nation's resources.

For his pioneering work in the development of economics as a field of study, Adam Smith is sometimes called the founder of "modern economics."

MICROECONOMICS AND MACROECONOMICS: WHAT'S THE DIFFERENCE?

For convenience, economists typically divide the study of economics into two main parts: microeconomics and macroeconomics.

Microeconomics

Microeconomics is the study of how the individual participants in the economy interact with one another. Participants include consumers, firms, workers, savers, investors, and others. These participants interact in the marketplace. Consumers, for example, seek to purchase the goods and services that they need for the lowest possible price. Firms, on the other hand, seek to produce goods and services that generate the largest possible profits. Workers offer their services to employers and hope to earn the highest possible wage. And so it goes. Microeconomics examines these behaviors in some detail.

You are an important part of the microeconomy. Suppose you wake up one Saturday morning and decide to have breakfast with friends at Betty's Diner. You and your friends each order the breakfast combination—two eggs, bacon, pancakes, biscuits, and a pot of coffee for the table. From the consumer's perspective, the $5 per meal purchase was an excellent use of your money.

Let's take a look at the same marketplace activity from the "other side" of the market—from the perspective of Betty, the owner of the diner. In the microeconomy Betty represents the producer. Betty must calculate all of her costs in the production of the breakfast combination—the cost of the food, the wage of the waitress, the rent on the diner itself, and all costs for utilities such as electricity. To stay in business Betty has to earn a profit from the sale of her meals, and this can only be accomplished if her total revenues are greater than her total costs (see chapter 5 for more on business costs).

The simple act of buying a breakfast at Betty's Diner illustrates the microeconomy in action. That is, it shows the interaction of a consumer and a producer in the marketplace. Much of the study of microeconomics deals with decisions of buying, selling, or producing goods or services.

Macroeconomics

Macroeconomics is the study of how the overall economy functions. Major macroeconomics topics include changes in price levels in the economy, and increases or decreases in unemployment. Macroeconomics also deals with changes in aggregate supply (the total supply of goods and services produced in the economy) and aggregate demand (the total demand for goods and services). National policies to stabilize the economy and to promote economic growth are also central to the study of the macroeconomy (see chapter 12 for more on stabilization policies).

READING CRITICALLY

The study of economics—whether microeconomics or macroeconomics—involves a careful analysis of information and data. These studies require that the student distinguish between "facts" and "opinions," and recognize fallacies in reasoning.

Positive and Normative Economics

Economists, like other people, have opinions and biases that sometimes enter into their theories, their writing, their teaching, and their policy recommendations. In effect, they sometimes merge their facts with their opinions. To become a more critical reader, it is important that you understand the difference between facts and opinions. In the study of economics, we do this by distinguishing between positive economics and normative economics.

Positive economics is concerned with reality, with "what is." Sometimes called descriptive economics, positive economics relies on statements that can be tested or verified with data. An example of a positive statement is, "In 1997 the Department of Commerce reported that 83,384 U.S. businesses had failed." In this case, the truth of the statement can be tested using data collected by the Commerce Department—a reliable federal department that oversees business activity in the nation.

Normative economics presents a viewpoint on an economic issue or problem. In many instances normative economics identifies actions or policies that "should" or "should not" occur. A normative statement might also address the problem of business failures in the U.S. economy, but would do so with a viewpoint attached. For example, a normative statement would be, "The government should provide additional financial assistance to companies that are in danger of failing." Note that in this normative statement, the economist is offering an opinion about what "should" be done to reduce the problem of business failures in the United States.

Recognizing Economic Fallacies

Another step in becoming a critical reader is to be able to recognize when an author or speaker is using faulty reasoning to arrive at a conclusion. Economic fallacies are incorrect conclusions that result from errors in reasoning. These fallacies are grouped in two general categories: cause-effect fallacies and evidence fallacies.

Cause-effect Fallacies

"Cause-effect fallacies" are errors in reasoning that stem from misreading connections between one event and another. For example, when two events occur at about the same time, some people might automatically assume that one caused the other. The critical reader, however, is able to distinguish the mere "correlation" of two events—the fact that they occurred at approximately the same time—with an actual "cause." The two events may or may not be related.

In the spring and early summer of 1999 the United States and its NATO allies conducted a massive air attack on Yugoslavia. The goal of the attack was to force Yugoslavia to stop persecuting ethnic Albanians in the southern province of Yugoslavia called Kosovo. At the same time, the world market price for oil was increasing steadily. Looking quickly at the two events you might conclude that the turmoil in Yugoslavia and in the surrounding regions caused the increase in oil prices. This conclusion would be incorrect, however. The air attack by NATO on Yugoslavia, and the increase in oil prices, were correlated because they occurred simultaneously. The NATO attack did not cause world oil prices to climb, however. The strengthening of the Organization of Petroleum Exporting Countries (OPEC), an organization of 12 major oil producing nations, could be viewed as a cause for rising oil prices in 1999.

Another cause-effect fallacy is the single cause fallacy. This type of fallacy occurs when one cause is identified to explain a complex problem or issue. In reality, there are likely multiple causes for the situation. Economists sometimes called the single cause fallacy "oversimplification." Have you ever heard anyone say, "The poor live in poverty because they are lazy"? Laziness may be one small piece in the larger puzzle about why nearly 36 million Americans live beneath the poverty line. There are numerous additional causes of poverty, however, including the poor quality of education some people receive, job loss due to layoffs, personal traumas such as chronic health problems or mental illness, divorce or other family disruptions, racism, ineffective government programs, and others. As you can see there are multiple causes for poverty in the United States. Oversimplification represents faulty reasoning and, not surprisingly, leads to incorrect conclusions.

Evidence Fallacies

"Evidence fallacies" occur when there is insufficient, irrelevant, or incorrect data to support the author's conclusions. The critical reader understands that in order to defend a viewpoint, an author might intentionally or unintentionally omit relevant information, use inappropriate examples, or misuse statistical data. If the evidence is tainted or inadequate, the author's conclusions are likewise suspect.

Suppose you read an editorial in your local newspaper that claimed that poverty was a "black problem" because the vast majority of America's poor were of African-American decent. Further, this editorial emphasized that virtually all of the people who fell beneath the poverty line were unemployed because they refused to work. The editorial concluded that all of the nation's poor should be required to work and thereby become productive citizens. If the reader checked the facts, however, she would discover serious evidence fallacies.

The first evidence fallacy is that a "vast majority" of the nation's poor are African-Americans. While vast majority is not a precise figure, it is clear that the author is claiming that African-Americans represent significantly more than 50% of the nation's poor. Recent government data

Figure 1.2
Production Possibilities Table (in millions)

		Points			
	A	B	C	D	E
Bushels of Wheat	35	32	25	15	0
Bushels of Corn	0	5	10	15	20

from the U.S. Bureau of the Census tells us that this statistic is grossly inaccurate. In fact, over two-thirds of America's poor are white (68.5%), while lower percentages are African-American (25.6%) and other (5.9%).

The second evidence fallacy is that "virtually all" poor people are unemployed and refuse to work. "Virtually all," we might reasonably assume, means close to 100%. In reality, the U.S. Bureau of the Census tells us that over one-half of all families living in poverty had at least one wage earner. Further, data from the Department of Health and Human Services shows that fewer than 8 million people were on the welfare rolls in 1998, and many of these were children.

Thus, the general conclusion that poverty is a "black problem," and that poverty can be fixed by requiring the poor to work is not supportable. You might be interested to know that a worker earning the $5.15 national minimum wage could work 40 hours per week, for all 52 weeks of the year, and still earn a total income substantially below the poverty line for a family of four. In addition, many of the poor who do not work are unemployable, most notably the children. Evidence fallacies in the form of inaccurate and incomplete data distort the author's conclusions.

MAKING ECONOMIC DECISIONS: CHOOSING AMONG PRODUCTION POSSIBILITIES

This chapter began by defining economics as the study of how people choose to use their scarce resources in order to satisfy their wants. The reality of scarcity is universal, and scarcity requires that people make choices. A **production possibilities curve** (PPC) is an economic model that illustrates the range of possible production choices that nations or firms might make, and shows the inevitable costs of these decisions.

To help illustrate how economists draw and interpret a PPC, assume that Macroland can produce the crops shown on the production possibilities table shown in Figure 1.2. Note that at point A on the table, Macroland can produce 35 million bushels of wheat and 0 bushels of corn. In this extreme situation, all of Macroland's resources are used to produce wheat, and none are used to produce corn. At point B, 32 million bushels of wheat are produced along with 5 million bushels of corn.

Figure 1.3
Production Possibilities Curve

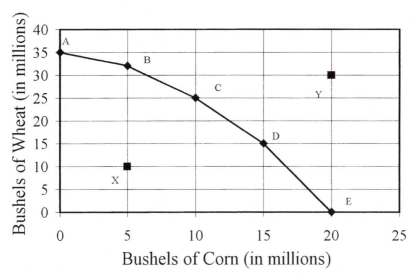

By the time Macroland reaches point E, 0 bushels of wheat are produced and 20 million bushels of corn are produced. What this table illustrates is that when resources are shifted from wheat to corn a trade-off occurs—more corn is produced, but less wheat is produced. That is, Macroland must sacrifice some bushels of wheat if it wants more corn. At point B, for example, Macroland must sacrifice 3 million bushels of wheat in order to get 5 million bushels of corn.

Economists call the sacrificed production, in this case the 3 million bushels of wheat at point B, the opportunity cost. To put it another way, the **opportunity cost** is the second best use of resources by society, by a firm, or by an individual.

The choices available to Macroland, as well as the related opportunity costs, are more easily seen by drawing a PPC for wheat and corn production, as shown in Figure 1.3. On the vertical axis is wheat production. On the horizontal axis is corn production. Note that the entire range of production possibilities for these two products is shown on the PPC that is labeled AE.

The opportunity costs are now apparent at a glance. For example, by reading the PPC in Figure 1.3 it is clear that at point C, 25 million bushels of wheat and 10 million bushels of corn are produced. You will recall, however, that opportunity cost measures what is not produced—the second best use of society's resources. At point C, therefore, the opportunity cost in terms of wheat is 10 million bushels of wheat (35 million − 25 million = 10 million). That is, 10 million bushels of wheat must be given up in order to produce 10 million bushels of corn. At point D, the opportunity cost in terms of corn is 5 million bushels of corn (20 million − 15 million = 5 million). This is because Macroland could have produced 20 million bushels of corn, but chose to sacrifice 5 million bushels so that some resources would be available to produce 15 million bushels of wheat.

Like all economic models there are assumptions attached to the PPC. The first assumption is that at any point along the PPC, resources are being used efficiently. A second assumption is that the factors of production are fixed at this moment in time. The amount of natural resources, human resources, and capital goods and technology cannot be changed.

You can see that two additional points are shown on the graph, point X and point Y. Point X is a point inside the PPC. All points inside of the PPC represent inefficient production. At point X, for example, only 10 million bushels of wheat are produced and 5 million bushels of corn. This output is far less than the possible combinations of wheat and corn production along the PPC AE. Labor strikes, waste of natural resources, or other inefficient use of resources could result in production at point X. Point Y, on the other hand, is a production impossibility at this moment in time. Point Y is outside of the PPC AE and, because the factors of production and technology are fixed, there is no combination of resources that would permit Macroland to produce at this high a level.

Opportunity cost is a basic economic concept that applies to decisions made by nations, firms, and individuals. Suppose Tom, a student at your high school, has four hours available after school to study for his math exam or to work at his part-time job. If Tom chooses to work during these four hours, the opportunity cost is four hours worth of study time. Tom made a choice and, in economics, virtually all choices have a cost. Wish him luck on his math exam!

2

HOW DO ECONOMIC SYSTEMS WORK?

Chapter 2 shows how different economic systems answer the basic economic questions of what to produce, how to produce, and for whom to produce. The study begins by examining the three models of economic systems: the traditional model, the command model, and the market model. In reality, all of the economies in today's world combine elements from each of these models and, therefore, are called mixed economies. Six major economies, some leaning toward the command model and some leaning toward the market model, are examined in some detail. These include the economies of the People's Republic of China, Russia, India, the United Kingdom, Japan, and the United States. All economies have certain economic goals, but scarcities often force nations to choose which goals are most essential at any moment in time.

THE BASIC ECONOMIC QUESTIONS

The **basic economic questions** are the questions that all societies, past and present, have had to answer. What to produce and in what quantity? How to produce goods and services? For whom to produce? How an economy answers these basic economic questions helps to distinguish one economic system from another.

What to Produce?

The "what to produce and in what quantity" question deals with decisions that people, firms, or nations make about which goods and services should be produced. A **good** is any physical object that satisfies a person's wants. A **service** is any productive activity that satisfies a person's wants.

In the U.S. economy individuals, ultimately, are responsible for answering the "what to produce" question. Consumers cast their "dollar votes" either for or against certain goods or services through their buying decisions. Today, consumers value automobiles and the skills of auto mechanics, so dollar votes are cast in favor of this good and this service. Dollar votes are no longer cast for horse-drawn carriages or blacksmiths, however, because consumers no longer desire them. Even in the realm of public goods and services it is individual taxpayers and voters who influence what goods and services the government will provide to the people.

How to Produce?

The "how to produce goods and services" question deals with determining how the factors of production should be used by firms to produce these products. In highly industrialized nations such as the United States, firms use sophisticated capital goods in the form of machinery, computers, and other equipment to increase efficiency in the workplace. In lesser developed nations, much of the production of goods and services is done by physical labor.

For Whom to Produce?

The "for whom to produce" question deals with the distribution of goods and services in the economy. In effect, this question asks who will receive what is produced. In the U.S. economy, the answer to the "for whom to produce" question is mainly concerned with the income of people and the prices of goods and services. For example, a household with an annual income of $250,000 dollars is able to purchase more goods than a household with an annual income of $25,000. The government also influences the distribution of goods in the U.S. economy by providing a variety of programs to help the needy—the poor, the elderly, and other groups (see chapter 13).

TYPES OF ECONOMIC SYSTEMS: THE MODELS

Each of the nearly 200 nations of the world answers the basic economic questions differently. Economists, however, have developed three models to help categorize these economic systems. The models include traditional economies, command economies, and market economies. Figure 2.1 compares and contrasts these ideal types of economic systems.

The models shown in Figure 2.1 are created by economists to catego-

Figure 2.1
The Models: Types of Economic Systems

Types of Economies	What to Produce?	How to Produce?	For Whom to Produce?
		Basic Economic Questions	
Traditional Economies	Dictated by custom or traditions; mainly concerned with satisfying survival needs	Traditional production methods; new technology, research, innovation is discouraged	Typically focused on the survival of the group; kinship ties are common, which promotes sharing
Command Economies	Centralized decision makers in the government, or a state planning agency dictate the types of goods to produce	Central authority dictates how resources will be used to satisfy society's needs; individual initiative is stifled	Central authority dictates wages or other compensation; government also controls prices and, therefore, many buying decisions
Market Economies	Decentralized decision making by individuals and firms; consumers' desires signal firms to produce profitable goods	Firms decide which production methods to use; firms are mainly concerned with increasing efficiency to cut costs	Household income is the most important factor in determining the individual's share of the nation's output

rize, or group similar economies. By using these ideal types of economies as a reference, economists can then make comparisons between economies in the contemporary world. For example, today there are very few traditional economies. This allows economists to focus their attention on economies that resemble the other two models—the command and market models. Today, most economies mix the characteristics from these models to fit their own needs.

MIXED ECONOMIES

Mixed economies are economies that combine the features from the traditional, command, and market models. All of the world's economies today are mixed economies. To illustrate the variety of mixed economies, a "continuum of economic systems" is shown in Figure 2.2. Note that to the far left of the continuum, the arrow points toward the command model. Hence, the further to the left an economy is placed on the continuum, the more it resembles the command model. Conversely, the further to the right an economy is positioned on the continuum, the more

Figure 2.2
Continuum of Economic Systems

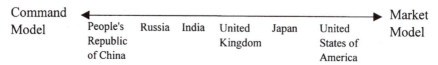

it resembles the market model. The following criteria were considered when placing the six economies shown in Figure 2.2 on the continuum of economic systems.

- degree of centralization (government control) in decision making in the economy
- degree of government ownership of the nation's industries, farms, or other businesses
- degree of government control over other resources, including labor and natural resources
- recent reforms or stated policies that indicate a change in direction for the economy

COMMUNISM: THE PEOPLE'S REPUBLIC OF CHINA AND "CHINESE SOCIALISM"

Definition

Communism is a type of economic system in which the government owns or controls the great majority of the means of production—the factories, farms, and other firms. In addition, the government dictates the answers to the basic economic questions of what, how, and for whom to produce. Thus, communism is a type of command economy.

Background

The roots of communism in the People's Republic of China can be traced back to the successful communist revolution that ended in 1949. Mao ZeDong, who headed this revolution, went on to lead his country for the next quarter century. During this period of time Mao tightened government controls over virtually all aspects of the economy and directed the use of resources through a series of five-year plans. **Five-year plans** establish goals for the economy and production targets for agricultural and industrial output. In agriculture the communists instituted the commune system, which brought an end to private property and reorganized farming so that peasants were forced to work the commune's land in production brigades. In industry, the communists tried to industrialize quickly with a program called the Great Leap Forward, but lacked the capital goods, technology and expertise to transform the economy. By the mid-1970s the economy was in ruins and, with the death of Mao in 1976, China embarked on its first steps toward market reform by adopting the Four Modernizations. This new program, which loosened some government controls over the economy, stressed the need to modernize agriculture, industry, science and technology, and defense.

The Economy Today

Even with the Four Modernizations, and significant economic reforms since the late 1970s, the People's Republic of China is still considered one of the few remaining communist nations in the world. Since 1978 when Deng Xiaoping (1978–1997) became China's leader, the Chinese economy has combined elements of both the command and market models to increase national output and improve the standard of living for the people. By the 1990s the Communist Party described China as a "socialist market economy with Chinese characteristics." Most economists have simply labeled this unique mixture of economic systems "Chinese socialism."

Elements of a command economy were evident in Chinese socialism during the 1990s. For example, in the mid-1990s there were still about 300,000 state-owned manufacturing firms in China which employed about 110 million workers, or about 70% of the urban labor force. Many of these state firms are in the unprofitable heavy industries such as steel, automobiles, and chemicals. The government still controls the major industries, such as banking, transportation, energy, and so on. State-owned firms even finance and run some public schools, colleges, hospitals, housing projects, and retirement homes. Currently, the Chinese economy is operating under its ninth five-year plan (1996–2000).

Over the past twenty years Deng Xiaoping also has initiated economic reforms to increase the role of market incentives in China's economy. As a result, by the late 1990s there were millions of smaller privately owned firms operating in China. These private enterprises accounted for about 17% of the nation's industrial output by 1997. In the agricultural sector, the people's communes that had dominated agricultural production under Mao's leadership, had been replaced by the more independent "township and village enterprises," cooperatives, and independent farms. In addition, the five-year plans during the 1980s and 1990s stressed market-oriented reforms and incentives including:

- increased emphasis on the production of consumer goods such as televisions and VCRs;
- increased freedoms to permit firms to earn profits;
- increased autonomy for plant managers to make their own hiring and production decisions;
- increased contacts with other nations through trade and through foreign investment in China.

Since Deng's death in 1997 the new Premier, Zhu Rongji, has continued policies that provide some market incentives to workers, managers, and foreign firms that operate in the nation. But many challenges remain, including how to operate two economies—one run by the government and the other by the market—simultaneously. This problem became more visible after the former British colony of Hong Kong was reunited with China in 1997. In addition, the massacre of pro-democracy protesters at Tiananmen Square in 1989 presents a question. Can China promote economic freedoms and market reforms with one hand, and maintain a totalitarian political system with the other?

Economic Thinkers: Karl Marx and Class Struggle

Karl Marx (1820–1895) was a German-born philosopher, economist, and revolutionary. In his pamphlet, *The Communist Manifesto* (1848), Marx and co-author Friedrich Engels called for an end to capitalism and the establishment of communism.

Marx believed that all of history was a history of class conflict. The ruling class at each stage of history, Marx argued, oppressed those who did not have wealth or property. With each conflict between the oppressor and the oppressed a new stage of history was born. Marx believed that another class conflict was about to occur—a conflict that would destroy capitalism. He theorized that the downtrodden working class, a group that Marx called the proletariat, would rise against the capitalists, whom Marx called the bourgeoisie.

Marx believed that the class struggle between the proletarist and the bourgeoisie would result in the creation of a new economic system—socialism. Under socialism, private property would cease to exist and a classless society would form. In time, even the temporary government, what Marx called the "dictatorship of the proletariat," would also "wither away." Once this occurred, Marx's vision of a perfect socialist society—communism—would be achieved.

Marx's revolutionary ideas spawned revolutionary actions, beginning with the overthrow of the Czar in Russia in 1917 and the creation of the Union of Soviet Socialist Republics a few years later. The collapse of the USSR in 1991 underscored some of the problems nations have had in trying to apply Marx's utopian views during the 20th century.

AN ECONOMY IN TRANSITION: RUSSIA

Definition

Economies in transition are economies that are moving away from their communist past and toward a market-oriented future. Russia, and the former communist nations of Eastern Europe, are currently making this transition.

Background

For most of the 20th century, communism had ruled Russia. From the successful communist revolution of 1917 to the mid-1980s, the communist economy of the Union of Soviet Socialist Republics was dominated by the government's central plans. These central plans were a type of economic blueprint that dictated the use of resources in the USSR. The first five-year plan was formed under Premier Joseph Stalin. It, like later plans, emphasized heavy industries and military goods over light industries. Thus, the economy focused on producing products such as steel, machinery, chemicals, and weapons, over consumer goods. In the agricultural sector private property was confiscated by the government, and large state-run farms were formed. This process was called the "collectivization of agriculture." During Stalin's harsh rule, virtually all industries were under the ownership and control of the government, and all resources—including laborers—were allocated to achieve the goals set forth in a series of five-year plans.

The Economy Today

The transition favoring market reforms began in 1985 when Russia was still one of fifteen Soviet "republics" that comprised the Union of Soviet Socialist Republics, or USSR. Its leader, Mikhail Gorbachev, initiated two types of reforms: glasnost and perestroika. **Glasnost** called for a new "openness" in the political arena, the end of the Communist Party's control over the government, and free elections. **Perestroika** supported a "restructuring" of the Soviet economy that included policies to crack down on corruption and alcoholism in the workplace, to establish incentives to increase agricultural and industrial production, and to create a "competitive atmosphere" among firms.

After the USSR collapsed in 1991, the newly elected President Boris N. Yeltsin expanded the nation's market reforms. **Privatization**, the process of selling or otherwise transferring state properties to private firms or individuals, continued. By 1997, 127,000 state-owned firms were privatized. Government controls over most prices were phased out. People were encouraged to start their own businesses, hire workers, and earn profits. Agricultural land was now freely sold to citizens and, through joint ventures, to foreigners. Largely due to Yeltsin's commitment to market reforms, Russia was also able to solicit loans and foreign aid from international organizations such as the International Monetary Fund (IMF) and from industrialized nations including the United States. The Russian Economics Ministry also reported a robust 8% economic growth rate for 1999, with growth in the chemical industry and in light industries leading the way.

Significant obstacles to Russia's successful transition to a market economy remained, however. Privatization of large and inefficient state-owned enterprises has been slow. In addition, the unstable Russian currency—the ruble—has contributed to the rise of a sizable **informal economy**—an "underground economy" based on barter or other exchanges without the government's knowledge. Under these conditions it was not surprising that the real Gross Domestic Product (GDP) declined steadily during most of the 1990s. The **real GDP** measures the value of all newly produced goods and services in an economy in a given year (adjusted for inflation). Tax revenues also declined, while the government debt mushroomed. The surprise resignation of President Yeltsin on December 31, 1999, created additional uncertainty about the future direction of the Russian economy—a future that will hinge on the actions of acting President Vladimir Putin and others in the coming years.

DEMOCRATIC SOCIALISM: INDIA AND INDICATIVE PLANNING

Democratic socialism is a type of economic system that combines socialist planning with free market economic activities. Nations that have adopted this type of economy have chosen democratic political institutions as the basis for their government. India, the second most populous nation in the world, practices democratic socialism.

Background

Under British rule, which began in the mid-1700s, industry was restricted. As a colony of the British Crown, India was expected to provide a number of raw materials such as cotton for processing in British mills. In agriculture, where the vast majority of the Indian population lived and worked, landlordism was the norm. Under this system landlords, with the support of the British authorities, controlled much of the arable land. Wealth and status were for the few—the British and a small Indian elite. Hundreds of millions of peasants, in the meantime, struggled simply to survive. After India gained its independence from Great Britain in 1947, the elected Indian government initiated reforms to strengthen its industrial and agricultural sectors.

The Economy Today

Soon after India achieved independence, reforms favoring democratic socialism were enacted. Over time the government nationalized many key industries, including the railroads, automobile manufacturing, and most of the banking, telephone, and airline industries. **Nationalization** occurs when the government takes ownership of an industry, but compensates the previous owner. In many of India's light industries, however, private ownership was encouraged. These light industries continue to produce a variety of consumer goods such as clothing, computers, televisions, home appliances, and fine jewelry. In addition, the great majority of India's agricultural land is in private hands, although in the more remote rural areas powerful landlords still dominate the local economies and government. In February of 2000, India announced plans to privatize 20 to 25, state enterprises, including Indian Airlines.

Another important feature of India's democratic socialist economy is indicative planning. **Indicative planning** is a type of government planning that sets economic goals and then makes recommendations about how the nation's resources should be used to meet these goals. Indicative planning is far less forceful than the rigid centralized planning of the Soviet Union under communism. India still devises five-year plans through its National Development Council. Recent five-year plans have stressed the need for job creation, investment in rural areas, and an annual economic growth rate of about 6%—a goal that was achieved during the mid-1990s.

Many challenges remain, including a rising population that today numbers close to 1 billion people according to the United Nations. While India is food self-sufficient, a growing population is cause for concern in terms of how to provide enough jobs, and how to reduce the flood of unskilled peasant labor from the countryside into India's already crowded cities.

Economic Thinkers: Thomas Malthus and Overpopulation

Thomas Malthus (1766–1834) is best remembered for his *Essay on the Principle of Population* (1798). In this essay, he warned of the dangers of an exploding population in a world of limited resources.

Malthus predicted that the world's population would grow at a faster rate than the food supply. The result, he reasoned, would be that a certain segment of the world's population would always live on the edge of starvation. After all, the supply of arable land was fixed, and even the soil currently under cultivation would someday be exhausted.

What Malthus did not foresee was technological innovations in agriculture, such as the "green revolution." The **green revolution** introduced new technology to agriculture in the form of advanced capital goods, fertilizers and pesticides, irrigation techniques, and hybrid (genetically engineered) seeds. All of these innovations have increased crop yields around the globe since the 1960s.

Today, as the world's population surpasses 6 billion, some people are again looking at Malthus' warnings as they debate the effects of population growth on the future of the planet.

PRIVATIZATING A DEMOCRATIC SOCIALIST ECONOMY: THE UNITED KINGDOM

The economy of the United Kingdom (UK) has undergone significant changes since the early 1980s, including the partial dismantling of Britain's democratic socialist economy—an economy that had enjoyed widespread support during the 1940s to the 1970s. Today, the British economy is moving toward an economic system that more closely resembles the market model.

Background

After World War II the government of the UK nationalized key industries, including energy resources, the railway system, the telecommunications system, the steel industry, health care, and others. The UK also created a comprehensive welfare system to ensure the economic well-being of the people. This welfare system included not just public assistance programs for the unemployed and the poor, but also free medical care, a free college education for qualified students, and other benefits. By the mid-1970s, labor unrest and other economic problems—including higher taxes needed to pay for its "cradle to grave" welfare system—eroded popular support for socialism and for the ruling Labour Party.

The Economy Today

Market-oriented reforms were initiated almost immediately after the Conservative Party victory in the 1979 elections. The Conservatives, under the leadership of Margaret Thatcher (1979–1990) and later John Major (1990–1998), proceeded to privatize many of the industries that were nationalized just a few decades earlier. For example, privatization in the telecommunications industry occurred in 1984, coal in 1994, and the passenger and freight operations of the railroads in 1994 to 1997. Reforming the cradle to grave welfare system proved more difficult as issues of the fairness and the expense of social programs were debated into the late 1990s without resolution. A national minimum wage, set at 3.60 pounds sterling ($5.83) per hour for workers aged 22 years or older, went into effect in the spring of 1999. While some elements of the UK's democratic socialist past remain in place, the nation continues to take steps toward a market-oriented future.

CAPITALISM: JAPAN AND "SOFT PLANNING"

Definition

Capitalism is an economic system based on private ownership and control over most resources, such as natural resources, machinery and equipment, and one's own labor. In addition, in capitalist economies consumers are free to choose which goods and services they wish to purchase, and firms are free to use the resources and methods of production that lead to business profits. Capitalism is often referred to as a free-enterprise system, or a market economic system.

Background

The roots of capitalism in Japan stretch back to the 1600s when merchants, artisans, and rich peasants became entrepreneurs and profited from growing markets in Japan. Under the watchful eye of the powerful military class of samurai, these entrepreneurs learned the value of self-discipline, education, and risk-taking. When Japan opened its doors to trade with the West in the mid-1800s—and to Western technology—the pace of Japanese modernization quickened. After the virtual destruction of the Japanese economy during World War II, the Japanese rebuilt their capitalist economy. To help guide Japan's economic recovery a powerful Economic Planning Agency, and the Ministry of International Trade and Industry (MITI), were created.

The Economy Today

Capitalism in Japan relies on private ownership of virtually all businesses. But the government has a role in planning how to use the nation's resources. Economic planning in Japan typically takes the form of recommendations or advice from the government, hence it is often called "soft planning."

Soft planning involves two groups. One is the Economic Planning Agency, which has cabinet rank. The mission of this agency is to map out long run strategies to keep Japanese firms profitable and competitive in world markets. In its 1996–2001 plan, the Economic Planning Agency stressed the relaxation of state controls in the economy and the creation of jobs. By the summer of 1999 the head of the Economic Planning Agency, Taichi Sakaiya, announced sweeping reforms to reduce the role of government in favor of free competition in an effort to create more efficiency in Japanese industries. The other group involved in economic planning is the Ministry of International Trade and Industry (MITI). MITI is considered a quasi-public institution because its membership not only includes government officials, but also business leaders, scholars, and labor union leaders. MITI's guidance is mainly based on providing or withholding incentives to businesses. For example, to encourage firms to enter certain markets, MITI offers firms tax breaks, financial support for the research and development of products, guaranteed low-interest loans from banks, and even protection from foreign competitors through quotas or tariffs. These incentives can be withheld from firms that do not heed MITI's advice.

Japan became the "economic miracle" of the industrialized world during the 1950s to 1980s. Japan's success stemmed from high rates of investment in new machines and equipment, a highly skilled labor force, and the ability to adapt and transform foreign technology into profitable business ventures. By the 1990s, however, Japan's economy had slipped into periodic recessions, the most severe of which occurred in 1997–1998. Public confidence in the economy continued to shrink in the late 1990s as unemployment increased and several major banks failed. The traditional network of powerful Japanese corporations, called the "keiretsu," also came under attack for pressuring banks to make large, risky—and ultimately unprofitable—loans to them. Traditionally, the "keiretsu" created strong corporate linkages with one another and with their Japanese suppliers and distributors—a practice that firms in other nations felt was unfair because it excluded "non-members" from competing for business contracts with these firms.

CAPITALISM: THE UNITED STATES AND THE MARKET MECHANISM

Definition

Like the capitalism that exists in Japan, American capitalism relies on private ownership and control over most resources, and protects the wide range of economic freedoms enjoyed by consumers, workers, savers and investors, and firms. Unlike the Japanese brand of capitalism, there is no government planning agency to "guide" the U.S. economy. Instead, the market mechanism guides most economic activity in the United States. The **market mechanism** is an informal network of signals that influences consumers' demand for goods and services, and firms' use of resources to supply goods to consumers. The most important of these signals is price. Prices coordinate the millions of individual buying and selling decisions in the American economy. That is, consumers seek the lowest priced good to satisfy their needs, while firms seek to produce items from which they are able to earn profits.

Background

The evolution of America's capitalist economic system dates back to its colonial past. Even then the basic features of capitalism were present—private ownership of property, freedom to make contracts, freedom to choose among competing goods, and financial incentives to work, produce, save, and invest. During the 1800s American capitalism took a different form as the industrial revolution spread and the factory system came to dominate industrial production. As the size and power of big businesses increased during the late 1800s and early 1900s, the government's role in the economy likewise expanded. This was because additional protections were required including the need to protect competitive markets from monopolies, to protect workers from dangerous workplaces, to protect consumers from unsafe products, and so on. Despite a larger role for government in the economy, the United States still has "limited government" compared to most other nations.

The Economy Today

The informal operation of the market mechanism has helped the American economy maintain its status as the world's largest economy through the post-World War II era. The size of a nation's economy is measured by the size of its **Gross Domestic Product** (GDP), which calculates the value of all newly produced goods and services in an economy in a given year. Recent GDP data for the United States is shown in Figure 2.3. According to the Department of Commerce, by 1999 the nominal GDP (GDP not adjusted for inflation) in the United States topped $9.2 trillion, far surpassing the GDPs of the leading industrial nations of Europe and Asia. In fact, the consistent increases in the nation's real GDP (GDP adjusted for inflation) from March of 1991 through February of 2000 marked the longest period of uninterrupted expansion since World War II (see chapter 12). The Bureau of Labor Statistics also reported that the nation's unemployment rate continued to decline to just 4% by January 2000, the lowest rate since 1970. Inflation crept along in an acceptable 1.5% to 3% annual rate during most of the 1990s. Most surprising were the surpluses in the federal budget in fiscal years 1997–1998 and

Figure 2.3
U.S. Gross Domestic Product, 1990–1999 (in $ billions)

Year	Nominal GDP	Real GDP (in 1996 $)	Real GDP (% Change)
1990	$5,803	$6,684	+1.7%
1991	$5,986	$6,669	-0.2%
1992	$6,319	$6,891	+3.3%
1993	$6,642	$7,054	+2.4 %
1994	$7,054	$7,338	+4.0%
1995	$7,401	$7,537	+2.7%
1996	$7,813	$7,813	+3.7%
1997	$8,301	$8,165	+4.5%
1998	$8,760	$8,516	+4.3%
1999	$9,248	$8,861	+4.0%

Source: U.S. Department of Commerce, Bureau of Economic Analysis.

1998–1999, which totaled $69 billion and $79 billion respectively, according to the Office of Management and Budget (OMB). Further, the OMB predicts budget surpluses to continue into the foreseeable future, with about $1 trillion in accumulated surpluses by 2004.

The United States was not without its share of economic problems, however. The national debt, which had grown steadily from 1970–1997, stood at about $5.5 trillion in 1998, according to the OMB. Personal savings plummeted during the late 1990s, and by 1998 it had dropped to almost zero, according to the *Economic Report of the President*. This report also noted that personal bankruptcies soared to a recorded breaking 1.4 million in 1998. Concerns about the future of the Social Security System, and Medicare—the federal health insurance for the elderly—also intensified as many workers in the "baby boom" generation approached retirement age.

MAKING ECONOMIC DECISIONS: CHOOSING AMONG ECONOMIC GOALS

Economic Goals

Economic goals are the broad objectives that a nation tries to achieve in its economy. The seven economic goals in the U.S. economy include:

- Economic freedom: Economic freedom refers to the freedoms of the marketplace—to buy, to sell, to save, to invest, and so on.
- Economic efficiency: Economic efficiency refers to producing the most goods or services per unit of input (the factors of production). Efficiency is increased by using sophisticated capital goods, new technology, worker training programs, and the like.
- Economic equity: Economic equity deals with what is fair or unfair, right or wrong in an economy. Equity issues often relate to income and its distribution in the economy.
- Economic security: Economic security deals with protecting people from situations that are beyond their control such as bank failures, poverty, and job layoffs.
- Full employment: Full employment exists when all of a nation's resources are used productively. That is, society's resources are "fully employed." Full employment applied to labor resources is achieved when 5% to 6% of the labor force is unemployed. By allowing some unemployment, the government takes into account the constant stream of job seekers in the U.S. economy who are in between jobs, or are new entrants into the labor force.
- Price stability: Price stability refers to the absence of inflation or deflation. **Inflation** occurs when the price level for all goods and services in the economy increases. **Deflation** occurs when the price level in the economy decreases.
- Economic growth: Economic growth refers to sustained increases in a nation's total output of goods and services. Economic growth is measured by tracking the growth of the real GDP.

Goals in Conflict

Economic goals sometimes come into conflict with one another. This is inevitable because of scarcity. That is, people simply cannot have everything that they may want. For example, in his State of the Union Address in January of 1999, President Clinton proposed to save the ailing Social Security system—a retirement system for the great majority of the nation's workers. He defended increased support for Social Security mainly on the basis of economic equity and security. Supporters of a strong Social Security system believed that it was "fair" to protect this retirement program that workers—especially the fast-maturing "baby boomers"—had contributed to during their working careers. The retirement income provided by Social Security, along with the Medicare health insurance, also increases the financial security of these retirees. Opponents of the current Social Security system pointed to the loss of economic freedoms, particularly the freedoms of workers who must pay 7.65% of their gross wage into the system, and the economic freedoms of the employers of these workers who must match this 7.65% payment. Further, they argue that money that is taxed away from the people cannot be invested in new capital or new businesses, thus reducing economic efficiency and growth.

Economic decision making is what the study of economics is all about. The next chapter takes a closer look at how the market decides on a fair market price for goods and services, and for resources used in production.

3

HOW ARE PRICES SET IN THE U.S. ECONOMY?

Chapter 3 discusses how the forces of demand and supply determine the market prices for most goods and services in the U.S. economy. You might be surprised by how much you already know about this topic. We will take a look at a hypothetical product, the Grandbar, to illustrate how the forces of demand and supply interact to set a market equilibrium price and quantity. We will also examine situations where the government sets prices in the U.S. economy through price floors and ceilings—policies that have costs as well as benefits for people.

DEMAND AND THE LAW OF DEMAND

Demand

Demand is the amount of a resource, good, or service that people are willing and able to buy at a series of prices in a given period of time. It is important to note that this definition requires both a willingness and ability to buy the item. That is, the buyer not only must desire the good but also have enough money to make the purchase. Further, economists put a special emphasis on a given time period because it is common for the demand for a resource, good, or service to change over time.

Law of Demand

The **law of demand** states that there is an inverse relationship between the price of a good and the quantity demanded of the good. This means that for most goods as the price increases, the quantity demanded de-

Figure 3.1
Demand Schedule for Grandbars

Price of Grandbars	Quantity Demanded of Grandbars (millions per month)
$1.50	0
$1.25	2
$1.00	6
$ .75	10
$ .50	16
$ .25	24

creases. Conversely, as the price of a good decreases, the quantity demanded increases. You have probably understood this relationship for many years. If you think about your everyday buying decisions this inverse relationship becomes clearer. Most Americans seek the lowest possible price for the goods that we buy. Ads that promise "25% Off," or "Buy 1 and Get the Second Free" tend to attract our attention because these items are a good buy. These ads also illustrate the law of demand in action.

When studying the impact that price changes have on the quantity demanded of a good, economists use the *ceteris paribus* assumption. **Ceteris paribus** means that all other factors that might affect the demand for the good are held constant. This allows the economist a moment to focus on a single variable—price. The law of demand can be illustrated in two ways, a demand schedule and a demand curve. A demand schedule is a table that shows the inverse relationship between price and quantity demanded, while a demand curve plots the same data onto a graph.

To construct a demand schedule assume the following hypothetical data for Grandbars, a new brand of health bars, shown in Figure 3.1. Note that as the price of Grandbars decreases, the quantity demanded increases, and vice versa.

A demand "curve" simply takes the data from the demand schedule and plots it onto a graph, as shown in Figure 3.2. The vertical axis of the graph always shows the price of the good, in this case the price of Grandbars. The horizontal axis always shows the quantity demanded of the good. Each point on the demand curve shows one of the relationships between the price of Grandbars and the quantity demanded. At point A on the curve, for example, zero Grandbars are demanded at a price of $1.50. As the price decreases, however, the quantity demanded increases. At point C, 6 million Grandbars are demanded when the price drops to $1.00. At point F, 24 million Grandbars are demanded when the price

Figure 3.2
Demand Curve for Grandbars

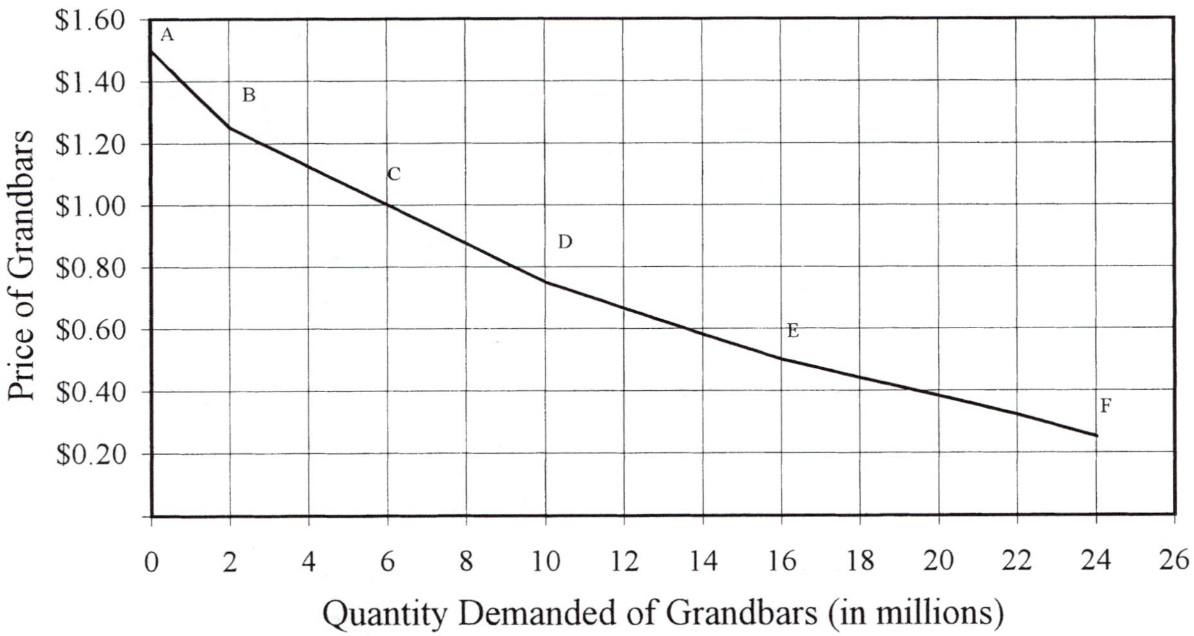

falls to just $.25. When these points are connected, the demand "curve" is formed. Note that the demand curve is downward sloping. This downward slope reflects the law of demand in graphic form. The key points to remember are:

- a change in the price of a good results in a change in the "quantity demanded" of the good, not a change in the "demand" for the good;
- a change in the price of a good will cause a "movement" along the existing demand curve.

CHANGES IN DEMAND

To create the original demand curve for Grandbars all other factors that could have had an impact on the demand for this good were temporarily held constant. In the real world, many factors affect the demand for resources, goods, or services. These other factors are called "determinants of demand."

When a determinant of demand changes, the entire "demand" for a good changes "at each and every price." What are these determinants of demand? You are already familiar with some. If you had a chance to watch television last night you most likely saw a large number of commercials. TV commercials are designed to inform you about a certain good or service, and then persuade you to buy it. In economic terms, TV commercials try to change your "tastes and preferences" in favor of a particular product. If the commercial is successful, consumers will be willing to buy more of the good at all of the prices listed on the demand schedule.

Using the earlier demand for Grandbars as a starting point, suppose consumer tastes and preferences—a determinant of demand—shifted in favor of Grandbars. Perhaps this was due to an effective advertising campaign, or perhaps because a recent government report noted special health benefits derived from its consumption. Whatever the reason, the result of consumers' new preference for Grandbars is that more people will buy Grandbars at each and every price. Now, perhaps 4 million Grandbars can be sold at a price of $1.50 rather than the original zero. Similarly, at a price of $1.25, the quantity demanded jumps from 2 million Grandbars to 6 million. And so it goes at all of the possible prices. Figure 3.3 expands on the original demand schedule to show how consumers' tastes and preferences increased the demand for Grandbars. Economists plot this new data onto a graph to create a totally new demand curve. Positive changes in one or more of the determinants of demand cause the entire curve to "shift" to the right, while negative changes in a determinant of demand cause the entire curve to shift to the left.

Figure 3.3
Impact of Tastes and Preferences on the Demand for Grandbars

Price of Grandbars	Original Quantity Demanded of Grandbars (millions per month)	New Quantity Demanded of Grandbars (millions per month)
$1.50	0	4
$1.25	2	6
$1.00	6	10
$0.75	10	14
$0.50	16	20
$0.25	24	28

Determinants of demand can shift in favor of a good or against a good. You have just seen in Figure 3.3 that when a determinant of demand such as tastes and preferences shifts in favor of a product, consumers will buy more at each and every price. If you took the time to plot this new data you would see that the entire demand curve shifts to the right. Determinants of demand can also shift against a good. If the advertising campaign for Grandbars lost its appeal, or the favorable government report about the health benefits of eating Grandbars was inaccurate, or consumers simply no longer enjoyed eating Grandbars, buyers would be willing to spend less for Grandbars at each and every price. Hence, then we can say that there is a decrease in the demand for Grandbars, and the demand curve shifts to the left.

In addition to consumer tastes and preferences there are five other determinants of demand, each of which can cause demand to shift in a positive or negative direction. In addition to tastes and preferences, these determinants of demand include: market size, people's income, the price of a substitute good, the price of a complementary good, and consumer expectations.

• Market size: Market size refers to the number of buyers for a good or service. When the market size increases the demand for goods tends to increase. Market size could increase through national advertising, opening trade with different nations, and so on. Hasbro's aggressive advertising of its Furby prior to the 1998 Christmas season dramatically increased the market size for this pint-sized fuzzy toy. The market size could decrease by eliminating advertising or by closing off trade with other nations.

• Income: When people's incomes rise they tend to buy more of just about everything, but when incomes fall so does demand.

Increases in income are common during periods of prosperity, but tend to fall off during economic downturns.

- Substitute goods: **Substitute goods** are goods that are similar to one another and could be used almost interchangeably. When the price of a substitute good increases, the demand for the related good tends to increase. For example, Coca Cola and Pepsi Cola are substitute goods. If Coca Cola increased its price you can be sure that the demand for a substitute good, Pepsi Cola, would rise because some consumers would switch to the lower priced Pepsi. Conversely, if Coke lowered its price, the demand for Pepsi would fall because some Pepsi drinkers would switch to the lower priced Coke.

- Complementary goods: **Complementary goods** are goods that are used in conjunction with one another. If the price of one complementary good increases, the demand for the other good will decrease. This is because the higher price for one will make using the other good more expensive. Flashlights and batteries are complementary goods. If the price of batteries doubles, this will cause the demand for flashlights to fall because it now costs more to operate the flashlight. If the price of batteries decreases, on the other hand, the demand for flashlights, boom boxes, and battery operated toys will increase.

- Consumer expectations: Consumer expectations are the beliefs people have about their own financial security and the financial security of the nation. When people are optimistic about the future they tend to buy more, thereby increasing the demand for many goods. High consumer confidence in the expanding U.S. economy from 1991 through 2000 helped fuel robust buying during this period. Conversely, when consumers' expectations turn gloomy people tend to reduce their spending, causing demand for many goods to decline.

SUPPLY AND THE LAW OF SUPPLY

Supply

Supply refers to the amount of a good or service that producers are willing and able to sell at a series of prices in a given period of time. Note that the entire perspective has changed from that of the consumer to that of the producer. Keep in mind that the producer must make a profit or the firm will go out of business. This fact influences producers' decisions about how much of a good they will produce or sell at a series of prices.

Law of Supply

The **law of supply** states that there is a direct relationship between the price and the quantity supplied of a good. That is, as the price of a good increases, producers will increase the quantity supplied. If, on the other hand, the price of a good falls, producers will reduce the quantity supplied. This behavior is not surprising. Higher prices could mean higher profits for the firm, or could be used to cover any additional costs of producing the product.

Like the law of demand, the law of supply can be illustrated in two ways—with a supply schedule and a supply curve. To construct the supply schedule and supply curve let's return to our earlier Grandbars example. On the supply schedule shown in Figure 3.4, note that as the price of Grandbars increases the quantity supplied increases, and that as the price of Grandbars decreases the quantity supplied decreases. At the highest price of $1.50, for example, the producer is willing to produce 26 million Grandbars per month. The producer is willing to produce fewer Grandbars as the price declines.

You can draw the supply curve by plotting the data from the supply schedule onto a graph, as shown in Figure 3.5. The process is identical to the plotting of the demand curve. When all of the points taken from the supply schedule are plotted onto the graph, the supply "curve" is formed. Note that the supply curve is upward sloping showing that as the price of Grandbars increases the producer will produce more of them. At point U on the supply curve, for example, producers will produce just 2 million Grandbars because the $.25 price is so low. At point Z, producers will supply 26 million Grandbars when the price jumps to $1.50. Hence, this upward slope reflects the law of supply in graphic form. The key points to remember are:

- a change in the price of a good results in a change in the "quantity supplied" of the good, not a change in the "supply" of the good;
- a change in the price will cause a "movement" along the existing supply curve.

CHANGES IN SUPPLY

Recall that all factors were held constant when constructing the original supply curve shown in Figure 3.5. But changes in the supply of a good, like the changes in demand for a good, occur all of the time. The factors that change the overall supply of a good are called "determinants of supply." These determinants of supply cause producers to supply more or less of the good "at each and every price."

Figure 3.4
Supply Schedule for Grandbars

Price of Grandbars	Quantity Demanded of Grandbars (millions per month)
$1.50	26
$1.25	20
$1.00	14
$.75	10
$.50	6
$.25	2

One determinant of supply is resource prices. Again, let's jump back to the original supply of Grandbars. Suppose the price for an important ingredient in the Grandbar such as raisins decreased in price. This decrease in a resource price would be viewed favorably by the producer of Grandbars because the cost of producing Grandbars would fall. The producer could now produce and offer for sale more Grandbars at each and every price. Instead of producing 26 million Grandbars at $1.50, the producer might now be willing to produce 30 million. As we move down the supply schedule, instead of producing 20 million Grandbars at $1.25, the producer might now produce 24 million. The impact of lower resource costs on the remainder of the supply schedule is shown in Figure 3.6. Economists would then draw a new supply curve for Grandbars to reflect the new supply data. Positive changes in one or more of the determinants of supply cause the entire supply curve to "shift" to the right, while negative changes in these determinants cause the entire curve to shift to the left.

Determinants of supply, like the determinants of demand, can work in favor of a product or against it. Figure 3.6 shows the positive impact of lower resource prices on the supply of Grandbars. That is, as resource prices decreased the producer was willing and able to produce more Grandbars at each and every price. Determinants of supply can also shift against a product. Suppose, for example, the price of the peanuts and caramel used in Grandbars increased. Then the story would be much different. Instead of producing more Grandbars at each and every price the producer would produce fewer.

In addition to resource prices there are four other determinants of supply, any of which could change the overall supply for a good. These include: advances in technology, the number of competitors, taxes, and expectations of future prices for the good.

Figure 3.5
Supply Curve for Grandbars

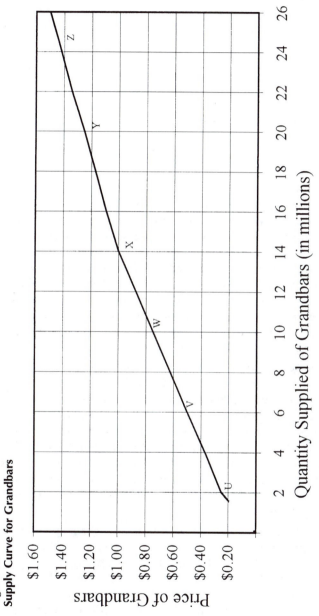

Price of Grandbars

Quantity Supplied of Grandbars (in millions)

Figure 3.6
Impact of Lower Resource Prices on the Supply of Grandbars

Price of Grandbars	Original Quantity Supplied of Grandbars (millions per month)	New Quantity Supplied of Grandbars (millions per month)
$1.50	26	30
$1.25	20	24
$1.00	14	18
$.75	10	14
$.50	6	10
$.25	2	6

- Technological advance: Advances in technology allow firms to produce goods more efficiently which, in turn, encourages firms to increase the quantity supplied at each and every price. For example, advances in microchip technology revolutionized the production of many products, including the pocket calculator that you probably have in your book bag. Technological advance can also reduce or eliminate the demand for certain products. Such was the case when the mass production of the automobile in the early 20th century reduced, and eventually eliminated, the demand for horse drawn carriages.

- Number of competitors: The more competitors that are in an industry the greater the supply of the product will be. Profits act like a magnet in an economy, attracting new competitors to profitable industries. Over the past twenty years, for example, many firms have entered the personal computer industry and have increased the supply of computers tremendously. IBM, Apple, Hewlett Packard, Dell, and other firms have become household names. At the same time firms have exited other industries, such as the typewriter industry, causing the supply of typewriters to drop to nearly zero.

- Taxes: As taxes rise the supply of goods fall, and as taxes fall the supply of goods rise. A payroll tax like Social Security costs the worker 7.65% of his wage, and the employer an equal amount. This payroll tax increases the cost of labor and obliges the firm to increase the price of the product. Higher production costs discourage production and, therefore, producers tend to supply less. A reduction in payroll taxes reduces the costs of production and the price of a good. In response, producers are likely to increase production and the supply of goods.

• Price expectations: Price expectations represent the best guess that a firm or industry can make about the future price of a good. If, for example, U.S. auto manufacturers expect the prices for most models of automobiles to drop during the next production year, you can expect these car companies to cut back on the number of autos they produce. That is, they will decrease the supply of domestic automobiles. If, on the other hand, signs point to higher prices for automobiles in the coming year you can expect U.S. car companies to increase the supply of automobiles.

ESTABLISHING AN EQUILIBRIUM PRICE AND QUANTITY

Take a look at the demand curve for Grandbars in Figure 3.2 and the supply curve for Grandbars in Figure 3.5. You immediately notice that consumers and producers are at odds with one another. On the one hand, the downward sloping demand curve tells us that consumers prefer to buy large quantities of goods when prices are low. On the other hand, the upward sloping supply curve shows producers' preference to sell large quantities of goods when prices are high. In a free market economy neither the consumer nor the producer has enough power to dictate the "right price" to the other. The **market equilibrium** is the compromise that must be reached so that both consumers and producers are satisfied with the price of a good and with the quantity available for purchase.

The market equilibrium for Grandbars is determined by placing the demand and supply curves onto the same graph, as shown in Figure 3.7. The point where the two curves intersect is the equilibrium point. This point represents the best compromise between consumers and producers at this moment in time. As you can see from Figure 3.7, the market equilibrium price for Grandbars is $.75 and the quantity is 10 million Grandbars per month. Note that the horizontal axis is now simply labeled "quantity." This means that the "quantity demanded" and "quantity supplied" are being studied on the same graph.

PRICE FLOORS AND CEILINGS

The forces of demand and supply determine most prices in the U.S. economy. There are situations, however, where the government gets involved in setting prices. In a sense, when the government sets prices for goods or resources it is overriding the invisible price signals that tell us what and how to produce.

Figure 3.7
Equilibrium Price and Quantity of Grandbars

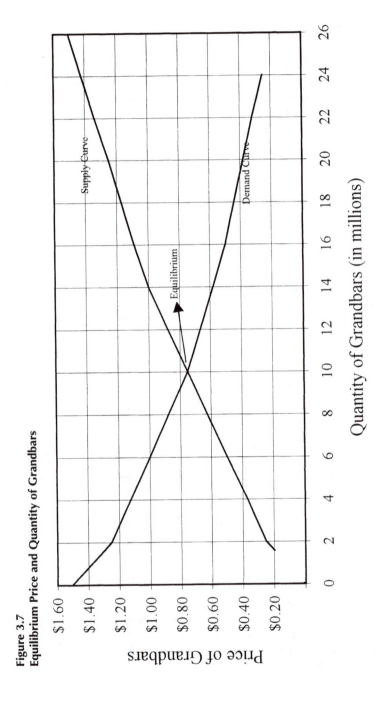

42

Figure 3.8
Price Floors and the Minimum Wage

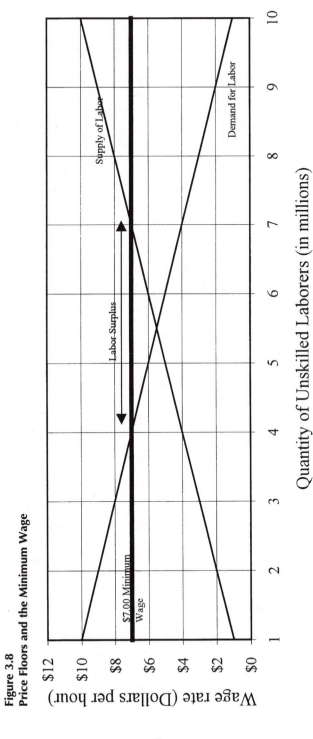

43

Price Floors

A **price floor** is a government guaranteed minimum price for a resource, good, or service. In effect, the government is determining the
price rather than the free market. For example, the minimum wage is a
price floor. What the federal minimum wage of $5.15 says is that most
firms must pay their employees at least $5.15 per hour in exchange for
the labor they provide. Let's take a look at some of the possible effects
of the national minimum wage by examining Figure 3.8.

Figure 3.8 shows a typical demand and supply curve for a resource,
unskilled labor. Note that the demand curve is downward sloping to
reflect the law of demand for unskilled laborers. At a high wage of $10
per hour, only 1 million laborers are demanded by firms, while at a low
wage rate of $1 per hour 10 million laborers are demanded by firms.
Predictably, on the supply curve far more laborers are willing to work
if wages are high. Ten million laborers are willing to work at a wage of
$10 per hour, while only 1 million workers are willing to work at the
low wage of $1 per hour. The intersection of these two curves creates
the market equilibrium wage of $5.50, and a quantity of 5.5 million la-
borers.

What a government price floor does is override the market's compromise on wages. For our example, let's suppose that a new minimum
wage of $7.00 per hour is enacted by Congress. Using the data from
Figure 3.8, the number of unskilled laborers demanded by firms will
drop to 4 million because of the higher minimum wage. At the same
time, the number of workers who are willing to work jumps to 7 million.
The problem is fairly apparent—the higher minimum wage has created
a surplus of 3 million laborers.

Price Ceilings

A **price ceiling** is a government imposed maximum price for a resource, good, or service. Again, it is the government rather than the
market that determines the price. Rent controls on apartments are a type
of price ceiling. Under rent controls the local government places a price
ceiling on the amount that a landlord can charge to tenants. The intent
of rent controls is to guarantee affordable housing. But, as was the case
with price floors, there are unintended consequences of ignoring supply
and demand, as shown in Figure 3.9.

Suppose a local government enacts rent controls that put a $500 limit
on rents for certain apartment units. This $500 price ceiling is drawn in
on Figure 3.9. The predictable consequence of this price ceiling is that
the quantity of apartment units demanded increases from 400,000 to
500,000 units, but the quantity supplied drops from 400,000 to 300,000

units. The effect of the government price ceiling, therefore, is a shortage of 200,000 apartment units in the city.

Economic Thinkers: Milton Friedman in Defense of Free Markets

Milton Friedman (1912–), an American economist, is among the most widely read and controversial economic thinkers in the contemporary world. He has consistently, and forcefully, defended the use of free markets to allocate society's scarce resources. Among his more popular books are *Capitalism and Freedom* (1962) and *Free to Choose: A Personal Statement* (1980), both of which were co-authored with his wife Rose Friedman.

In many respects Friedman's defense of free, competitive markets mirrors that of Adam Smith. Both of these economists would agree that where competition exists efficient markets emerge. Efficient markets, in turn, not only build a prosperous economy but also create a high standard of living for the people. Friedman argues that consumers and producers who are driven by their own self-interest are in the best position to allocate society's scarce resources. It follows that government interference in free markets—such as imposing price floors and ceilings—are harmful to the economy.

For his many contributions to the field of economics Milton Friedman was awarded the Nobel Prize in Economic Science in 1976.

ELASTICITY OF DEMAND AND SUPPLY

A change in the price of a good or service will change the quantity demanded or the quantity supplied. What still needs to be determined is how much of a change in these quantities will occur when the price of a good changes. This, to the economist, is the study of the elasticity.

Elasticity of Demand

The **elasticity of demand** measures the impact of prices on the quantity demanded of a good. The demand for a good is "elastic" when even a relatively small change or difference in price causes a large change in the quantity demanded. The demand for a good is "inelastic" when even a large change or difference in price has a relatively small impact on the quantity demanded.

Consider the inelastic demand for gasoline. Consumers cheered when the price of regular unleaded gasoline dipped beneath $1 in the fall of 1998, but winced when gasoline prices jumped by over 50% by early 2000. And through these ups and downs in price, consumers continued to buy gasoline. Why? The buying continued because the demand for gasoline is basically inelastic. Demand for gasoline is inelastic because it is a necessity and there are no close substitutes for it. The demand for

Figure 3.9
Price Ceilings and Rent Controls

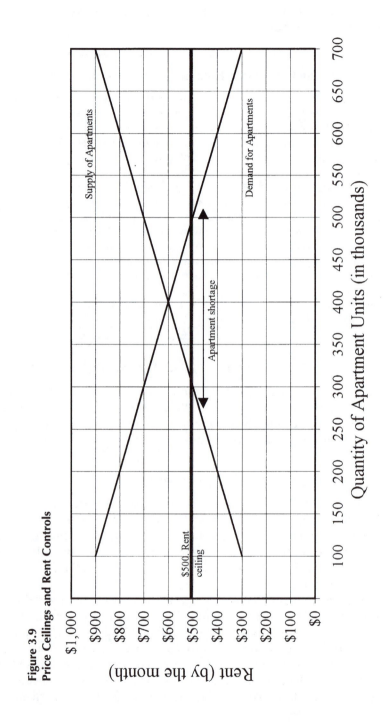

home heating oil and many medicines is also inelastic for the same reasons.

The demand for many other products is more elastic or flexible. This means that the price of a good or service will have a major impact on the quantity demanded. These types of goods are usually not viewed as necessities, or at least there are close substitutes. Consider the demand for a particular car. While a car is a necessity for many people, the demand for a particular car is elastic because there are numerous substitutes available. Other goods with an elastic demand range from European vacations to roast beef.

Elasticity of Supply

The **elasticity of supply** measures the impact of prices on the quantity supplied of a good. The supply of a good is "elastic" when a change in its price has a major impact on the quantity supplied. The supply of a good is "inelastic" when price changes have little effect on the quantity supplied.

The supply of a good or service tends to be more elastic in the long run than in the short run. This means that the supply of most goods or services can be increased or decreased more easily over time. Suppose the price for a brain operation unexpectedly jumped from \$100,000 to \$200,000. The number of operations, however, cannot be significantly changed due to the fixed number of brain surgeons. The higher price for brain operations sends a signal to the marketplace that there is lots of money to be made in brain surgery. It is reasonable to predict that more people will train to become brain surgeons in the long run, and that the services of brain surgeons will become more elastic.

Other products have an elastic supply simply because the factors of production can easily be adapted to produce the good. Suppose consumers suddenly wanted more red T-shirts and were willing to pay an additional \$.50 for red T-shirts. Producers of T-shirts could almost instantly change the quantity supplied of red T-shirts by changing the color of the dye. Within a few days, the small increase in price would cause a large increase in the quantity supplied of red T-shirts. From your own experience think how quickly producers can supply T-shirts that sport the latest rock group, championship sports team, or other artwork—and how quickly the production of these specialty items can be stopped once they become unpopular or outdated.

The supply of some goods is perfectly inelastic, or fixed, regardless of the price. If you had a chance to watch the nationally televised Women's World Cup Soccer Championship Game on July 10, 1999, you would have seen the U.S. women capture the championship. You also would have seen 88,000 enthusiastic soccer fans packed into the Rose Bowl's

88,000 seats. Undoubtedly more tickets could have been sold to this historic event—it certainly was the hottest ticket in town. Despite high demand for game tickets, ticket sales were limited. Why? In economic terms, the fixed number of seats represents a perfectly inelastic supply of seats. At $10 per ticket, $20 per ticket, or $100 per ticket, the number of seats could not be changed due to the constraints of the stadium.

SUPPLY AND DEMAND IN EVERYDAY LIFE

It might be difficult for you to believe that something you can't see has so much of an influence over your everyday decisions. Yet the invisible signals that surround us, especially those that relate to the prices of goods and services, affect our economic behaviors every day.

The forces of supply and demand influence the price we pay for almost every good or service in the American marketplace, from collector baseball cards to your home. Did you know that in the spring of 1998 Mark McGwire's 1985 Topps baseball card was selling for $35? By September of that year the same mint condition card was selling for $250, and by the end of the baseball season that fall the card was worth ten times this amount. What happened? The forces of supply and demand "happened." The supply of the 1985 Topps card is fixed or, as economists would say, the supply is perfectly inelastic. The demand for the card, on the other hand, increased in a near-frenzied manner during Mark McGwire's record breaking season. His 70 home runs during the 1998 season made baseball history—and made holders of the 1985 Topps Mark McGwire card a little richer!

4

WHY DO CONSUMERS BEHAVE AS THEY DO?

Chapter 4 further examines the factors that shape consumer behavior in the American economy. Chapter 3 discussed consumer demand. Chapter 4 digs deeper into some of the forces that underlie people's demand for goods and services. It explores consumers' buying decisions, and the role of advertising in shaping consumer tastes and preferences. It also acquaints you with a number of handy consumer skills, and introduces you to your consumer rights and how they are protected in the United States today.

CONSUMERS IN THE U.S. ECONOMY

Consumers buy goods and services for their personal use. Thus, all people are consumers. To make these purchases, consumers must first have an income. In most cases, people have more than one source of income.

Sources of Income

In 1999 nearly $8 trillion in income poured into American households. Even after taxes, we still had nearly $7 trillion left to save or to spend. Households get their income from a variety of sources—usually some combination of wages and salaries, interest or dividend payments, rents, profits from business ventures, or transfer payments. A retiree, for example, may collect a Social Security check (a public transfer payment), work at a part-time job (for a wage), and receive semi-annual dividend payments (from stock that he owns).

Figure 4.1
Sources of Household Income, 1998

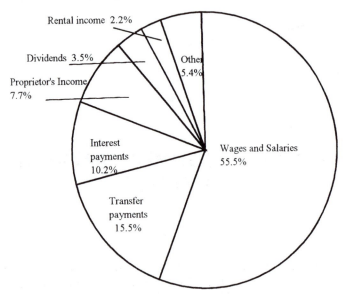

Source: U.S. Department of Commerce, Bureau of Economic Analysis.

It may surprise you, but only a little over one-half of our income is from wages or salaries, as shown in Figure 4.1. Still, wages and salaries account for over $4 trillion, or 55.5% of our personal income. Ranking second is transfer payments (15.4%). Transfer payments are government payments to individuals in need of assistance and include the payments to individuals from programs such as Social Security, Temporary Assistance for Needy Families, unemployment compensation, and food stamps. Transfer payments account for over $1 trillion in household income. Interest (10.2%) and dividend (3.5%) income represents the income that comes from saving or investing your money. Over $1 trillion is added to household income through interest and dividend payments. And over $1 trillion more in income comes from the earnings of proprietors (7.7%), usually small business owners and farmers, rents from properties (2.2%), and other sources (5.4%). You will read more about wages and other sources of income in chapter 13.

Spending Money

American consumers spend money, and lots of it. In 1999 Americans spent nearly $7 trillion on goods and services—that's about $18.5 billion dollars a day! To look at consumer spending from a different angle, households spend 99.5% of their income on goods and services. This

Figure 4.2
Consumer Spending, 1998

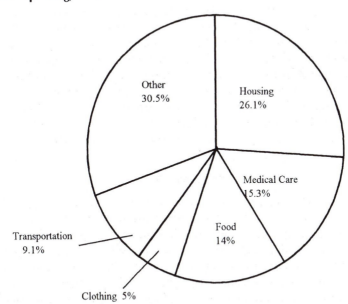

Source: *Economic Report of the President, 1999.*

means that less than one-half of one percent of our incomes is saved. Interestingly, almost 60% of our incomes is spent on services, and the remaining 40% on goods. Some of the categories of spending are shown in Figure 4.2.

The largest single category of spending for American consumers is housing (26.1%). Housing expenses include mortgage or rent payments, utilities such as electricity or gas, and purchases of furniture and household equipment. Medical care (15.3%) is another major expense—an expense that is growing due to the rising costs of medical care, and the longer life expectancy for Americans. Spending on food (14%), transportation (9.1%), and clothing (5%) round out the top categories, while other expenditures (30.5%) completes our picture of how we spend our money.

MAXIMIZING UTILITY: GETTING THE MOST FOR YOUR MONEY

Utility is a measure of how much satisfaction you get from consuming a good or service. By looking at the utility of goods you are better able to decide which uses of your money will give you the highest amount of satisfaction.

Utility

Joshua likes donuts, jelly donuts in particular. He also likes apples, but not as much as jelly donuts. Let's use this information as a starting point for our study of utility. Let's also assume that the price of a jelly donut and the price of an apple are each $.50. If Joshua had just $.50 in his pocket, and had to choose between buying a jelly donut or an apple, which would he choose? Based on what you know about his tastes and preferences, you've probably guessed correctly—he would choose the jelly donut! In economic terms, Joshua receives higher utility from the consumption of a jelly donut than he does from an apple.

Marginal Utility

Suppose Joshua had time to sit down at the coffee shop to enjoy a jelly donut with a cup of coffee. After eating the first jelly donut he decided to buy another. It also tasted good but, after having already eaten one donut, the second one wasn't quite as satisfying as the first. In other words, the utility, or satisfaction derived from the second donut was less than the utility gained from eating the first. How much less? Now we need a unit of measurement—a "util"—to compare the satisfaction of eating the first donut with that of eating the second donut. A util is a unit of utility. Economists know that assigning a number of utils to the consumption of a good is not scientific, and that the number of utils would vary from person to person. But utils will help us to illustrate an important point about consumer behavior. For our case, let's assume that when Joshua ate his first jelly donut he received ten units of satisfaction, or ten utils. When he ate his second jelly donut, however, he received only six additional units of satisfaction. Thus, the additional utility, also called the **marginal utility** (MU) of eating the second donut, is six utils. In economics, the term "marginal" usually refers to the additional or next unit. The total amount of satisfaction, or total utility (TU) gained from eating the two donuts, measured in utils, is 16.

Diminishing Marginal Utility

Because the second donut added just six utils to Joshua's overall satisfaction—compared to ten utils for the first donut—economists say that the utility is diminishing. **Diminishing marginal utility** occurs when the consumption of an additional unit of the same good—in this case jelly donuts—offers less utility than the consumption of the previous one.

If Joshua decided to linger for a while longer at the coffee shop he might order additional jelly donuts—a third, a fourth, and a fifth. And if he ate them all right there at the coffee shop diminishing MU would continue. The third donut gave Joshua a little more utility, perhaps two utils. Thus, while the marginal utility dropped from six utils to two utils, his TU actually rose by two utils, from 16 utils to 18 utils. But this was not so with the fourth donut. Eating the fourth donut added nothing to Joshua's overall satisfaction. In this situation, the MU was zero, and his TU remained the same. As he forced himself to eat the fifth donut he began to feel sick. That is, by eating the fifth donut Joshua experienced negative MU of four utils. In this situation, his TU dropped from a high of 18 utils to 14. A summary of Joshua's experience with utility is shown in Figure 4.3.

Getting the Most for Your Money

Fortunately you don't have to choose between eating one donut or eating five donuts. In making economic decisions there are few black or white choices. Instead, there are many shades of gray. Your choice can be any number of donuts, or none at all. By looking at the marginal utility—the additional satisfaction or benefit—of eating additional donuts you can make better choices about the use of your money. Your goal is to get the greatest amount of satisfaction from each dollar that you spend. In Joshua's case, he certainly could have spent his money more wisely. The MU of his third, fourth, and fifth donuts were very low—the fifth donut even reduced his TU! The $1.50 Joshua spent on these final three donuts surely could have been spent on items with a higher MU, such as a soda later that night at the movies, or video games at the mall. Marginalism refers to people's decisions to purchase an additional unit of a good, to work an additional hour, or to produce an additional unit of output. In economics, many decisions are made "at the margin."

THE ROLE OF ADVERTISING IN CONSUMER DECISION MAKING

Advertising is a paid announcement by a firm. It is designed to provide information about a product to consumers, and to persuade them to purchase the product. In 1996 $173 billion was spent on advertising in the United States according to the *Statistical Abstract of the United States*. The six major types of media used in advertising were television (24%), newspapers (22%), direct mailings (20%), radio (7%), the Yellow Pages (6%), and magazines (5%). Other forms of media accounted for the remaining 16%. By the late 1990s advertising on the Internet had begun. While still in its infancy, Internet advertising allows the advertiser to count the number of people who see the ad. It also is able to measure those who click through to get additional information from the firm's

Figure 4.3
Utility from Jelly Donuts

Number of Donuts	Total Utility	Marginal Utility
0	0	0
1	10	+10
2	16	+6
3	18	+2
4	18	0
5	14	−4

Web page, and even to see how much of the product people bought as a result of the ad.

Thousands of advertising agencies operate in the United States to create advertisements. Ad agencies combine the art and the science of advertising to create a message colorful enough to hold your attention. This applies to all types of ads—TV commercials, print ads, and so on. To accomplish this goal advertisers conduct research that assists them in the use of advertising appeals and techniques. Informed consumers should be able to recognize these appeals and techniques.

Advertising Appeals

Advertising appeals try to influence buying decisions by targeting consumers' emotions, fantasies, reason, or other feeling. The four main types of appeals include the rational appeal, sex appeal, humor, and a variety of emotional appeals. As the name implies, the rational appeal centers on the consumer's reason, logic, and intellect, and tends to explain ways that the product can improve the buyer's life. Sex appeal connects the advertised product with sexy people and exciting lifestyles, and hints that by purchasing the advertised product the buyer could experience a similar lifestyle. Humor creates comical situations or actions that the consumer then associates with the product. Emotional appeals relate the product to the consumer's psychological needs such as the need for acceptance, friendship, or love. This appeal might also focus on the consumer's fears of failure, personal inadequacies, or loneliness. Often, an advertisement uses more than one appeal to attract the consumer's attention.

Advertising Techniques

Advertising techniques are the specific strategies that advertisers use to strengthen their appeals—to make them believable. Advertising techniques include:

- testimonial, which uses a trusted or popular person—often a celebrity—to endorse the product;
- bandwagon, which asks the consumer to join the crowd by purchasing the product;
- cardstacking, which lists a number of positive features or benefits of the product;
- comparison, which shows the advantages of the advertised product over similar substitute goods;
- demonstration, which shows how the product works, or how the product can improve your life;
- problem solving, which shows how the product can fix a problem, or prevent one from occurring;
- scientific test, which provides impartial evidence that your product can deliver on its claims;
- symbolism, which builds trust in a brand name, usually by connecting the product with a logo or trademark; and
- life-style, which associates the product with a way of life compatible with that of likely buyers.

CONSUMER SKILLS: BECOMING A WISE SHOPPER

After you graduate from high school you may head off to college or to work. You will be more independent and more responsible for your own financial affairs. Two important consumer skills that you will need are how to budget your money, and how to comparison shop for products.

Your Personal Budget

Your personal budget is your plan to balance your monthly income with your monthly expenses. To create your personal budget, list your monthly income on the left-hand side of the budget. Next, on the right-hand side of your personal budget, list your anticipated expenses. Some expenses do not change from month to month. These are called "fixed expenses" and include such items as your car payment, rent for your apartment, and car insurance payment. To help you prepare for unexpected expenses, you should also put a portion of your income aside in a savings account and, thus, treat savings as a fixed expense. The other monthly bills are called "flexible expenses," which can vary from month to month. Food, for example, is a flexible expense. This doesn't mean that you can choose to go without food. It simply means that the kind of food that you buy can be changed to fit a tight budget. Other typical flexible expenses include your purchases of clothing, entertainment, long-distance telephone service, and electricity.

To complete your personal budget you must add all sources of income in the left-hand column, then do the same for all of the expenses in the right-hand column. If your income is equal to or greater than your expenses, you should be able to run your household. If your income is less than your expenses, you have a choice to make—either earn more income or reduce some expenses. By devising a personal budget you will see clearly the types of choices that must be made as you work to pay your bills.

Comparison Shopping

Comparison shopping occurs when a consumer considers the purchase of alternative goods to satisfy a need. It is one of the best ways to stretch your scarce financial resources. Consumers comparison shop for goods and services all of the time. There is one caution—the least expensive product may not be the best buy for you.

When comparison shopping you want to compare the quality and price of one product with those of substitute goods. You also want to check on the warrantees that come with these products. Suppose you wanted to buy either a traditional VCR or one of the newly marketed digital VCRs for your new apartment. Before you buy either a comparison must be made. With the traditional VCR you can tape your favorite programs for replay at your convenience, and play movies that you rent or those you already own. The price of the VCR is reasonable, in part, because a number of companies are competing for your business. The new digital VCRs, which were introduced to the American market by pioneering companies such as Replay Networks and TiVo in 1999, have the features of the traditional VCRs plus some. With a little simple programming the digital VCR can scan local program schedules for your favorite shows, actors or actresses, directors, and so on and then automatically record them during the week—two at the same time if necessary. Nice features! But will you use these features? Are you willing to trash your existing video collection? Can you afford the more expensive digital VCR?

Before we leave the topic of comparison shopping it is important to mention the role of warrantees in your buying decision. A warrantee is a written guarantee of the product, its components, its lifespan, and its performance. Federal laws state that the seller must explain the terms of the warrantee to you when you buy a product. You should be familiar with different kinds of warrantees, however. Here are a few questions you might ask the seller. First, which parts of the product are covered under the warrantee? Many warrantees list a number of exemptions—parts that are not covered. Have the seller point these out to you. Second, under what conditions is the warrantee null and void? For example, will the warrantee still be in effect if you misuse or neglect the product? Third, how long is the warrantee in effect? Remember, the length of a warrantee might be stated in units other than time. A car's warrantee might cover three years or 30,000 miles—whichever comes first! Fourth, if the product breaks down, who will repair it? Will the seller service the product, or does it have to be mailed back to the manufacturer? Who pays for the mailing or transportation costs if a product is sent to the manufacturer for repair? And is the labor included in the warrantee, or are just the parts under warrantee?

THE CONSUMER: PAWN OR KING?

Over the decades there has been debate over who really decides the "what to produce" question in the U.S. economy. In the 1950s and 1960s economists such as Vance Packard, author of *The Hidden Persuaders, The Waster Makers,* and numerous other books, claimed that producers reigned supreme in the American marketplace. Advertisers, he argued, create demand for goods and services. Hence it was business that answered the "what to produce" and "how to produce" questions. Popular as this theory was at the time, mainstream economists today hold a very different view of the consumer's power in the American economy. That is, they believe that consumer sovereignty is the norm. The consumer's power stems from his power to cast "dollar votes" for a product by purchasing it, or against a product by purchasing a substitute instead.

To demonstrate the power of the consumer, consider Ford Motor Company's Edsel—an automobile that was introduced to American consumers in the fall of 1957. Ford constructed an Edsel plant, solicited over a thousand car dealerships to sell the car, and spent a terrific amount of money on advertising, yet it flopped in the marketplace. Why? The specific reasons are still a mystery even today. What can be said is that consumer tastes and preferences were not swayed by the extensive advertising campaign that accompanied the Edsel. Another legendary flop was the introduction of New Coke in the 1985. The Coca Cola Company spent millions of dollars on advertising to convince the American consumer that by changing its 99-year-old formula the company had created "the best Coke ever." Instead, the change in formula created a consumer rebellion, and the original Coca Cola was returned to store shelves as Coke Classic. Later, the production of New Coke was quietly discontinued. The consumers spoke, and these firms listened!

CONSUMER RIGHTS AND CONSUMERISM

In the early 1960s the consumer movement, or consumerism, was born. **Consumerism** combined the efforts of government, consumer groups, and individuals to work in the interests of American consumers. Most of the efforts of consumerists were designed to protect consumers from unhealthy or unsafe products, or from misleading or false advertising and sales practices. Some consumerists also targeted the business practices of natural monopolies such as utility companies, environmental problems resulting from production, and excessive interest rates charged to borrowers.

Consumerism was given a boost by President John F. Kennedy in the early 1960s. In his 1962 "Special Message to the Congress on Protecting the Consumer Interest," President Kennedy outlined four basic consumer rights. These rights included the right to safety, the right to be informed, the right to choose, and the right to be heard. With the support of President Kennedy and other public officials, a path was cleared for the consumer movement to grow.

Economic Thinkers: Ralph Nader—Giving Consumers a Voice

Ralph Nader (1934–　) was one of the early champions of the consumer movement in the United States. As a consumer activist since the 1960s, Nader investigated cases of consumer abuse, instigated action against offenders, and lobbied Congress for legislation to protect consumers.

Ralph Nader became a national celebrity in the mid-1960s when he published his landmark book *Unsafe at any Speed* (1965). In this book Nader attacked the General Motors Corporation for producing dangerous cars and for withholding safety problems from the public. After Nader testified before Congress on auto design flaws, Congress passed the National Traffic and Motor Vehicle Safety Act in 1966, which increased the government's say in the design of cars produced in the United States. A couple of years later he organized youth groups that were comprised mainly of college students to investigate the action—or inaction—of the federal government to correct consumer abuses. These student groups soon took on the nickname, "Nader's Raiders," and operated under the Nader's Center for Study of Responsive Law.

In 1971 Nader organized Public Citizen, Inc., a consumer lobby group dedicated to protecting the basic consumer rights named by President Kennedy nearly a decade earlier. While controversial at times, Nader's voice rang through the offices of business leaders and elected officials alike and, in doing so, reinforced the individual's right to instigate change in our democratic society.

Consumer Protection

Did you ever have a consumer complaint? Most likely you brought the complaint to the attention of the business that sold you the product or provided the service. This is an excellent first step in resolving a personal consumer problem. But what about larger concerns you might have about a product's safety, or products that do not live up to the advertiser's claims? What can you do?

Virtually every state has an office or bureau of consumer protection. If you suspect fraud or illegal activities such as the "bait and switch" sales technique, you might also contact the Attorney General in your state. Bait and switch is an illegal practice that lures the unsuspecting consumer into a business with a low-priced advertised product. The salesperson immediately switches your attention away from the sale item to a higher-priced item, which you are then pressured to buy. Local officials are in the best position to handle these types of complaints.

The federal government also has a number of agencies and departments that can be contacted depending on the nature of the complaint, including:

- The Consumer Product Safety Commission (CPSC), which investigates products that have posed a danger to people, including items such as unsafe baby cribs, toys with detachable parts that could be swallowed, and flammable fabrics. The CPSC has the power to ban the sale of dangerous products and can order a recall of dangerous products. In 1999, for instance, the CPSC ordered the recall of more than 19 million dive sticks because they impaled some children who dove to retrieve them in pools. Certain makes of Star Wars Lightsabers—products that became very popular after the release of the movie *Star Wars: The Phantom Menace* in 1999—were also recalled because some children were burned by them. In 2000, recalls were ordered for some Tommy Hilfiger socks because the logo might detach and become a choking hazard for infants. In 2000, the CPSC, in cooperation with Burger King, asked consumers to "immediately destroy and discard" Pokemon balls that had been distributed by Burger King in the fall of 1999 (choking hazard).

- The Federal Trade Commission (FTC), which deals with complaints involving fraud, price fixing, false or misleading advertising, and abuses of consumer credit laws.

- The U.S. Postal Service, which deals with any questionable business practices or schemes that are carried on through the mail, including unordered items sent to you. Did you know that you can keep unordered merchandise as a gift?

- The Food and Drug Administration (FDA), which deals with complaints or concerns involving the nation's food supply, drugs and other medications, and cosmetics; and

- The U.S. Office of Consumer Affairs, which serves as a clearinghouse for consumer complaints, an advocate for consumer legislation, and a source of information for citizens on a variety of consumer topics.

Private Organizations

There are also a number of private groups at work to protect consumer interests. Perhaps the best known private, non-profit organization is The Consumers Union of the United States. You might already be familiar with this organization through its popular magazine, *Consumer Reports*. Because *Consumer Reports* accepts no advertising, it can investigate consumer issues and evaluate the effectiveness of many consumer goods without being pressured by major advertisers. Millions of consumers purchase this monthly magazine to see how specific goods or services are rated—whether they are good buys, acceptable, or poor. In this way, *Consumer Reports* helps people get the most for their money.

Closer to home, there are a number of local non-profit groups that might assist you with consumer issues, questions, or complaints. Most cities or regions have a local Better Business Bureau (BBB). The BBB is sponsored by local businesses. Among its functions are to provide information to people about local firms, and to keep track of consumer questions and complaints. Some even offer consumer education programs. Another local business association is the Chamber of Commerce. While the local Chamber of Commerce is mainly concerned with promoting business interests, it is aware of the importance of favorable relations between businesses and the consumers they serve.

Finally, there are many professional associations comprised of people who work in a specialized occupation. These associations are designed to improve the profession, the skills of members, and their public image. Many doctors, for example, belong to the American Medical Association (AMA), and lawyers belong to the American Bar Association (ABA). These associations are sensitive to public opinion and care about how they are perceived by consumers. Directly related to our study of consumer behavior is the American Advertising Federation (AAF), which has issued a Code of Ethics for the nation's advertisers. Stressed in this code are truth and decency in advertising. In a sense, professional associations are self-policing in that they try to ensure a high standard of performance for all members.

MAKING ECONOMIC DECISIONS: BUYING A CAR

In most cases the largest buying decision you will face as a teenager will be buying a car. Let's apply the personal decision-making process that you were introduced to in chapter 1 to this major purchase.

Your first step in the decision-making process is to define the problem. In this case, your problem is that you need a car and, at the moment, you don't have one. The second step is to identify the alternatives. The alternatives in this case refer to different makes and models of cars, both new and used. The third step is to establish a number of criteria for your purchase. That is, what goals or expectations do you have for the car? In this case you have listed nine criteria. These criteria should serve as a checklist as you comparison shop for the car. They include:

- Gas mileage: You may want a car that gets at least 30 miles per gallon, especially as gas prices climb.
- Reliability: You may need the car to get you to work, to class, and so on. Can it get the job done?
- Appearance: You want to drive a car you are comfortable in. Can it satisfy your "tastes" in an auto?
- Safety features: You may want a car that has dual air bags, lap belts and shoulder harnesses, and that stands up well in crash situations.
- Warrantee: You may want a warrantee that will cover most parts and labor costs for at least six months after the purchase.
- Quality of service: You may want to build a relationship with the service department, for repair work and routine maintenance on the car. Does the auto dealership have a quality service department?
- Price: You have limited resources. Can you afford to make the monthly payments on the car?
- Related costs: How much will the monthly auto insurance cost you? How much will the yearly property tax be?
- Resale potential: You may want to use this car as a "trade-in" at some point in the future. How well does the car hold its value over time?

Step 4 in the decision-making process is to consider how well each alternative meets the nine criteria. Recall that each of the criteria may be weighed differently. Which criteria are the most important to you? Is there a single criterion—price, for example—that could automatically disqualify one or more of the alternatives? Step 5 is to make your decision! In all likelihood, your final selection may be the car that satisfies most, but not all, of your criteria. But by having the checklist of criteria in place before you begin shopping, you can better assess the strengths and weaknesses of each option.

5

HOW ARE GOODS AND SERVICES PRODUCED?

Chapter 5 examines how goods and services are produced and distributed in the American economy. The chapter begins by reminding us that production can only take place by using the factors of production—natural resources, human resources, capital goods, and entrepreneurship. Businesses use these factors efficiently in order to increase production and the productivity of their workers. This makes good economic sense as these factors are not free resources. Instead, they represent the costs of production that businesses must incur. While production enables us to enjoy a wide variety of goods in the American marketplace, economic development sometimes comes into conflict with another social goal—protecting the natural environment.

THE FACTORS OF PRODUCTION

The **factors of production** are the resources that are used to produce goods or services. These factors of production include natural resources, human resources, capital goods, and entrepreneurship.

Natural Resources

Natural resources, or land, are the gifts of nature that are used in production. Take a look around you. You might be sitting in a classroom or in a library right now. The wooden desks, chairs, book shelves, and paper you are writing on, and the pages in this book—even the wood on your pencil—comes from trees, a natural resource. If you are using your solar powered pocket calculator to work on a math assignment, it might be powered by sunlight coming through the window. Because the sunlight helped produce your education, this gift of nature is a natural resource. Similarly, the aluminum trash can sitting in the corner of the room probably came from bauxite, and the steel pencil sharpener near the doorway used iron ore. These minerals are also natural resources.

In recent years the use of some natural resources has become controversial. Much of the controversy centers on the use of renewable and nonrenewable resources. As the name implies, **renewable resources** can be replenished. That is, these resources such as plants, animals, sunlight, and the wind are replaced by nature. **Nonrenewable resources**, on the other hand, are simply used up in the production process. Significantly, the supply of nonrenewable resources is also fixed. You may enjoy the warmth of your classroom during the winter months, but if your school is heated with oil, coal, or natural gas, once the supply is depleted it needs to be replaced with a fresh supply. Recent Earth Day activities illustrate people's concern for their environment. As a guideline for the conservation of these finite resources people can practice conservation, reuse rather than replace goods, and recycle products such as glass, paper, and plastic.

Human Resources

Human resources, or labor, represent the human element in production. Traditionally when we think of "labor," physical effort comes to mind. In our usage of the term, labor also includes intellectual efforts of people. At your school there are many productive human efforts that show the manual and intellectual labor of workers. The custodians' manual labor provides a valuable service to the school by attending to its cleanliness. The cafeteria staff's manual labor provides necessary food services for students and staff. The teachers, counselors, social workers, and administrators perform mainly intellectual labor in the production of your education.

Nations look to both the quantity of labor and the quality of labor in their economies. The quantity of labor is measured by the size of the labor force. In 1999, according to the Bureau of Labor Statistics (BLS), the U.S. labor force totaled 139.3 million workers. The labor force is comprised of those who are employed and those actively seeking employment. The BLS also reported that the U.S. employment rate, or percentage of the labor force working, was 95.8% in 1999, while the unemployment rate was 4.2%. Strange as it may sound, this 4.2% unemployment rate is considered better than "full employment" (see chapter 2). The quality of labor refers to the skills and attitudes of the workers. In the U.S. economy, for example, the 97% literacy rate is one indicator of a competent labor force. In addition, one-quarter of the entire labor force has a bachelor's degree or more, and more than 80% of the labor force has at least a high school diploma. Other factors that contribute to a quality work force include a sound work ethic, proper diet, availability of health services, a well-developed infrastructure, and intensive training in the use of new technology.

Capital Goods

Capital goods, or capital, are items made for the purpose of producing other goods. If you take another look around your classroom, there are numerous examples of capital. You wouldn't be very comfortable sitting in the classroom without a desk and chair. The desk and chair assist in the production of your education and, therefore, are capital goods. Other capital goods nearby include the school's computers, VCRs and monitors, and the classroom pencil sharpener. Tractors, harvesters, office buildings, subways, taxicabs, and department stores are other examples of capital goods.

For resources to be productive they must be used. "Having" and "using" capital resources are not the same thing. The "capacity utilization rate" measures how much of the nation's capital is actually being used. During times of recession, the capacity utilization rate typically dips beneath the 80% mark. For example, the *Economic Report of the President* reported that the capacity utilization rate had dipped below 75% during the recession of 1982. The capacity utilization rate has averaged over 82% from 1992 to 1999. Are economists worried about the 18% of the nation's capital that is idle? The answer is no. Routine maintenance on plants, retooling, and other natural down times account for much of the 18%.

Entrepreneurship

Entrepreneurship represents the actions of innovators in an economy who create new products, new ways to produce products, or new firms. Entrepreneurs recognize opportunities in the marketplace, and then act on this insight. Many of the advances in our material well-being stem from the creative energy of entrepreneurs. When you walked into the classroom this morning you most likely turned on the lights. In part, you can thank Thomas Edison, an entrepreneur who not only invented the light bulb but also pioneered the whole concept of a research laboratory—a place where investors, scientists, and even entrepreneurs could develop their ideas. By the turn of the century, Henry Ford was applying his entrepreneurial skills by adapting the concept of the moving assembly line from meat production to car production. In doing so, Ford was able to produce quality automobiles for the average American.

So what personal qualities make the entrepreneur successful? While it is difficult to offer a formula for entrepreneurial success, entrepreneurs are confident in themselves, persistent, organized, achievement oriented, and willing to accept responsibility for business successes and failures.

Economic Thinkers: Steven Jobs, the Entrepreneur

Steven P. Jobs (1955–   ) is among the best known, and most successful business-persons in the United States. As an inventor, corporate CEO, and entrepreneur, Jobs has been an agent for change in the computer industry since the 1970s and, today, in animated motion pictures.

Steven Jobs co-founded Apple Computer with Steve Wozniak in the mid-1970s, a process economists call "venture initiation." By the late 1970s Jobs and Wozniak had introduced a novel product—the personal computer—to the American market-place. It was called the Apple II. Apple had fired the first shots in a spirited battle for consumers' dollar votes for this new product. Soon, rival IBM launched its own comparably priced personal computer, the PC.

Jobs, now working from the inside of the established Apple corporation, responded by assembling the "Mac Team"—a talented group of computer whiz kids whose job it was to build a sophisticated, but easy-to-use successor to the Apple II. The "Mac Team," aided by Jobs, created the Macintosh. This type of innovation from within an existing company is often referred to as "intrapreneurship."

Jobs was ousted from Apple in 1985, but returned to Apple as interim CEO in 1997. His mission was to rescue the failing corporation. Again assembling a talented and energetic team, Jobs returned Apple to profitability with its flashy, Internet-friendly iMac. Steven Jobs, the entrepreneur, helped change the face of the computer industry in the United States and in the world. The history of Apple is the history of product innovation, but then again, isn't this what you would expect from an entre-preneur?

PRODUCTION COSTS

The factors of production are used by firms to produce goods and services. But these resources are not provided to firms for free. They must be paid for.

The Costs of Production

The **costs of production** are the payments made in exchange for the factors of production. If you have a job, for example, you exchange your labor for a wage or salary. Your labor is a factor of production. The wage is the firm's cost of production. Wages and salaries are the largest category of costs to the firm. But there are three other costs of production—rents, interest, and profits. Rents are payments made by firms in exchange for land or other properties that the firm uses. Interest represents the payments that firms make for money they borrow in order to buy capital—new equipment, the factory or farm, or machinery. Profits, in this context, represent the extra money that must be paid to the entrepreneur. Entrepreneurs take above-average risks, and expect above-average profits if they are successful.

Recording Production Costs

When people make a household budget, they often separate their fixed expenses from their flexible expenses. In much the same way firms tend to divide their expenses, or costs, into categories. These include fixed costs and variable costs.

Fixed costs (FC) are the costs that do not change as the rate of output changes. Imagine for a moment that Grandbars, Inc. has a plant in your town. The fixed costs—those that remain constant regardless of how many Grandbars are produced—would include the rent on properties used by Grandbars, interest payments to creditors, local property taxes, and insurance premiums.

Variable costs (VC) are the costs that change as the rate of production changes. The two most important variable costs are wages and materials. Materials might be natural resources or "intermediate goods"—goods that have already been processed so they can be assembled onto a larger product.

To distinguish between FC and VC, suppose consumer demand for Grandbars is expected to jump from 10 million to 15 million units next month. Extra workers must be hired, and more materials—in this case raisins, caramel, peanuts, and assorted grains—must be purchased to reach the new production goal. What happens to the costs of production for Grandbars, Inc.? Despite an increase in the rate of production—from 10 million to 15 million Grandbars—there is no change in the FC. This is because the FC are constant no matter how many Grandbars are produced. The VC will change, however, because additional wages must be paid to the new workers, and additional payments to the suppliers of materials must be made. If you add the firm's FC to its VC, this equals the firm's **total costs** (TC).

THE PRODUCTION PROCESS

Production occurs when firms transform the factors of production into goods or services. The production of goods and services is a complex process. Generally, there are five interrelated components of the production process—product design, process design, plant design, job design, and management design. Let's apply these five elements in the production process to Better Athletic Shoes (BAS)—a firm that produces quality sneakers for the competitive athlete.

Product Design

Product design is the process of transforming an idea into a marketable good or service. At this stage of production, the firm determines the features and benefits of the product. Suppose BAS designs a new sneaker for competitive high school and college athletes. The "features," or physical composition of this sneaker, would include a good quality of leather, extra supports for arches, and other materials that make a quality product. The use of expensive materials to make this product is acceptable because the competitive athlete expects to pay a high price for sneakers. The "benefits" of a product are the things the product can do for the athlete. The new BAS sneaker could stress comfort and how it would contribute to the player's performance on the court.

Process Design

The process design illustrates how the firm will make the product. BAS must decide on what machines and equipment are necessary to produce a quality sneaker and on how this equipment should be arranged within the plant. It would be poor planning if BAS machines designed to test the strength of the stitching were placed ahead of the leather cutters and sewing machines. Obviously, the strength of the stitching can't be tested until after the cut leather is sewn together. BAS also needs to decide on the degree of mechanization its plant will employ. If BAS anticipates a large demand for its sneaker, it can be mass produced using the traditional assembly line method of production, or the more sophisticated robotized techniques. One advantage of using robots is that computers are used to control the machinery. This allows BAS to make changes in the product design more easily.

Plant Design

The plant design considers the structure of the building, as well as its size and location. The structure of the building considers the "process" needs as well as the general appearance of the facility. That is, the building must be suited to the type of machinery and the number of workers employed. The plant's size is determined by the anticipated demand for the product. If BAS expects to sell 1 million pairs of sneakers per year, the amount of machinery and the number of workers must be up to this task. Finally, finding the best location for the building is important. What makes a location suitable? Most firms consider the costs of land and materials, the availability of skilled workers, access to transportation, and tax breaks or other incentives offered by local authorities. If the firm is selling its goods directly to consumers, as in the case of a department store or a supermarket, the building must also be conveniently located for consumers.

Job Design

The job design refers to the types of jobs workers will do. During much of the 20th century many manufacturing jobs in the United States were done along an assembly line. Under this job design, each worker performed a specific, repetitious task day in and day out. Automation changed some workers' responsibilities in the industrial sector by replacing routine jobs with machines or robots. Under these conditions, the job design changed so that more highly skilled workers were needed to operate and to program the machines. In today's service-oriented workplace, many additional changes are occurring in the job designs of employees including flexible hours, the ability to work at home, and team approaches to tasks. Many of these new methods of production are enabled by the use of computer technology.

Management Design

Management is responsible for coordinating workers, machines, and resources into an efficient production unit. In many smaller businesses, usually sole proprietorships and partnerships, the owners of the firm also manage it. In larger corporations, ownership and management are separated. The owners of corporations are the stockholders, while the managers are hired professionals such as the Chief Executive Officer (CEO), President, and a series of Vice Presidents (see chapter 6 for the differences in these businesses). During the first half of the 20th century the most widely used management design was based on "scientific management," which was introduced by Frederick Winslow Taylor (see Economic Thinkers: Frederick Winslow Taylor). Today, however, the management designs for most workplaces have rejected the authoritarian nature of Taylorism. In its place are styles of management that encourage participation and teamwork. This new approach still deals with the traditional problems of purchasing resources at reasonable prices, managing inventories of these resources and finished goods, and ensuring that quality controls are in place—to evaluate the final product and the quality of workers' performance in making the product (see chapter 14 for more on management).

Economic Thinkers: Frederick Winslow Taylor and Scientific Management

Frederick Winslow Taylor (1856–1915), also known as the "father of scientific management," helped give birth to a new profession in the U.S. economy—the "efficiency engineer." In his *Principles of Scientific Management* (1911), Taylor explained how to organize resources—including labor—to increase efficiency.

Taylor's studies often involved little more than keen observation of a production process and a stopwatch. With these tools he organized production around a complex **division of labor**—a system whereby workers specialize in a narrow range of tasks in the larger production process. For example, on an assembly line Taylor could break down virtually any job into smaller pieces and then rearrange the pieces in a more productive way. His practical experience came not from a classroom, but from the floor of a Philadelphia machinist shop where he worked in the early 1880s. Under Taylor's system of scientific management the time required to perform even the smallest task was calculated, and then each worker's job was integrated into the larger production process. Soon, the terms "scientific management" and "Taylorism" were being used interchangeably.

Taylor had an enormous influence on production in American factories for decades and his "time and motion" studies produced some dramatic gains in efficiency. But scientific management also treated laborers more like machines than people. While the management design for many firms today differs from those of the early century, Taylor's scientific management helped establish the United States as the world's leading industrial nation.

PRODUCTIVITY

Firms try to use their resources efficiently. Economists measure a firm's efficiency by calculating its productivity. **Productivity** is the amount of output that is produced by a firm, per unit of input (factor of production). In most cases economists figure a firm's productivity in terms of the labor "input." This is why they often speak of the "productivity of labor."

Production and Productivity

Production and productivity are sometimes confused. The rate of production simply refers to how much of a good is produced. If BAS, Inc. produced 100,000 pairs of sneakers last month, we can say that the firm's production was 100,000. Productivity, on the other hand, refers to the amount of a product that is produced per unit of input, such as labor. If BAS employed 100 workers last month, then we can say that its productivity is 1,000 pair of sneakers per worker (100,000 pairs of sneakers divided by 100 workers = 1,000). Productivity can be measured in any unit of time—in hours, days, weeks, or longer.

Now suppose that another 100 workers are hired by BAS and, as a result, the total production of sneakers jumps to 150,000 pairs of sneakers. Did production increase? Yes, by 50,000 pairs of sneakers. Did productivity increase? No! It actually fell to 75 pairs of sneakers produced per worker during the month (150,000 pairs of sneakers divided by 200 workers = 75).

Increasing Productivity

Increasing productivity is an important goal for firms and nations. This is because higher productivity means that a greater amount of goods and services can be produced with the same, or even lesser amounts of resources. As a result, scarce resources can be conserved, and people's standard of living—measured by the availability of goods and services in the economy—can rise.

One way to increase productivity is by increasing the nation's capital stock. The **capital stock** is the total amount of capital goods that a country has to produce goods and services. In the private sector, firms that employ sophisticated capital increase each worker's output. We could reasonably predict that if the precision cutting of leather, and the stitching of these pieces of leather in the BAS plant were done by machine, the job could be done faster and with fewer workers. Productivity, measured in output per worker, would increase because the rate of production increased while the number workers—the inputs—decreased. The government's investment in capital—roads, airports, seaports, railway service, and so on—also improves productivity by making it easier for firms to conduct normal business operations.

Another way to increase productivity is by investing in the skills of workers. Firms do this by providing proper job training, particularly in the use of new technology such as computer systems. Many business functions, from keeping track of inventories to tabulating business receipts, have been made more efficient through technology. The government also encourages the development of workers' skills by providing public education for its people, subsidizing public universities, offering worker training or retraining programs, awarding research grants, and the like.

A third way to increase productivity is through specialization. **Specialization** occurs when individuals, firms, regions, or nations, produce a narrower range of goods in which they have a natural advantage. In a nation the size of the United States there are many regions with varied resources that encourage specialization. Alaska, for example, has oil. New York does not. It makes sense, therefore, for Alaska to develop its oil industry and for New York to produce something else. The government can assist specialization by promoting international trade. There are some products that Americans want that can be produced more efficiently in other parts of world such as bananas from Central America or coffee from Brazil. Trade with other nations encourages them to specialize and allows American firms to make better use of their own resources.

The productivity of labor has increased steadily during the 1990s. According to the Bureau of Labor Statistics, the productivity of the Amer-

Figure 5.1
U.S. Productivity, 1990–1999

1990	1991	1992	1993	1994	1995	1996	1997	1998	1999
+1.3%	+1.5%	+4.3%	+0.1%	+1.3%	+0.7%	+2.9%	+2.2%	+2.8%	+3.0%

Source: Bureau of Labor Statistics.

ican worker increased every year during the 1990s, with some of the healthiest productivity gains coming in the later part of the decade. These productivity gains are shown in Figure 5.1. Part of this success can be attributed to the booming economy of the 1990s. But the positive changes in the American workplace, including an estimated $2 trillion investment in computers, software and other technologies during the 1990s, have made the U.S. economy the envy of the world.

DISTRIBUTING PRODUCTS

When we enter a department store, a grocery store, or a specialty store we expect the shelves to be well stocked with our favorite products. There are several channels of distribution that help bring us the goods that we demand.

Channels of Distribution

A **channel of distribution** is the path that a product travels to move from the producer to the consumer. The path may be a long one, with "middlemen" assisting in the move, or it may be a direct path from the producer to the buyer.

For many goods, manufacturers rely on middlemen to handle the distribution of their products. A major jeans producer, for example, might produce 10 million pairs of jeans in a year. Instead of trying to sell the jeans to individual consumers around the world or to individual stores, the producer sells the entire supply to a wholesaler. Wholesalers are businesses that buy huge quantities of goods, and then move them to the next stop—the retailer. The wholesaler's profit comes from the fee it charges for distributing the goods. Retailers, who purchase the jeans from wholesalers, also add a sum to the price before they sell the jeans to consumers. Some of the nation's leading retailers include Sears, WalMart, and JC Penney.

Other channels of distribution are shortened by cutting out one or both of the middlemen. Producers, for example, might sell directly to large retailers and by-pass the wholesaler completely. Or, in some instances, the producer might be able to sell the product directly to the consumer through factory outlet stores or even local markets. Before deciding which channel of distribution is the best one to use, the manufacturer considers the type of product that it produced, the distance to the intended market, and the cost of transporting the product. Our jeans producer, for example, makes a product with wide appeal. Thousands of retailers, large and small, might want to sell this brand of jeans. Because of the huge market size, and the distance the product might have to travel to reach the consumer, it is likely that the producer would employ the services of a wholesaler. A local producer of vegetables, on the other hand, may be able to sell the vegetables directly to the consumer at local farmer's markets or even from a vegetable stand at the farm itself.

Channels of distribution are also used by businesses to get the resources they need for production. This channel of distribution starts with a producer of raw materials and ends with a producer of goods. Many agricultural products are purchased this way. Wholesalers, for example, purchase huge amounts of wheat from thousands of independent farmers (the resource producer). Then the wholesaler re-sells the wheat to producers of bread, pastries, cereals, health bars, and other products that use wheat as an ingredient.

In recent years some of the traditional channels of distribution have been altered by technology. Today, the use of the Internet's "on line" shopping has permitted an immediate link between the producer, or other supplier of goods, and the consumer. Some people have already grown accustomed to shopping for goods and services as varied as books, airline tickets, antiques, and clothing on the Internet. Other innovations have included direct marketing through catalogs. For twenty years, this popular way of shopping is as easy as using your credit card to phone in an order. A few days later the order arrives in the mail— but be prepared to pay additional shipping and handling costs! Also growing in popularity during the 1990s have been the club warehouses, which sell a limited variety of goods at low prices. To shop at a club warehouse you must be a member, which usually requires a small annual fee. BJ's and Sam's Club are a part of this growing discount market that blurs the distinction between wholesaler and retailer.

MAKING ECONOMIC DECISIONS: ECONOMICS AND THE ENVIRONMENT

The production of goods and services is essential to our standard of living. If production stopped, no one would have a job, no products would be produced, and the entire economy would grind to a halt. While everyone agrees that the economy must produce products, there is less agreement about how much destruction of the natural environment can be tolerated as a result the production process. Two recent cases are representative of the conflict between economic development and the environment.

Production versus the Environment

Pollution is a side-effect of many types of production. There are many types of pollution including water pollution, air pollution, and land pollution. The problem of acid rain creates all three types of pollution.

Acid rain occurs when factories and automobiles spew sulfur and nitrogen oxides into the atmosphere. When these gases mix with water vapor, acid rain is formed. Acid rain is carried by the wind often for hundreds or even thousands of miles. It falls to the earth with the rain, snow, hail, or fog. When it hits the ground, it contaminates the soil, robbing it of its nutrients. It also kills wildlife, trees and other vegetation, and even the fish in lakes. Humans are directly affected by the health hazards connected to acid rain. It destroys crops, contaminates drinking water, and corrodes homes or other structures. To complicate the problem, emissions from U.S. firms and cars have created the acid rain that has been swept by the winds into neighboring Canada. Economists refer to this situation as a social cost of production. **Social costs** occur when a neutral third party—in this case Canadians—is harmed by pollution that it had no role in creating. Economists sometimes refer to social costs as "negative externalities."

For decades the acid rain issue has been a sore spot in relations between the United States and Canada. Canada wanted this pollution to stop. In 1990 a revision of the landmark Clean Air Act (1970) identified acid rain as a problem that had to be reduced. Soon many U.S. producers had agreed to restrict their pollution to specific levels. The acid rain issue continues to spark controversy, and more permanent solutions to the problem—such as the installation of smokestack scrubbers or the burning of low-sulfur oil and coal—will be expensive. Hence, there must be a trade-off. Do we want higher prices for some goods and services in the United States, or do we want a cleaner environment? Think about it. As a future voter you may help decide this issue.

Production versus Endangered Species

During the 1990s the conflict between the logging industry and the survival of an endangered species—the northern spotted owl—revived the debate about acceptable versus unacceptable consequences of production.

The logging industry is an important part of the economy of the northwestern section of the United States. Thousands of jobs rely on logging directly. Many thousands of additional jobs in related industries—such as home construction—also rely on the supply of lumber. Home construction, in turn, creates demand for home appliances, furniture, and other household products. Needless to say, Americans place high value on the many uses of timber produced by loggers.

Americans also place high value on the preservation of the environment, and the plant and animal life living in the natural environment. In recent decades particular attention has been paid to species of wildlife that have become endangered—the bald eagle, the buffalo, the grizzly bear, and the northern spotted owl. In 1990 the U.S. Fish and Wildlife Service placed this owl on the threatened species list and thereby extended to the owl protection under the Endangered Species Act. What this meant was that additional acres of forests—about 3 million additional acres of private, state, and federal forests—would be closed to the logging industry in order to protect the spotted owl's natural habitat.

In economics it is easy to measure the price of a piece of wood. You can drive to the nearest lumberyard and see the price, usually calculated by board foot. The price of the wood is influenced by its type and quality. But this type of price calculation is not possible with wildlife. What is a northern spotted owl "worth"? The fact is, we cannot assign a price to an owl. But the northern spotted owl still has value to us. While controversial, the decision to limit the harvesting of trees in the Pacific Northwest raises an interesting point about our economy. That is, price and value are not the same. Some things that we value have a high price tag, a Mercedes for example. Other things that we value don't have a price tag, such as our enjoyment of a scenic landscape or a spotted owl. The challenge is to preserve what we value, whether or not it has a price tag, in an informed manner.

6

HOW ARE BUSINESSES ORGANIZED?

Chapter 6 discusses the three main types of business organizations—sole proprietorships, partnerships, and corporations. Each type of business has advantages and disadvantages. The chapter also examines franchises and other forms of business organization—including cooperatives and nonprofit organizations. Recent issues involving business organizations are addressed, including the recent wave of mega-mergers, the rapid pace of downsizing in American industry, and the business practices multinational corporations (MNCs).

THE FIRM

All economies face the same three basic economic questions of what to produce, how to produce, and for whom to produce (see chapter 2). In the American mixed economy the private sector—individuals and firms—are mainly responsible for answering these basic questions. The consumer answers the "what to produce" question by casting his "dollar votes" for certain products. Firms answer the "how to produce" question by making production decisions (see chapter 5).

Firms

A **firm** is an organization that uses the factors of production to produce goods or services that consumers want. The terms "firm" and "business" can be used interchangeably. There are about 22.5 million firms operating in the U.S. economy.

An **industry** is the entire group of firms that produce a similar product. For example, the Coca Cola company is a firm. The Coca Cola and Pepsi Cola companies are two of the dominant firms in the carbonated soft drink industry. The only time you might consider a firm and an industry to be the same is in the case of a monopoly (see chapter 7).

Suppose you were an entrepreneur who wanted to start a business. Which type of business organization would you establish—a sole proprietorship, a partnership, a corporation, or a franchise? Let's view the advantages and disadvantages of each to help you make a decision.

SOLE PROPRIETORSHIPS

A **sole proprietorship** is a business that is owned by one person. The owner of a proprietorship may be the only employee, perhaps operating a small convenience store, barbershop, or specialty shop. Or, the owner may hire many employees to staff a larger business such as a restaurant, an auto service station, or a home construction enterprise. The sole proprietorship is the most common type of business in the United States. According to the Internal Revenue Service (IRS) nearly 16.5 million sole proprietorships operate nationwide—that's 73% of all firms! Because proprietorships are typically smaller firms, however, they account for only about 5% of all sales in the United States. For our convenience, say that you are interested in starting a gourmet coffee shop in town. At this specialty shop, "Coffee 4 All," you will sell many varieties of coffee beans. Let's see some of the advantages and disadvantages of becoming the sole proprietor of Coffee 4 All.

Advantages

The sole proprietorship is the easiest type of business to form. To set up Coffee 4 All you must comply with local zoning laws, which tell you where the firm can or cannot be located in your town. You also discover that state and local authorities have standards for cleanliness that your firm must follow because you are selling a food product.

Another advantage to the proprietorship is your ability to make decisions quickly. You are the owner and the boss! This gives you the authority to make virtually all business decisions about how to organize your shop and sell your gourmet coffee beans. It also gives you an enormous sense of satisfaction when the business prospers.

Finally, as the owner of Coffee 4 All you are in line to reap all of the profits from the sale of your product. Profits occur when your firm's total revenues are higher than its total costs. This is your reward for starting the business! As an added bonus, the tax rates for proprietors are lower than they are for corporations. This allows you to keep a larger percentage of your profit than the owners of corporations can.

Disadvantages

Proprietorships are not particularly easy to finance. This is because banks are hesitant to extend a loan to you unless you are willing to put up some collateral—most likely your home—as a guarantee that you will repay the loan. But borrowing money to cover initial expenses such as rent payments for the shop, wages for your employees, and so on is common for proprietors.

Next, you have unlimited liability. This means that if Coffee 4 All does fail, you as the proprietor are personally responsible for all of the firm's debts. If your firm fails you may have to sell your house, or dig into your personal savings account to pay your creditors.

Finally, you cannot be an expert in all phases of running a business. That is, as the proprietor you will make decisions about hiring and firing workers, keeping enough office supplies on hand, monitoring inventories, attending to customers in the shop, making deliveries on schedule, keeping records, paying taxes, and so on. Suppose you fall ill or are involved in a serious accident that prevents you from doing your job for weeks, months, or longer. What would happen to the business? Because the success of the sole proprietorship rests mainly on the shoulders of the proprietor, proprietorships are considered the least stable type of business organization.

PARTNERSHIPS

A **partnership** is a business that is owned by two or more people, each of whom has a financial interest in the firm. The types of firms that ordinarily form into partnerships are very similar to those that become sole proprietorships. Professionals often form into partnerships such as law firms and medical practices. Partnerships are also common in the skilled trades areas such as plumbing, home construction, and electronic repair services. In the United States today there are about 1.6 million partnerships, or 7% of all businesses. Like sole proprietorships, partnerships tend to be smaller than corporations and, thus, account for just 5.5% of the total sales of goods and services in the U.S. economy.

There are two main types of partnerships—the general partnership and the limited partnership. In a "general partnership" the partners are involved in running the firm and, therefore, share in the day-to-day decision making. In a "limited partnership," some of the partners run the firm while others simply invest money in it. If you were considering a partnership for your new firm, Coffee 4 All, a necessary first step would be to draw up a "partnership contract" between you and your partners. Expert legal advice is needed to specify the responsibilities of each partner, to determine how the firm's profits will be distributed, and to state how you will dissolve the firm if things just don't work out.

Advantages

Partnerships are fairly easy to organize. Certain zoning and licensing codes must be complied with, but the paperwork is fairly simple. Your partnership contract should also be drawn up before the business opens. It is also easier to get the start-up funding for a partnership than it is for a proprietorship. For example, you could take on one or more silent partners to supply the necessary funds. You are also more creditworthy in the eyes of the bank because the collateral that you and your partners can bring to the table is greater than that of the proprietor.

Secondly, decision making is more expert in a partnership than that in a sole proprietorship. Each of your partners will, most likely, bring a special talent or skill to the firm. If Coffee 4 All is organized as a partnership different partners may be skilled in customer service, accounting and payroll, maintaining inventories and supplies, and so on. And if each partner performs as you expect, all can achieve the sense of pride and accomplishment that is derived from owning a successful business.

Finally, you realize that the fruits of your labor—the firm's profits—belong to you and to your partners. Your share of the profits, and that of your partners, was carefully spelled out in the partnership contract. And your tax rates, like those of the proprietor, are lower than those faced by corporations.

Disadvantages

One disadvantage is that partners in a general partnership have unlimited liability for business losses. In this respect you have the same disadvantage as the proprietor. But in a partnership you are also responsible for the business debts of your partners. This is a sobering thought as you consider possible partners for Coffee 4 All! On a related note, also consider that if you create a limited partnership, your silent partners have limited liability. That is, the most they can lose in this business venture is the amount they originally contributed to it. Creditors cannot come knocking at their doors for the debts that you have created.

Another disadvantage of a partnership is that disagreements among partners can reduce the stability of the firm. Ideally, the partnership contract should specify each partner's role in the firm. But this piece of paper cannot account for your partners' personality or other character traits. Suppose one of your partners decides that his voice is more important than yours in the decision-making process, or one or more partners are slacking off? These questions concern you as you consider the best structure for your firm.

CORPORATIONS

A **corporation** is a business that is a legal entity in itself. In a corporation, ownership of the firm (stockholders) is separated from the operation of the firm (management). Many types of firms organize into corporations, such as manufacturing companies, financial institutions, retailers, and so on. There are about 4.5 million corporations operating in the United States, which is about 20% of all business firms. Corporations account for about 90% of all sales of goods and services, however, which makes the corporation the dominant form of business enterprise in the country.

The division between owners and management occurs because a corporation sells shares of itself to many investors. These shares are also called stocks; hence stockholders are the owners of the corporation. Because there are so many stockholders, they select a Board of Directors to oversee and set goals and policies for the corporation. The Board of Directors, in turn, hires professional management to run the company. The top official in most corporations is the chief executive officer (CEO). Beneath the CEO in the chain of command is the company President, followed by a series of Vice Presidents—each of whom has a specific responsibility in the production, marketing, or distribution of the good. It has been said that corporations are like people—no two are exactly the same. There is some truth to this statement. The CEO and the President, for example, might be the same person. One corporation may have six vice presidents while another might have a dozen. There is no "correct" structure for a corporation.

Advantages

One advantage to starting a corporation is that start-up funds are easier to get. Corporations are the only form of business organization that can raise funds by selling stocks and bonds to investors. If you sell stock in Coffee 4 All, you are selling a piece of your company to somebody else. This is because stocks represent ownership in the corporation. If, on the other hand, you sell bonds to investors you are simply borrowing money from them. This is because bonds represent debt—the corporation is the debtor and the investors become its creditors.

Secondly, expert managers can be hired to run the business—the CEO, President, and Vice Presidents in charge of production, marketing, and so on. And you, the founder of the firm, might occupy an important position on the Board of Directors—perhaps even "chairman" of the board.

A third advantage is limited liability for the stockholders. That is, the maximum amount of money that you could lose in your business is the amount that you invested in it. If Coffee 4 All is organized as a corporation your home and personal assets are protected.

Next, your financial rewards can be substantial—if the firm is profitable! You can see three ways to make money if you start a corporation. The first is through stock ownership. As the founder of Coffee 4 All you most likely reserved a number of shares for yourself, and sold the rest to investors. These shares offer dividends to investors, including you, when the firm earns profits. Dividends are the regular payments made to investors by profitable corporations. The higher the firm's profits, the more the firm can afford to distribute in dividends. Stock ownership offers a second way to earn money—capital gains. Capital gains represent the difference between the purchase price of a stock and its selling price. When an investor sells a stock for more than its purchase price, the investor earns capital gains. A third way you might reap financial rewards is through the ownership of corporate bonds. Bonds pay interest to investors (see chapter 10 for more on stocks and bonds).

Finally, a corporation is the most stable type of business. This stability comes from the wide distribution of the firm's stock. What does this mean for Coffee 4 All? Because many people own shares of your company, sickness, accidents, even the death of a stockholder, have no impact on the company itself. If a stockholder dies, the shares of stock are simply passed along to the stockholder's heirs.

Disadvantages

One disadvantage is that forming a corporation is a complex process. You first must apply to your state government for "articles of incorporation." This application lists some of the details about your proposed business including what it will produce, where it will be located, how start-up funds will be raised, and who can be contacted if problems arise. Legal fees and other expenses could also be substantial.

A second problem is the length of time it takes for a corporation to make decisions. Corporate decisions are sometimes examined and re-examined at different levels of the corporation—by department heads, by vice presidents, and so on. As the corporation grows you, like other investors, might also feel less attachment to the business. This is because stockholders contribute nothing to the actual production of the good. Thus, there is little sense of satisfaction or pride in your personal contribution to the firm's success.

Third, taxes on corporate profits are higher than the taxes on the incomes of proprietors or partners. Consider your tax burden if you own stock in Coffee 4 All. First, corporations pay corporate income taxes on the firm's profits. Once these taxes have been paid, the corporation's after-tax profits can be distributed to shareholders in the form of dividends, or can be kept by the firm as "retained earnings" (to reinvest in the business). But what happens when these dividends are distributed to investors? The dividends are taxed again! This is because dividends are a type of income for people, and income is subject to the federal personal income tax. Economists sometimes refer to this as "double taxation" because the same corporate profits are taxed twice. And if at some later date you sell your stocks for a profit, a capital gains tax is in place to let you share your good fortune with the government (see chapter 11 for more about taxes).

Corporations: Going Public, Going Private

According to the Commerce Department corporate profits in the United States totaled $818 billion dollars in 1997—$572 billion after taxes. Of this sum, shareholders received $275 billion in dividend payments. During the 1990s advances in the value of many stocks have added trillions of dollars to the paper wealth of investors on the nation's stock markets. So why are some corporations so happy and others so glum about their status as publicly traded corporations?

Corporations can choose to sell stocks to the general public, or can choose to restrict the sale of stock to a small group—perhaps to the members of a family. For some the decision to "go public"—to sell stocks to the general public—provided the necessary funds with which to build profitable corporations. To go public, corporations issue an Initial Public Offering (IPO). An IPO places a specific number of stocks up for sale. Investor demand for the stock then sets the price per share—when demand is high the stock's price increases, and when the demand is low the stock's price falls (see chapter 10 for more on trading stocks). CEOs and other executives can put aside large quantities of stocks for themselves also—a practice that has created enormous personal fortunes for the founders of these companies. These fortunes are part of the reward for their entrepreneurial skills, risk-taking, and business savvy. Bill Gates, for example, earned the lion's share of his $80 billion or so fortune through his holdings of Microsoft stock!

For others, such as Black Entertainment Television's (BET) founder and CEO Robert L. Johnson, the stresses and unpredictability of the stock market was more a hindrance than an asset. After spending most of the 1990s as a publicly traded corporation, Johnson reversed the process—and took BET Holdings "private" once again. To accomplish this feat, Johnson purchased all outstanding BET shares at $63 each in 1998. In Johnson's view, the increased scrutiny of analysts and others on Wall Street was not compatible with his ambitions to create what he called "black America's brand of choice." The flagship of BET Holdings remains its profitable cable channel BET. But Johnson's entrepreneurial vision is much grander—to tap into black America's $500 billion in annual spending for other goods and services including restaurants, hotels and casinos, magazines, clothing, skin care products, financial services, and more. In his view, this vision can better be achieved on his own without the distractions of investors, and Wall Street analysts, looking over his shoulder.

FRANCHISES

A **franchise** is a business that uses a parent company's name to sell a product while maintaining a degree of independence from the parent. The parent company is called the "franchisor," and the person opening one of these satellite firms is the "franchisee." To set up a franchise, a franchise contract is drawn up between the franchisor and the franchisee. This contract specifies quality standards for the product, service standards for management and employees, and the financial conditions under which the franchise is formed and operated. The franchisor, after all, must be certain that its reputation is protected as the franchise chain expands.

A franchisee takes certain business risks, just like other entrepreneurs do. But thousands of entrepreneurs have chosen to set up shop as independently owned and operated franchises. For example, there are tens of thousands of gas stations operating under parent companies such as Mobil, Getty, and Citgo. Many thousands of franchisees have also entered the fast-food industry under such familiar names as McDonalds, Burger King, Wendy's, KFC, Subway, Taco Bell, and Domino's Pizza. You might be interested in becoming a franchisee one day. Before you sign a franchise contract, consider the advantages and disadvantages of this type of business organization.

Advantages

One advantage is that franchises are fairly easy to organize. Like other businesses, the franchisee must abide by local zoning rules. Negotiating the specific terms of your contract with the franchisor should also be a routine task because the franchisor, most likely, has a standard set of expectations for all franchisees who join the franchise chain. As an added bonus, your creditworthiness typically gets a boost from being associated with a major franchise chain such as McDonald's, Radio Shack, or H&R Block. The franchisor may even help you finance the start-up costs for your business. This is important because the range of start-up costs runs from thousands of dollars to hundreds of thousands of dollars.

Secondly, franchisors offer technical assistance to franchisees. This type of assistance includes the training of a franchisee in effective management techniques, linking the franchisee with suppliers of materials or resources that are needed in production, and so on. And you are still the boss, entitled to the same inner satisfaction felt by successful proprietors or partners.

A third advantage is immediate name recognition. Franchisors spend freely on national advertising and marketing for their product line. The purpose of this advertising is to promote sales for the entire franchise chain, and you benefit from this publicity.

Disadvantages

One disadvantage is your obligation to pay a franchise fee to the franchisor. "Franchise fees" vary from firm to firm, but the dollar amount—which could be measured in a percentage of the franchisee's profits—is clearly stated in your franchise contract. These fees, coupled with the start-up costs, represent a considerable sum of money.

Finally, the stability of the business falls on the back of the franchisee. In this respect, the franchisee shares a burden similar to that of the sole proprietor. What would happen to the firm if the franchisee suffered from a prolonged injury or sickness? As was the case with all other types of businesses, there are no guarantees of success.

OTHER FORMS OF BUSINESS ORGANIZATIONS

Two additional types of businesses also have an important role to play in the U.S. economy: cooperatives and nonprofit organizations. One feature of these types of business organizations that immediately stands out is that they are not organized to earn profits! This sets them apart from all other types of businesses where profit is the primary motive for their existence.

Cooperatives

A **cooperative**, or co-op, is a voluntary association of people that conducts a business activity to serve its members rather than reap a profit. Members of co-ops usually belong to a group, such as producers within a certain industry, workers in a labor union, or the like. In addition, members of co-ops are usually required to pay a small fee to join the co-op. Co-ops exist all around us. For example, a food co-op allows members to shop at the co-op store, where prices for some food items are lower than those at supermarkets. Agricultural co-ops help members negotiate better prices for their output. Financial co-ops, such as credit unions, permit members to deposit and borrow money, write checks (called share drafts), and conduct other financial transactions. You may even bump into a consumer co-op at college. Many bookstores on college campuses are organized as student co-ops.

Nonprofit Organizations

Nonprofit organizations provide important services to people, but do not do so for profits. Because they do not seek profits, issue stock, or pay dividends, they are exempted from paying taxes to Uncle Sam! Many groups involved in charitable, humanitarian, or community service activities are nonprofit organizations. Examples include the American Red Cross, the Cancer Society, and the Boy Scouts and Girl Scouts of America. It may seem strange to think of these organizations as "producers," but they all use resources to provide goods and services. And while profit is not their incentive to produce, the fact that they continue to thrive—mainly on voluntary donations—hints that Americans value what they produce!

CURRENT ISSUES IN AMERICAN BUSINESS

There has been no shortage of controversial issues in the realm of business and business practices during the 1990s. Two of the biggest controversies of the period include the costs and benefits of corporate mega-mergers and corporate downsizing.

Corporate Mega-Mergers

A **merger** occurs when two corporations are legally joined under single ownership. During the late 1990s an unprecedented wave of mergers between major firms, or "mega-mergers," occurred. In fact, in a one year period (1998–99), deals were struck for the ten largest mergers in the history of the United States. Multibillion dollar mega-mergers were negotiated in many industries—Chrysler and Daimler-Benz ($41 billion) in the auto industry, Mobil and Exxon ($86 billion) in the oil industry, Sprint and MCI ($129 billion) in communications, and BankAmerica Corp. and NationsBank Corp. ($62 billion) in banking, to name a few. The $93 billion merger between Pfizer and Warner Lambert in the pharmaceutical industry in early 2000 signaled that the wave of mega-mergers was continuing into the 21st century.

Supporters of mega-mergers tend to focus on five main benefits. First, mergers increase efficiency by eliminating costly duplication of facilities and personnel. Secondly, costly building projects can be avoided by expanding the firm through a merger, rather than by building new facilities. Third, a skilled work force is already in place in the merged plants, thus eliminating the need to hire and train new workers. Fourth, because of its larger size, it may be easier for the merged firm to raise additional money by selling bonds or issuing new stock. Finally, larger firms may be more competitive in international markets. That is, to compete against the industrial giants of Europe and Asia, American firms need more size and muscle.

Opponents of the recent wave of mega-mergers paint a different picture. They argue that mega-mergers result in plant closings, unemployment, and related economic hardships for individuals and their communities. Opponents argue that plant closings are inevitable because merged firms must eliminate duplicate facilities—and personnel—for efficiency reasons. In addition, opponents argue that because of the enormous size of corporations involved in mega-mergers, competition in U.S. markets is reduced. As a consequence, they forecast that less competition will result in higher consumer prices in the long run.

Downsizing

Downsizing is the process a firm goes through to eliminate waste and become more efficient. Downsizing has gone by several names since the mid-1980s. Firms sometimes refer to this process as restructuring, or streamlining. By the late 1980s and early 1990s American industry had embraced downsizing as a necessary step to restore the competitiveness of American products in world markets. This concern to increase competitiveness was fueled by intense foreign competition, particularly in key industries such as automobiles, motorcycles, steel, televisions, textiles, and electrical equipment.

Supporters of business downsizing argue that its main benefit is increased productivity (see chapter 5). Inefficient plants or departments within the firm are systematically downsized or even shut down. Firms in many industries have downsized during the 1990s. Among the largest was General Motors. GM closed plants and laid off thousands of workers in the early 1990s. Supporters argue that a modern, dynamic economy must adapt to new consumer demands, new competition, and new technologies. Downsizing is viewed as one way to become "leaner and meaner" in pursuit of these goals.

Opponents focus on the costs of downsizing, especially unemployment. During the 1990s millions of workers lost their jobs—678,000 in 1998 alone! Some of these lost jobs were due to downsizing. Also consider the related costs. When plants close down there is less taxable property in towns and cities, thus local governments collect lower tax revenues. Lower tax revenues, in turn, translate into reduced public goods or services—such as financial support for schools, police and fire protection, and so on. Other likely costs to communities include lower business revenues for local merchants, reduced donations to local charities or civic organizations, and an increased crime rate.

MAKING ECONOMIC DECISIONS: CLEANING UP THE IMAGE OF MULTINATIONALS

A **multinational corporation** (MNC) is a corporation that has production facilities in more than one nation. Most often, a MNC's headquarters is located in an industrialized nation. The spread of MNCs into the less industrialized nations of the world—also called developing nations—has been a source of controversy since the 1960s.

One issue concerns the treatment of foreign laborers by MNCs. For decades there have been concerns about the harsh treatment of child labor and the use of political prisoners as slave labor in some countries. More recently, the working conditions, wage rates, and length of the work week have been added to the list of concerns. These labor concerns have captured the attention of American labor unions, which see job competition with inexpensive foreign labor as a threat to their members' livelihoods. These concerns have also sparked protests from human rights activists and local authorities in developing nations.

Many prominent companies from the United States and from other industrialized nations invest in the developing world. The advantages of locating in these nations vary—but most look to use the less expensive resources in these countries, including inexpensive labor. The benefits of cheap labor are rather obvious. Lower resource costs contribute to lower production costs. And, in competitive markets, these cost savings to firms typically mean lower prices for consumers.

By the late 1990s the images of some MNCs were tarnished by reports of mistreatment of their foreign laborers in faraway places—like China, Vietnam, and other nations. In many cases the abuses involved subcontractors hired by major MNCs. Subcontractors are firms contracted to produce goods for another firm. The abuses included substandard pay, 16-hour work days, and authoritarian bosses. Most sensitive to these criticisms were MNCs that produced consumer goods because these firms rely on good relations with consumers. The most famous consumer outcry against worker exploitation occurred in 1997, when activists organized protests against the Nike corporation and its subcontractors and staged a widely publicized consumer boycott against Nike products. Similarly, subcontractors that produced toys for Disney and for Mattel— America's largest toy producer—were criticized because of alleged abuse of workers. A public relations nightmare resulted, and these businesses had to decide how to deal with the crisis.

Some MNCs in 1998 and 1999 actively investigated the reported abuses of workers and took action to prevent future problems. It was just plain good business sense to make the needed reforms. For example, both Disney and Mattel made significant improvements in the working conditions in their plants, and created written "codes of conduct" to guide business practices. They also arranged for regular inspections, called "social audits," of their overseas plants. Similarly, Nike initiated new policies to improve wages and working conditions—especially in the realm of safety procedures—and to reduce the number of hours laborers were required to work. To MNCs, it seems the benefits of these reforms have outweighed the costs.

7

HOW DO BUSINESSES COMPETE?

Chapter 7 examines the four main types of market structure in the U.S. economy—perfect competition, monopolistic competition, oligopoly, and monopoly. The term market structure deals with the number of firms in an industry and how competitive the industry is. For the past century the government has sought to protect competition in the American mixed economy through antitrust laws and regulations. While U.S. antitrust rules have supported competitive markets within the United States, they do not apply to non-competitive business practices by other nations—including the actions of the Organization of Petroleum Exporting Countries (OPEC)—the world's most powerful cartel.

MARKET STRUCTURES

Market structure refers to the way an industry is organized. The main feature used to separate one market structure from another is the degree of competition that exists in an industry. The most competitive market structure is perfect competition, while the least competitive is a monopoly. Six characteristics are used to determine an industry's market structure, including:

- the number of buyers (consumers) and sellers (firms) in the industry
- the type of product produced by the industry (identical or differentiated)
- the amount of information available to producers and consumers about the market and the product

- the ease of entry into the industry and exit from the industry
- the role of government in the industry
- the degree of market power (control over price) held by individual firms in the industry.

PERFECT COMPETITION

Perfect competition is a "model" market structure in which thousands of firms, acting independently, produce an "identical" good to sell to consumers. The forces of supply and demand are the major determinants of which goods firms will produce, and at what price. In reality, no industry completely satisfies all of the requirements of perfect competition. There are a number of industries in the agricultural sector of the U.S. economy that resemble this model, however. To examine a perfectly competitive industry, let's begin at Kevin's corn farm in Kansas.

Thousands of Sellers and Buyers

Kevin's 5,000 acre farm is one among thousands of farms that produce corn. In fact, while 5,000 acres is a large area to cultivate, it is a tiny portion of the 73 million acres of U.S. farmland that is devoted to growing corn. Let's assume that Kevin's farm can produce 125 bushels per acre which, according to the Department of Agriculture, is about the national average. This means that Kevin's total output of corn is 625,000 bushels (125 bushels × 5,000 acres). This is an impressive number of bushels, but it is a very small percentage of the overall corn production in the United States. U.S. corn producers harvested over 9 trillion bushels of corn per year in the mid-1990s—more than any other nation in the world! Kevin could stop producing corn today and it wouldn't make a noticeable dent in the nation's overall supply.

Identical Products

Kevin is also aware that the corn that his farm produces is identical to the corn produced by his neighbors in Kansas, and by farmers in Iowa, Nebraska, and elsewhere. The production of identical products—sometimes called homogeneous products—is a second feature of the perfectly competitive industry. Because there is no difference between his corn and that of other producers, buyers have no preference for one farmer's corn over another farmer's corn. This information is important to Kevin because when it comes time to sell his crop buyers will expect to pay the same price for corn, regardless of who produces it.

Perfect Information

The third feature of the perfectly competitive industry is that information about the market and the product is available to producers and consumers. Producers, for example, have the same information about production methods, new technology in agriculture, advances in high-yield seeds, and so on. This information comes from many sources including farm equipment producers and dealers, farm journals and bulletins, the mass media, and the government. They also know the current market price for corn. Consumers of corn are also well informed about the quality of the product, its availability, and price through many of these same sources. Because Kevin's corn is identical to other corn, he does not need to provide this information to consumers through advertising.

Easy Entry and Exit

A fourth characteristic of the perfectly competitive industry is the ease with which firms can "enter" or "exit" the industry. Currently, Kevin's farm is producing corn. If profits from corn production rise dramatically this season, Kevin can expect additional firms to "enter" the corn industry during the next growing season. Conversely, if profits from corn production fall, it is reasonable to predict that some farmers that had previously produced corn would "exit" the industry and grow a different crop. Economists say that there is an easy entry into and exit from perfectly competitive industries because there are no significant "barriers to entry" in these industries. A **barrier to entry** restricts or even prevents firms from entering an industry.

Small Role of Government

The role of government is slight in a perfectly competitive industry. Usually, government regulations seek to prevent firms from unlawfully organizing to set prices or restrict supplies of a product. Because there are thousands of independently operating firms in a competitive industry, there is little chance that any firm or combination of firms will be able to dominate the industry.

No Market Power

Finally, firms in perfectly competitive industries have no market power. That is, individually, they have no control over the price of their output. Instead, firms in competitive industries are "price takers." Price takers must accept the market price for the goods they produce. In Kevin's case, the market price for corn is determined by the overall supply of corn produced by thousands of farmers across the nation (the market supply) and the overall demand for corn by both individuals and firms (the market demand). The intersection of the supply and demand curves for any product—including corn—determines the market or equilibrium price (see chapter 3). If Kevin tries to increase profits by raising the price of his corn, consumers will simply buy corn from another producer.

In reality, American agriculture strays from the perfect competition model in a number of ways. It is common, for example, for U.S. farmers to organize farmer's cooperatives. These co-ops are designed to increase the bargaining power of farmers—the producers of corn and other agricultural products—in their negotiations with major buyers of agricultural products. By allowing the co-op to bargain on behalf of a group of farmers, Kevin and other members of the co-op increase their market power. On the buyer's side of the market, wholesalers also purchase corn and other agricultural products in large quantities. This increases the buyer's bargaining power and control over prices in much the same way as the co-op does for farmers.

MONOPOLISTIC COMPETITION

Monopolistic competition is a type of market structure in which many firms produce differentiated products. "Differentiated" products are goods or services that are similar, but not identical. In a monopolistically competitive industry, firms actively compete for the consumer's dollar votes. Many industries in the United States are monopolistically competitive, including the industries that produce fast-foods, cosmetics, clothing, soap, and high school textbooks. Let's examine a monopolistically competitive industry through the eyes of Clara, a restaurant owner in a small Florida city.

Many Sellers and Buyers

In a monopolistically competitive industry there are many sellers and buyers of a good or service. What does "many" mean? In Clara's case, her business is one of 50 restaurants in her area. If Clara had opened her restaurant in Miami, "many" would have been a much larger number of restaurants because Miami is a larger city.

Differentiated Products

Clara is also aware that product differentiation is important to her success. She differentiates her product by producing a fine Italian cuisine and superior service. Clara also advertises in the local newspapers and in the Yellow Pages of the telephone book. These print advertisements differentiate her product by emphasizing the strengths of her restaurant—good food and superior service. In other industries products can be differentiated through the use of logos or trademarks, which are symbols used to represent a product. Athletic equipment and clothing, for example, is often marked with the symbols of competing firms such as Nike, Adidas, Converse, Wilson, and others. On the national level "product differentiation" is important if a firm wants to create consumer loyalty to its brand name.

Good Access to Information

A third feature of a monopolistically competitive industry is that sellers and buyers have access to a good deal of information about the market. Producers like Clara have a reasonably good idea about the costs of production incurred by rival firms in the industry, and the price that competitors are charging for their output. Clara, like other restaurant owners, researches the costs of the ingredients that go into her dinners and purchases quality ingredients from the lowest cost supplier. Clara also gathers information about competitors' prices, special offers, discount coupons, menu choices, and so on from their advertisements. Clara then uses this information to adjust her menu or prices. On the national level, it is common to see firms in larger monopolistically competitive industries behave as Clara does. For example, advertisements for McDonald's, Burger King, and Wendy's often try to differentiate their products, and offer price discounts or other promotions to get your business.

Relatively Easy Entry and Exit

A fourth characteristic of a monopolistically competitive industry is the relative ease of entry into and exit from the industry. Clara owns and manages a successful restaurant, but she has seen restaurants come and go. This is because in a monopolistically competitive industry, individual firms face few barriers to entry. Their investment in capital, natural resources or intermediate goods (semi-finished goods), and labor is minimal compared to the larger firms.

Small Role of Government

In monopolistically competitive industries the role of government is slight. This is because no one firm in the industry has the ability to control prices or otherwise distort the market. Clara's firm, for example, is one of 50 restaurants in her area. While she can alter her product and prices some, she has no influence on the output or prices of rival firms. Thus, there is little chance that Clara, or other firms in monopolistically competitive industries, will be involved in anti-competitive behaviors.

Limited Market Power

A sixth feature of a monopolistically competitive industry is that firms in the industry have limited market power. That is, these firms have some influence over the price they charge for their product. This limited control over price occurs because these firms produce differentiated products, not identical products. Clara, for example, understands the value of distinguishing her food and service from that of other restaurants as a way to create a loyal clientele. Similarly, when major firms are able to create brand loyalty to the product they are likewise able to exert more control over prices.

OLIGOPOLY

Oligopoly is a type of market structure in which a small number of firms produce most of the industry's output. There are two different kinds of oligopolies. Firms in a "pure oligopoly" produce an identical product, steel or copper for example. Firms in a "differentiated oligopoly," on the other hand, produce differentiated products such as breakfast cereals and automobiles. Let's continue our comparison of market structures by examining why the U.S. auto industry is a differentiated oligopoly.

Few Firms

The single most important feature of an oligopoly is that a small number of firms dominate the industry's production. Again there is the problem of defining what "small number" of firms actually means. Most economists tend to define oligopolies as having from three to a dozen firms that produce 70% or more of the industry's output. For many years the U.S. domestic auto industry (automobiles produced by American firms) was dominated by the "Big Three"—General Motors, Ford, and Chrysler. By the late 1990s the picture was clouded by two major mergers. In 1998 the German auto giant Daimler-Benz merged with Chrysler, creating DaimlerChrysler. In 1999 Ford Motor Company purchased the auto division of Sweden's Volvo. So, what does this do to the market structure of the U.S. auto industry? Some economists would say that just two major U.S. auto producers remain, GM and Ford, and that this "oligopoly" has turned into a "duopoly"—a lesser used term to describe a market structure in which two major firms dominate an industry. Other economists would broaden the field by including all of the world's major auto firms into the oligopoly, with the world's five dominant firms leading the way—GM, Ford (with Volvo), Toyota, DaimlerChrysler, and Volkswagen.

Differentiated or Identical Products

A second feature unique to oligopolies is that they can produce differentiated products or identical products. The auto industry is a good example of a differentiated oligopoly because the major car producers each produce a wide variety of automobiles in economy, mid-sized, and luxury classes. Further, the auto giants have numerous "divisions" within the company, each trying to carve a niche for itself with consumers. The Ford Motor Company, for example, produces and sells cars not only under the Ford name, but also under the names of each of its divisions—Aston Martin, Jaguar, Lincoln, Mazda, Mercury, and now Volvo. In the case of a pure oligopoly, a few major firms produce an identical (homogeneous) product. Pure oligopolies in the United States include copper, aluminum, steel, and flat glass.

Limited Information

A third feature of an oligopoly is that "oligopolists"—the major firms in the industry—are better able to withhold information from competitors. Rival oligopolists are secretive about many aspects of their production, believing that the less their competitors know the better. In the U.S. auto industry, for example, if GM is able to buy its parts in greater quantities than its rivals, GM will likely pay a lower price per part. This is true in many business dealings in the economy—buying in bulk is often cheaper than buying in lesser quantities. GM will guard this information, and other secrets related to its costs of production, new auto designs, and pricing. Why is secrecy so important? In an oligopoly there are just a few producers, and the competition among them is fierce. By guarding information related to its products, GM may gain an advantage over its rivals with innovative changes in design, accessories, warrantees, financing options, or other factors that sweeten the sale. Of course, once the product is released for sale to consumers, GM will advertise heavily to inform consumers about the features and benefits of its product.

Difficult Entry or Exit

A fourth feature of an oligopoly is that it is difficult for a new firm to enter the industry, and also difficult for an existing oligopolist to exit the industry. This is mainly due to high barriers to entry—factors that restrict or prevent entry into an industry. Some major barriers to entry include the high costs for capital goods, research and product development (R&D), and skilled labor. Another barrier is **patents**—legal protections granted by the government to inventors, researchers, or others who develop new products or processes. In short, it is very expensive for a new firm to break into an established oligopoly such as the auto industry. On the flip side it is also difficult for a firm to exit from an oligopoly to produce a different product for many of the same reasons. The expense of converting plant and equipment, retraining a work force, developing new technology, applying for new patents, and so on would be staggering.

Larger Role of Government

The role of the government increases in an oligopolistic market structure. This is because the government must guard against anti-competitive behaviors by oligopolists. For example, "rival" oligopolists might engage in **collusion**—an illegal practice where "competing" firms work together to make production and pricing decisions. If unchecked, collusion would allow oligopolists to increase their prices and profits by acting like a single company. Federal watchdogs, such as the Federal Trade Commission (FTC) and the Antitrust Division of the Department of Justice, monitor oligopolies to ensure that collusion does not take place.

Greater Market Power

A sixth feature of an oligopoly is that the market power of rival firms is substantial. Part of the reason for this increased influence over price is that oligopolists are free to respond to their rivals' prices, or changes in prices. It is common practice, for example, for rival oligopolists to use "price leadership" to set the price of a product. If GM announced that its new economy car will sell for $10,000 this year, Ford and Daimler-Chrysler might follow GM's price lead and charge about the same price. Ford and DaimlerChrysler might also decide not to follow GM's lead, however, and price their basic economy cars at $9,000. As you might imagine, GM would have to respond quickly to this lower price by reducing its price or by offering rebates (cash-back offers). If GM did not respond, many consumers would choose to buy the less expensive Ford or DaimlerChrysler cars because they are substitute goods for GM's economy car. Thus, while an oligopolist has some say in the price of its product, it must always look over its shoulder to see what its rivals are doing!

MONOPOLY

Monopoly is a type of market structure in which one firm produces virtually all of the industry's output. Economists sometimes say that because one firm is so dominant, the firm is the industry. We will discuss the four main types of monopoly in the next section of this chapter.

One Firm

The most striking feature of a monopolistic market structure is that a single firm produces all, or nearly all of the industry's output. Historically, leading industrialists such as John D. Rockefeller (see Economic Thinkers) created monopolies through mergers, acquisitions, cut-throat competition, and other tactics. Today, most monopolies operate in the United States simply because it is more efficient for one large firm, such as an electric power company, to produce an essential good or service.

Unique Product

A second feature of monopolies is that they produce a "unique" product for which there is no ready substitute. The electricity provided by the local power company, for example, is likely the only source of electric power available to consumers in a region. Every time consumers turn on the lights, television sets, or personal computers they are making a purchase of this essential service from this electric power company. Other local monopolies in your area might include cable television, local telephone service, local water supplies, and garbage collection.

Perfect Information

A third feature of a monopoly is that that it has "perfect" information about the market. This is because the monopolist is the market. The monopolist knows what inputs are necessary for production to take place, and what each of these inputs costs. The monopolist also knows about the consumer of the good or service, including the number of consumers in the market and the anticipated demand for the product. There is little need for the monopolist to advertise, or otherwise share information about the product, because there are no competing firms.

Extreme Difficulty of Entry or Exit

A fourth characteristic of a monopolistic market structure is that it is nearly impossible for a competitor to enter the industry, or for the monopolist to exit the industry. This is due to the high barriers to entry and to government regulations. The high barriers to entry include expensive capital goods, R&D, skilled labor, and patents. Another barrier is that a monopolist may control the raw materials necessary to produce a good. The DeBeers company in South Africa, for example, not only controls some of the most productive diamond mines in the world but also purchases large quantities of rough diamonds from other producers. As a result, DeBeers controls a substantial segment of the resource necessary to produce fine gems—uncut stones. Added to these barriers are government regulations that prohibit other firms from entering the industry, or prevent the monopolist from exiting the industry!

Significant Role of Government

The role of government is substantial in monopolies because there is a real danger that a powerful monopolist might abuse consumers. Therefore, the government often regulates the monopolist's prices, and mandates that the monopolist produce a sufficient quantity of the product to meet consumer needs. State regulatory agencies join with the FTC to monitor the behavior of monopolies.

Significant Market Power

The monopolist enjoys more market power than firms in any other type of industry. The high degree of market power stems from the fact that the monopolist is the industry. There are two major constraints on the price that the monopolist can charge for its product, however. The first is that government regulators have a significant say in both the price and the availability of the monopolist's product. Increases in electric power rates, for example, must first receive the approval of state authorities. The second main constraint on the monopolist's power to set prices is consumer demand. If the monopolist's rates are permitted to increase too high, consumers can reduce their demand for electricity through conservation—turning off lights or appliances when they are not needed, turning down the air conditioner in the summer or the electric heat in the winter, and so on. Over a period of time, high electric rates might even cause consumers to convert heating systems in their homes or offices from electric heat to a substitute—such as oil, natural gas, or solar powered systems.

Economic Thinkers: John D. Rockefeller and the Standard Oil Monopoly

John D. Rockefeller (1839–1937) was a leading American businessman—a captain of industry—in the late 1800s and early 1900s. By creating the Standard Oil Company, Rockefeller was able to monopolize the oil industry in the United States.

The rise of the Standard Oil Company proceeded steadily during the 1870s, 1880s, and 1890s. During the early stages of the company's growth, Rockefeller concentrated on bringing one phase of the production process under his control—the oil refineries. Thus, he planned a series of "horizontal mergers," takeovers, and acquisitions to gain control over this phase of the larger oil industry. To build his monopoly, Rockefeller engaged in ruthless competition. For example, secret deals with railroads reduced his shipping costs and permitted him to undercut his competition with lower prices for consumers. This type of business practice forced many competitors from the market. By 1890 Rockefeller controlled over 90% of the oil refining business in the United States and, thus, had created an oil monopoly.

During this same time period Rockefeller's corporate empire building also involved the purchase of related businesses. He aggressively bought oil wells, ships, railroads, and barrel companies. He also built oil pipelines. Before the end of the century Standard Oil had significant holdings in all phases of the production of oil. This type of top to bottom consolidation is achieved through "vertical mergers" and acquisitions.

TYPES OF MONOPOLIES

The four main types of monopolies that exist in the U.S. economy today are natural monopolies, government monopolies, technological monopolies, and geographic monopolies.

- Natural monopolies: A **natural monopoly** exists when a single firm can produce a good or service more efficiently than a number of competing firms could. This efficiency stems from a natural monopoly's ability to spread its costs over a large number of units produced. Economists use the term **economies of scale** to describe how average production costs fall as additional units of a good are produced. The economies of scale argument is the primary justification for the existence of natural monopolies. Some economists today question the need for some natural monopolies. This is because advances in technology or changes in other market conditions make it possible for smaller firms to provide comparable service at a comparable price to consumers. Today some states, including California and several states in the Northeast, allow competing power companies to produce and sell electricity to consumers on a competitive basis. In some areas there is also competition for local telephone service—another time-honored natural monopoly.

- Government monopolies: A **government monopoly** exists when any level of government grants itself exclusive right to produce a good or service. Perhaps the best known government monopoly is the U.S. Postal Service's monopoly on "first class" mail delivery. This monopoly is justified by the need to protect the postal delivery system from any disruptions, and to maintain the quality services provided by what is arguably the most efficient national postal service in the world. At the local level, many towns and cities are the exclusive providers of certain services to residents. Water and sewer services, and garbage collection are often government monopolies.

- Technological monopolies: A **technological monopoly** exists when a firm develops new technology that, in turn, is used to produce a new product—or a new way to produce a product. To protect the newly developed product or production process, a firm applies to the U.S. Patent and Trademark Office (PTO) for a patent. Patents protect the firm's new technology by prohibiting others from using it for a period of 17 years. So important were patents to the framers of "The Constitution of the United States" that patents were mentioned specifically in the document (Article 1, Section 8). Patents are vigorously protected in the United States. In one famous 1980s patent case, Polaroid sued Kodak for infringing on certain "instant photography" processes that had already been patented by Polaroid. After a lengthy trial, the courts agreed with Polaroid, and Kodak was obliged to stop its production of the product, to recall cameras that used the patented processes, and to pay a monetary sum to Polaroid. By the mid-1990s the PTO reported that it was receiving over 200,000 patent applications per year. And, in 1996 alone, the PTO granted 122,000 patents.

- Geographic monopolies: A **geographic monopoly** occurs when one firm is the sole provider of a good or service in a geographic region—a town, a city, a metropolitan area, or other region. It typically results when a market is unable to support two firms that produce essentially the same good or service. If, for example, a small town has enough consumers to support just one hardware store, this store would be a geographic monopoly. Geographic monopolies are far less important today than they were a century ago. Consumers, even in remote areas, are better linked to sellers through mail-order retailers, and "on line" shopping via the Internet. Some of the 70 million Americans who now have access to the Internet have already made buying "on line" a multibillion dollar activity. In addition, transportation on the nation's highways has improved over the years, and today provides a more convenient link between sellers and buyers than ever before.

MAKING ECONOMIC DECISIONS: THE OPEC OIL CARTEL

A **cartel** is a formal agreement or organization among firms that produce an identical product. By joining a cartel, members are expected to make joint decisions about the price and quantity of their product. The limits on supply are called production quotas.

The most important cartel in the world today is the Organization of Petroleum Exporting Countries (OPEC). The 12 member nations are all major producers of oil and are spread across the globe: Venezuela in South America; Algeria, Gabon, Libya, and Nigeria in Africa; Indonesia in Asia; and Iran, Iraq, Kuwait, Qatar, Saudi Arabia, and the United Arab Emirates in the Middle East. Created in 1960 by its five original members—Iran, Iraq, Kuwait, Saudi Arabia, and Venezuela—OPEC's goal was to stabilize world oil prices. By the 1970s, however, the cartel had grown to 13 members (Ecuador withdrew from OPEC in 1993), and its clout likewise expanded. The increase in OPEC's power stemmed from the discipline of its members to stick to their individual production quotas, and the fact that the lion's share of the world's known oil reserves rested safely within their borders. What happened to the price of oil on world markets during the 1970s? The price increased from just a few dollars per barrel in the early 1970s to about $35 per barrel by the end of the decade.

The 1980s and 1990s have not been as successful for the OPEC cartel. Disagreements among member nations on price and production quotas weakened the organization over the past 20 years. In addition, new sources of oil were discovered by the British (in the North Sea), the United States (in Alaska), Mexico, and by other nations. Thus, a greater share of the world's output of oil was in the hands of non-OPEC nations. By early 1999 the price of oil dropped to about $11 per barrel. After adjusting for inflation, this represented the lowest price for oil in a generation.

But many experts are not ready to nail the coffin shut on OPEC just yet. The oil ministers in member nations, who guide oil policies in their countries, began serious negotiations in 1999 to resolve their differences and to strengthen their cartel. In part because of the growing unity among the OPEC nations, oil prices rose to over $30 per barrel in some markets by February of 2000. This price hike was due, in large measure, to the willingness of OPEC members to withdraw over 4 million barrels of oil per day from world markets in 1999 and early 2000.

ANTITRUST LEGISLATION—PROTECTING COMPETITIVE MARKETS

Antitrust legislation refers to a series of laws passed by Congress over the past century to protect competitive markets in the U.S. economy. Today, the enforcement of antitrust laws has been shared by two federal agencies, the Antitrust Division of the Department of Justice, and the Federal Trade Commission (FTC). Some of the key pieces of antitrust legislation include:

- Sherman Antitrust Act (1890): prohibited competing firms from acting "in restraint of trade" and prevented attempts to form monopolies.

- Clayton Act (1914): prohibited "horizontal" mergers (of firms that produce the same product, or a single phase in the production of a product) if they "substantially lessen competition."

- Federal Trade Commission (1914): prohibited "unfair methods of competition" and increased the government's power to investigate antitrust violations.

- Wheeler-Lea Act (1938): prohibited deceptive and unfair trade practices, including misleading and false advertising.

- Celler-Kefauver Act (1950): prohibited "vertical" mergers (of firms that gain control over different phases of the production of a good) and "conglomerate" mergers (of firms in unrelated industries) if they result in substantially reduced competition.

8

WHY IS MONEY USED IN THE ECONOMY?

Chapter 8 explores the topic of money and its importance to a modern economy. Money is a "medium of exchange" that allows people to buy and sell products. While many items have been used as money throughout history, the one common feature of money is that people will accept it in payment for goods and services, or for other financial obligations such as taxes, debts, and so on. The origins of money can be traced back thousands of years. Even then, the advantages of exchanging goods and services using money rather than barter—the direct exchange of one good for another good—were apparent. In the American economy today economists have several definitions for what constitutes our money supply. This chapter examines money and its uses in the U.S. economy. It also surveys the impact of technology on the use of electronic money (e-money) in the growing field of electronic commerce—the variety of ways we make transactions without the use of cash.

MONEY AND ITS HISTORY

Money is any item that can be used to purchase goods or services or settle other financial obligations—including the payment of taxes. You are already familiar with many of the uses of money because you use U.S. currency—paper money and coins—for transactions on a daily basis. Let's examine money from a broader perspective to see where it came from and how it assists business activity in an economy.

For much of human history barter, rather than money, was used as a means of exchanging goods or services. **Barter** is the direct exchange of one good for another. Barter satisfied some of the needs of early peoples, but as civilizations grew the inconveniences of barter became more apparent. Barter, for example, required a "double coincidence of wants." This means that before a trade can take place, the two people involved in the exchange must want the item the other has to offer. Suppose a farmer produces corn, and a herder raises goats. For a trade to take place, the farmer must want a goat and the herder must want some corn. Otherwise, the exchange will not take place. And there is another complication. They must also agree on how much of one good is equal in value to a second good. Is one goat worth one bushel of corn, two bushels of corn, or five bushels of corn? Making exchanges of goods in this manner was time consuming and the results of the bargaining process were unpredictable.

To overcome the inconveniences associated with barter, civilizations have used "money" to exchange goods and services. Money has taken many forms over the past several thousand years. In ancient times the Maya and Aztecs used cloth and cocoa beans as money. A number of West African kingdoms used gold and cowrie shells as money. Wheat was used as money in ancient Egypt and Mesopotamia. Silk was used in China. In each case, these items were accepted in payment for goods and services by people in the region. And, in each case, these items were scarce. Scarcity tends to increase the value of money, regardless of the form of the money. While these early uses of money did not replace barter completely, they did make some transactions easier and more efficient.

Another major step in the use of money was the introduction of coins in the seventh century B.C. by the kingdoms of Asia Minor and by the Greek city-states. The Kingdom of Lydia, located in present-day Turkey, produced a coin called the STATER. This coin was originally comprised of a mixture of gold and silver. Later, the STATER was minted in two forms, one gold and one silver. Soon, the nearby Greek city-states were minting their own coins. The Athenian tetradrachma, for example, was widely circulated by the early sixth century B.C. The tetradrachma was used not only for day-to-day transactions within Athens, but also was used in commerce between other Greek city-states and their colonies throughout the Mediterranean region. For this reason, it is sometimes called the world's first international money. It was mainly through Greek influences that the use of coins spread to other civilizations, including the later Roman Empire. The use of coins made all types of exchanges easier and, thus, stimulated business activity within and between civilizations.

FUNCTIONS OF MONEY

These early forms of money, whether African cowrie shells or Lydian STATERS, improved upon the cumbersome barter system. And each satisfied, to some degree, the three main functions of money. These functions include money's role as a medium of exchange, a unit of account, and a store of value. While you may not be familiar with these terms, you will likely recognize each function in your day-to-day buying decisions. Let's suppose you just received $100 in cash as a birthday present from your parents, and you are now shopping at your local mall to spend some of this money.

As a "medium of exchange," money permits you to purchase an item at a price. After doing some window shopping at the mall, you decide to make your first purchase—a $15 CD at a music store. The cashier accepts your $15 in payment for the CD, and the exchange is completed. The process was accomplished quickly and efficiently. Neither you nor the cashier needed to haggle over the price or whether your money would be accepted in payment for the CD. This is because your dollar— the standard unit of money used in the United States—was accepted as the medium of exchange. As you might imagine, the exchange would have been a bit more complicated if you had tried to barter for the CD!

As a "unit of account," money is also important because it allows you to compare prices of goods and services. That is, prices permit you to judge the relative value of goods in the marketplace. Suppose on your shopping trip you stopped for a quick bite to eat at a deli in the mall. A glance at the menu options and prices posted above the deli counter tells you the relative value of each item. Suppose the six-inch hot pastrami sandwich is priced at $4, and the six-inch hot corned beef sandwich is priced at $8. Because there is a price attached to each type of sandwich, you can see that the price of the corned beef sandwich is twice that of the pastrami sandwich. As a unit of account, money can tell you the relative value of each type of sandwich in that particular marketplace— in this case the deli shop. It is still your decision about which sandwich to buy.

Finally, as a "store of value" money holds its value over time. Consider your shopping trip once again. Suppose you decided to spend just $40 at the mall, and save the remaining $60 from your original $100. You would want to be sure that the $60 you saved would not lose its value in the future. That is, the money that you put away for future use should have about the same purchasing power in the future as it does today. Purchasing power is measured by what your dollar can buy over time. If, for example, prices for most goods rose dramatically in the future the result would be a lower purchasing power for your dollar—your dollar would buy less in the future than it does today. How money might lose some of its value over time is explained later in this chapter.

CHARACTERISTICS OF MONEY

As you might imagine there are different characteristics that make money more or less suited to fulfilling each of the three functions of money. For example the cowrie shells of ancient West African kingdoms, the cocoa beans of the Aztecs, silk of China, and other forms of money all had strengths and weakness. The money used in the United States today, however, fulfills all of the basic requirements for a sound form of money. Let's examine how the U.S. dollar satisfies the four basic characteristics of money.

- Accepted: The most important characteristic of money is that it is accepted by the people in the region that it serves. This includes people living in the region, and people who do business in the region. Today, the U.S. dollar is the most universally accepted money in the world. Hence it satisfies the medium of exchange function of money. Earlier forms of money, such as cocoa beans and cowrie shells, were accepted only in specific regions.

- Stable: Connected to the acceptability of money is its stability—its ability to hold its value over time. While there have been periods of inflation when the general price level for goods rises, the U.S. dollar has consistently held its purchasing power. This fact has created confidence in the U.S. dollar in America and abroad. Some products that have been used as money, especially those that can be harvested such as cocoa beans and wheat, are less stable because a bountiful harvest will expand the amount of money too quickly—and the result will be a decline in its value. In short, money must remain scarce if it is to hold its value. Also related to the stability of money is its durability—it cannot rot, break, or otherwise become useless over time.

- Divisible: A third feature of money is that it must be divided into units. This division into units permits people to determine the value of goods and services with precision. The U.S. dollar is divided into 100 units, the smallest being the penny. Through the use of coins, any combination of "cents" can be figured. Different denominations of paper money can also be used to make larger transactions possible. Paper money includes denominations of $1, $2, $5, $10, $20, $50, and $100. Several centuries B.C., the city-state of Corinth was the first to produce coins in different denominations. Other items used as money, such as the cowrie shells and silk, cannot be so easily subdivided.

- Portable: A fourth feature of money is that it must be easy to carry from place to place. The U.S. dollar, like other paper money, is transported with relative ease by consumers and businesses alike. Recent technology has also expanded the people's ability to transport large amounts of money electronically—a topic that is more fully discussed later in this chapter.

TYPES OF MONEY

From its colonial period to the present, America has experimented with a number of different types of money. These types include commodity money, representative money, and fiat money. During some periods in our nation's history, we have used two types simultaneously. To begin this story, let's jump back to the 1600s when America was still in its infancy as a colony of Great Britain.

Commodity Money

Commodity money is a good that is also commonly accepted as a medium of exchange. That is, the good has value even if it was not being used as money. During America's colonial period, particularly during early English settlement, many items served as money. These items were usually the one or two main products produced by the colony. In colonial Virginia and Maryland, for example, tobacco was often used as a medium of exchange. Further north in the Massachusetts Bay Colony, beaver skins and corn were commonly accepted as money. Other commodities that served as money during the period included rice, livestock, gunshot and powder, and animal skins.

There were some significant problems with the use of commodities as money, even in the early years of English settlement in the New World. First, while this commodity money was often accepted as a medium of exchange within these early settlements, they were rarely acknowledged as money outside of the colony. For example, tobacco could be used to buy almost anything in colonial Virginia, but was not accepted as money in Connecticut or New Hampshire. Secondly, commodity money lacked stability in value. This is because its value fluctuated with the supply of and demand for the commodity. Tobacco, for example, became a leading "cash crop" in several southern colonies during the 1600s. As smaller tobacco farms grew into plantations by the mid-1600s, the supply of tobacco increased. In effect, tobacco was becoming less scarce, causing its value to decrease. To put the situation another way, people could literally grow their own money! A third weakness was that many commodities were not divisible. It was difficult, for example, to subdivide a cow or an animal skin without decreasing the value of the commodity. Finally, many types of commodity money were bulky, heavy, or otherwise inconvenient to transport. Thus, in most cases commodity money was not considered portable.

Representative Money

Representative money is an item that has no value in itself, but is accepted as a medium of exchange because it represents something of value—such as silver or gold. Representative money usually takes the form of a paper certificate that states its value. During America's colonial period, several New England governments issued "bills of credit" to pay their debts. In the late 1600s and early 1700s these bills of credit were redeemed for goods such as grain or cattle. Later, these colonial governments promised to redeem these bills for specie—gold or silver. The inexperienced colonial governments tended to print too many bills without the proper backing by specie, however. As a result, the bills of credit were difficult—often impossible—to redeem. It is easy to see why American colonists soon lost confidence in bills of credit, and refused to accept them in payment for goods and services. While these bills of credit were portable, and usually divisible, they were simply not stable in value.

The use of representative money in the United States continued into the 20th century, with varying degrees of success. During the late 1800s, the national currency in the United States was linked to specie—both gold and silver. The passage of the Gold Standard Act of 1900, however, created a "gold standard" for the United States. That meant that the national currency was tied to a single metal—gold. People could redeem paper money at a local bank for a specific amount of gold at any time. But the Great Depression of the 1930s eroded people's confidence in the banking system and in the nation's paper currency. Many people flocked to the banks to convert their paper money into gold, which put a strain on existing gold supplies. Finally, the Gold Reserve Act of 1934 removed the United States from the gold standard, and ended the use of representative money.

Fiat Money

Fiat money is a medium of exchange that has value because the government declares it to be valuable. In essence, fiat money is given value by government decree! Immediately after the U.S. government took the United States off the gold standard in 1934, fiat money came into use—and it is still in use today. In addition to removing the United States from the gold standard, the Gold Reserve Act of 1934 allowed the government to purchase the gold reserves held by all banks, and forbade the use of gold coins. The nation's gold supply was now held by the federal government.

Today, the fiat money in the United States is considered "legal tender." That is, by government decree the nation's currency, both paper notes and coins, must be accepted in payment for all kinds of transactions. If you look at the face of a $1 bill—officially called a Federal Reserve Note—you will see the following statement printed on it, "This note is legal tender for all debts, public and private." As long as the government is in power, and the people have confidence in the government, the national currency will remain as the nation's medium of exchange.

THE U.S. MONEY SUPPLY

Thus far we have examined the concept of money, and the types of money that have been used in the United States. This description has focused on the nation's currency—its stock of paper money and coins. But economists have a number of broader measures of the "money supply." These broader measures are used by economists and the government to help them track the progress of the economy and to recommend policies to stabilize the economy (see chapter 12). In this section we will introduce these different measures of the money supply.

Components of the Money Supply

A nation's **money supply** is comprised of its currency, financial instruments that function as money, and "near moneys." Near moneys include a wide variety of assets that can be converted into money. The four main measures that economists use to measure the money supply in the United States are the M1, M2, M3, and L.

The M1 is the narrowest measure of the nation's money supply. The M1 consists of four types of assets. The largest component is currency that is in the hands of people. The money that has been deposited in savings accounts or money being held by agencies of the government—such as the Treasury Department—is not included in the M1. A second component of the M1 is travelers checks. Travelers checks are purchased by people who are traveling for business or recreation. The travelers checks protect their money from loss or theft and can be used as money in many locations. A third component of the M1 is demand deposits. Demand deposits represent the money currently sitting in people's checking accounts. Finally, the fourth component of the M1 is other checkable deposits (OCDs). OCDs are different kinds of accounts people have at banks that checks can be written against, such as NOW accounts. Each of these components of the M1 is considered "liquid." That is, these assets can be turned into cash quickly without losing value. Currency is 100% liquid because it is cash and can be spent immediately. Travelers checks and checks drawn on a variety of bank accounts are also very liquid because they, too, can be spent almost like cash. In 1998 the combined monetary value of M1 totaled about $1.1 trillion, as shown in Figure 8.1.

A second, broader measure of the nation's money supply is the M2. The M2 consists of all four components of the M1, plus a number of near moneys. Near moneys are the assets that are highly liquid (easily con-

Figure 8.1
Components of M1, 1998

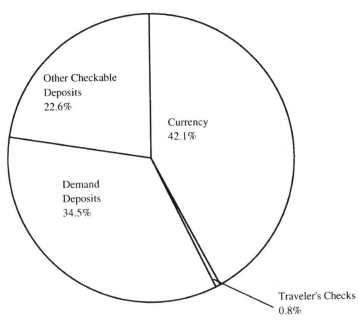

Source: Board of Governors of the Federal Reserve System.

verted into cash), but not as liquid as the components of M1. Some of
the most important near moneys that are included in the M2 are people's
savings deposits, small denomination time deposits, money market deposit accounts, and money market mutual funds. Savings deposits are
the regular bank accounts—statement and passbook accounts—that savers have to hold idle cash. Savings deposits are highly liquid because
savers can withdraw money from them at any time. Time deposits are
savings accounts that the saver has agreed to hold in a bank for a specified period of time, usually ranging from a few months to several years.
Time deposits are still assets of the saver, but are less liquid because of
the time restriction on withdrawals. Only small denomination time deposits—amounts less than $100,000—are included in the M2. The third
near money in the M2 is the money market deposit accounts (MMDAs).
Unlike other savings accounts, however, MMDAs offer variable interest
rates and some restrictions on the number of withdrawals the savers can
make each month. A fourth near money in the M2 are money market
mutual funds. These mutual funds are companies that purchase stocks
and bonds of other firms and then manage this collection of securities
for people who invest in the mutual fund. These investors are stockholders rather than savers because they own a piece of the mutual fund.

Combined, the components of the M2 total about $4.4 trillion ($1.1 trillion of the M1 + $3.3 trillion of near moneys). The government is most interested in the growth rate of the M2 when forming policies to maintain economic stability (see chapter 12).

The M3 and L are the final two measures of the U.S. money supply. The M3 is comprised of the M2 and a number of financial assets that are less liquid than those found in the earlier measures. Some of the most important additions to M2 include large-denomination time deposits ($100,000 or more), and money market mutual funds purchased by institutions rather than by individuals. Combined, the components of M3 total nearly $6 trillion ($4.4 trillion of M2 + $1.6 trillion of less liquid assets). The broadest measure of the money supply, L, includes all of M3 plus the money people have invested in a number of U.S. government securities, such as U.S. savings bonds and other short-term securities issued by the U.S. Treasury. When these final components are added to M3, the L measurement of the money supply tops $7 trillion.

Money versus Credit

It should be noted that credit cards are not considered a part of the nation's money supply. This may be surprising to you because millions of people who have credit cards often refer to them as "plastic money."

So, what is the difference between the money and near moneys of the money supply and credit? The money and near moneys that are listed in the M1, M2, M3, and L measurements of the money supply already belong to people. Money is in their wallets, in their checking accounts, in their savings accounts, and so on. Credit cards, on the other hand, are used to purchase goods or services with borrowed money rather than with the card user's personal assets. In effect, the credit card user takes out a "loan" each time the card is used (see chapter 9). Each month, when the issuer of the credit card sends its bill to the cardholder, payment of at least a part of the debt is required. People can then tap into their wallets, checking accounts, savings accounts, and so on to pay this debt.

Getting Currency into Circulation

The broad definitions of the money supply, from M1 to L, are useful to economists and political leaders when they formulate national policies. From our earlier discussion of money, it should be clear that the supply of money in an economy cannot grow too quickly or it will lose its value. Recall that this lesson was learned in the mid-1600s when the commodity money of colonial Virginia decreased in value as the supply of tobacco money grew. So who watches over the U.S. economy to make sure the money supply grows at a reasonable rate?

The answer to this question is the Federal Reserve System, or the Fed. The Fed serves as the central bank of the United States. Among its many roles, the Fed is responsible for distributing the nation's currency to the public. The two main reasons for issuing additional currency are to replace worn out paper money, and to meet the nation's expanding needs for currency. The Fed issues currency through the thousands of banks that comprise the U.S. banking system. Almost all paper money in the United States takes the form of Federal Reserve notes. While these Federal Reserve notes are issued by the Fed, they are printed by The Bureau of Engraving and Printing in Washington, DC. Today, Federal Reserve notes are printed in six denominations: $1, $5, $10, $20, $50, and $100. The U.S. Treasury Department also prints a tiny fraction of the nation's paper currency, called United States notes, in one denomination—the $100 bill. Coins, which are produced by the Bureau of the Mint, are also issued by the Fed. In contrast to the early years of our republic, neither state governments nor individual banks have the authority to issue currency today. You will read more about how the Fed increases or decreases the money supply to stabilize the economy in chapter 12.

MONEY IN AN ELECTRONIC AGE

During the 1990s technology made an enormous impact on the use of money to buy goods and services, and on our ability to gain access to money. Much of the new technology involves the instantaneous transfer of money from one location to another—from a bank to a business, from a savings account to a checking account, from an employer to a financial institution, and so on. Let's survey some of the most significant technological advancements involving money and its uses during the 1990s, and then explore some possible future directions for money in an electronic age.

Money and Technology in the 1990s

The technological advances of the 1980s and 1990s have transformed the way firms conduct their businesses and the way consumers use money. In some cases, the new technologies have already become part of their normal day-to-day routines.

One way technology has changed people's perception of money is by the different ways they can now buy or sell goods and services. A generation ago nearly all transactions were made with cash or checks. Today, there are numerous "cashless" ways to buy or sell goods. Let's examine some of the major ways that "money" can flow through the economy without ever leaving a bank vault.

- Debit cards: A debit card is a plastic card that is used to pay for purchases at grocery stores, gas stations, and other shops. To pay for the item or service, the debit card is inserted into a point-of-sale (POS) terminal. The amount of the purchase is then electronically communicated to the buyer's bank, and the amount of the purchase is subtracted from the buyer's account and sent to the merchant's account. To access an account, the buyer must punch in his or her personal identification number (PIN). This is to protect the buyer in case the card is misplaced or stolen. By the late 1990s consumers were able to use their debit cards at hundreds of thousands of stores and shops across the United States. Some experts believe that debit cards will eventually replace the use of personal checks because debit cards are more convenient—and they automatically balance the card holder's account as each transaction is made!

- Electronic checks: Electronic checks are automatic payments that people make through their banks to pay their bills. The process is rather simple. People must first deposit money into their bank account, and set up a schedule about when each bill should be paid. The bank, in turn, sends electronic checks through its "automatic clearing house services (ACH)," transferring funds from the customer's account to the creditor's (or other firm's) account. People who use the ACH system find it more convenient to pay their monthly bills this way.

- Credit cards: Credit cards are plastic cards that permit people to "buy now" and pay at the end of the billing cycle. Credit cards can be used at most businesses in the United States to purchase goods and services. Some major credit cards are household names, including MasterCard, Visa, Discover, and American Express. While credit cards have been in use for decades, they illustrate the same trend as the other forms of electronic payments—the trend toward a cashless society.

- Smart cards: A smart card is a plastic card with an embedded microchip. This microchip can store your personal financial information and can be used to make purchases or get cash from special smart card terminals. Interestingly, major credit card companies, such as MasterCard and Visa, have already entered the smart card business. The Visa smart card was used in Atlanta during the 1996 Summer Olympics! Smart cards have been in use in Europe and Asia for years.

- CyberCash: CyberCash is a system that permits the user to pay bills from a personal computer. The system consists of an "electronic wallet" that can be loaded into a person's personal computer. Then, the consumer can do business, such as pay bills or order merchandise, with firms that are likewise linked to CyberCash. Some experts see great potential for this system as Internet on-line shopping grows in popularity.

E-money and a Cashless Economy

New vocabulary has filtered into the economist's language in recent years to describe recent technological developments in money and its uses. **Electronic commerce** has come to mean the many cashless ways transactions can take place in the economy, such as the POS and the ACH systems. **Electronic money** (e-money) describes the new "currency," not made of paper and coin but instead made of electrically transmitted messages.

Will the United States and the world move into a cashless economy in the next millennium? Will all purchases be made with plastic cards that instantaneously debit one account and credit another? It is certainly difficult to imagine the absence of cash in our everyday lives. But then again, it wasn't so long ago that the thought of landing a person on the moon was unimaginable.

9

WHY DO PEOPLE SAVE, BORROW, AND USE CREDIT?

Chapter 9 examines why people save money, borrow money, and use credit in the U.S. economy. While there are good reasons for saving money—including the security of deposits and interest income—Americans tend to forego saving in favor of consumption. Money that is saved is usually deposited in one of four main types of depository institutions: commercial banks, mutual savings banks, savings and loan associations, or credit unions. In these depository institutions numerous savings options are available. Depository institutions also make loans to individuals and to firms. Americans have borrowed and have used credit freely in recent years. This trend has contributed significantly to the record number of bankruptcies that were declared in 1998. But savings, borrowing, and credit have also stimulated economic growth in the United States.

SAVING MONEY

Saving is the nonconsumption of disposable income. Over $7 trillion in income poured into American households in 1998, as shown in Figure 9.1. Some of this income was earned income, derived from wages, interest, rents, and entrepreneurial profits. Other income was unearned, mainly coming from transfer payments. Even after these sources of income were taxed by the government, households still had about $6 trillion left in their pockets. This after-tax income is called "disposable income." There are two things that a household can do with its disposable income—spend it or save it! Let's take a look at the main reasons why people might choose to save a portion of their disposable income.

Figure 9.1
Income and Savings in the United States, 1990–1998 (in billions)

					Years				
	1990	1991	1992	1993	1994	1995	1996	1997	1998
Personal Income	$4,792	$4,969	$5,264	$5,480	$5,758	$6,072	$6,425	$6,784	$7,126
−Personal Taxes	−$625	−$625	−$650	−$690	−$739	−$795	−$891	−$989	−$1,098
=Disposable Personal Income	$4,167	$4,344	$4,614	$4,790	$5,019	$5,277	$5,534	$5,794	$6,028
Personal Savings	$209	$246	$273	$214	$177	$180	$159	$121	$28
Savings Rate (% of disposable income)	5.0%	5.7%	5.9%	4.5%	3.5%	3.4%	2.9%	2.1%	0.5%

Source: U.S. Department of Commerce, Bureau of Economic Analysis.

Reasons for Saving Money

There are many reasons why people choose to save money in a **depository institution**—a bank, savings institution, or credit union that accepts deposits and grants loans. These reasons include: interest income, the safety of deposits, meeting household expenses, and preparing for retirement.

Money saved in a depository institution earns interest. **Interest** is the return that savers receive for their deposits. The interest rate is stated as a percentage, hence the interest rate could be expressed as 2%, 3%, and so on. Interest rates vary depending on the type of savings account you choose to open and on the depository institution that you do business with. In 1998 alone, the Commerce Department reported that American households earned over $750 billion in interest income!

Money saved in a depository institution is secure. In a bank, the depositor's savings are protected from theft, fire, or other misfortune. Savings are also federally insured to protect them from bank failure through the Federal Deposit Insurance Corporation (FDIC)—at least up to $100,000 per account! This federal insurance program, which was begun during the Great Depression, has served to build confidence in the American banking system since the mid-1930s. While the FDIC is the largest deposit insurance program, others exist to serve the savings institutions—such as savings and loan associations and mutual savings banks—

and credit unions. In effect, the FDIC and the other deposit insurance programs have eliminated the risk of saving. It is the absence of risk that separates "saving" money from "investing" money.

Money saved at depository institutions helps households prepare for a wide variety of expenses. These household expenses range from home repair to college tuition payments. Some of these expenses can be anticipated, while others cannot. For example, it is difficult to predict when your furnace or refrigerator will stop working, or when the roof on your house will need to be replaced.

Finally, money saved at depository institutions prepares people for their retirement. Some Americans believe that the Social Security and Medicare systems will provide the necessary financial security for their golden years. The reality is that these systems were designed to supplement, not replace, people's own incomes from savings accounts or personal investments. There are many savings plans specifically designed to help people prepare for their retirement. Individual Retirement Accounts (IRAs), for example, allow employees to deposit from $2,000 to $2,250 per year into a tax-deferred account. This means that the person pays no taxes on the money until it is withdrawn from the account at retirement. Similarly, a Keogh Plan is a savings option for the self-employed. Under this savings program, a self-employed person can save 15% of her income (up to a certain limit) in a tax deferred account. Saving for retirement is one of the wisest financial decisions a person can make!

U.S. Savings Rates

There are two main savings rates that need some explanation—the personal savings rate and the gross savings rate.

The **personal savings rate** is the percentage of a person's disposable income that is saved in a depository institution. Throughout the 1990s, the trend has been toward a decline in the personal savings rate, as shown in Figure 9.1. Since 1992, when the personal savings rate was about 6%, personal savings have dipped to about one-half of one percent of people's disposable income. This means that households spend over 99% of their incomes! Historically, the personal savings rates in the United States have been low compared to those in other highly industrialized nations. For example, the Commerce Department reported that in 1996 the personal savings rate in the United States was 2.9%, while in most other industrialized nations it was substantially higher, including France (12.5%), Germany (12.4%), Britain (11.6%), Japan (13.2%), and Italy (13.4%).

Much of the reason for the low personal savings rate in the United States can be attributed to consumer spending habits. America is a consumer society. During the prolonged economic expansion of the 1990s consumer confidence increased. This confidence, in turn, fueled consumer buying. After all, when people feel secure in their jobs and in the future of the economy, many conclude that there is little need to save "for a rainy day." Further, the availability of a wide variety of consumer goods, the dream of home ownership, and other attractive spending options continued to tempt consumers during the 1990s. The accelerated use of credit added to the spending binge. But credit is not "free money." When credit card bills appeared each month, people found themselves spending not only their disposable incomes on these bills, but also their savings! The decline in personal savings is a cause for some concern, particularly for households that have no savings cushion for emergencies or unanticipated expenses. Despite the decline in the personal savings rate there are other sources of savings in the nation's gross savings rate.

The **gross savings rate** includes the savings by individuals (the personal savings rate), businesses, and the federal and state governments. The gross savings rate is expressed as a percentage of the nation's Gross Domestic Product (GDP). The GDP measures the dollar value of all newly produced goods and services in the U.S. economy during a given year. In 1998, for example, the GDP was over $8.5 trillion, while gross savings was nearly $1.5 trillion—virtually all of which was due to savings by businesses ($1,066 billion) and government ($395.7 billion) according to the *Economic Report of the President*. Thus, the gross savings rate was over 17% of our GDP! Added to this figure was foreign investment in the United States, which has consistently brought hundreds of billions of dollars per year into the U.S. economy. Foreign investors rightfully believe that investing in the United States is as safe as it is profitable. In short, while personal savings was down during the 1990s there were still savings from other sources available to fuel continued expansion of the U.S. economy.

TYPES OF DEPOSITORY INSTITUTIONS

Depository institutions are the financial institutions that accept people's deposits and grant loans. Thus, people use depository institutions for both saving money and borrowing money. Today, the main types of depository institutions are commercial banks, savings institutions (mutual savings banks and savings and loan associations), and credit unions. The FDIC reported in 1997 that there were over 22,000 depository institutions in the United States with combined assets of $6.4 trillion, as shown in Figure 9.2.

Commercial Banks

Commercial banks are the largest type of depository institution, and provide a wide variety of financial services to businesses and to individuals. Commercial banks, like all depository institutions, accept deposits

Figure 9.2
Types and Assets of Depository Institutions

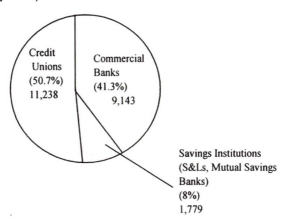

Credit Unions (50.7%) 11,238

Commercial Banks (41.3%) 9,143

Savings Institutions (S&Ls, Mutual Savings Banks) (8%) 1,779

Assets of Depository Institutions

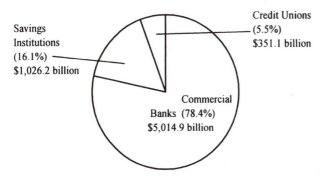

Savings Institutions (16.1%) $1,026.2 billion

Credit Unions (5.5%) $351.1 billion

Commercial Banks (78.4%) $5,014.9 billion

Source: Federal Deposit Insurance Corporation.

and grant loans to their customers. They also offer checking accounts, issue credit cards, lease safe-deposit boxes, and work to meet the individual needs of customers. The FDIC protects depositors' savings in commercial banks up to $100,000 per account.

Individuals use commercial banks to borrow money to purchase consumer durables (major home appliances), to finance home renovations or repairs, to buy a car, or to make other major purchases. The largest type loan an individual is likely to apply for is a home mortgage loan. A mortgage is a long-term loan granted by a bank to an individual for the purpose of buying property—such as a house. A mortgage loan is typically 15 to 30 years in length. In exchange for the mortgage, the borrower agrees to repay the principal—the amount of the original loan—plus interest for the duration of the loan. The interest rate can be fixed at a specific percentage. During the late 1990s, for example, some fixed rate mortgages dropped to below 7%. Mortgages can also carry variable rate mortgages (VRM), where the interest rate varies with the ups and downs of other interest rates in the economy.

Businesses use commercial banks more than any other type of depository institution. In fact, commercial banks were created in the 1800s to serve the business community. Banks extend loans to businesses expecting to earn a profit on the deal. Larger, well-established businesses—those that present the least risk—receive loans with lower interest rates, sometimes called the "prime rate." In February of 2000, for example, the prime rate was 8.75%. Loans to other firms—those where the risks are greater—pay a higher rate of interest for their business loans.

Mutual Savings Banks

Mutual savings banks are depository institutions that specialize in granting home mortgages and consumer loans to individuals, rather than in making business loans. They offer checking and a variety of other services to their customers. Most of their depositors hold small savings accounts. The board of directors for a mutual savings bank is concerned with how the bank can best serve the needs of depositors. Since 1989 the FDIC has managed the Savings Association Insurance Fund (SAIF), which provides deposit insurance to savings institutions including mutual savings banks.

Savings and Loan Associations

Savings and loan associations (S&Ls) are depository institutions that serve essentially the same customers as mutual savings banks. That is, they specialize in mortgage and consumer loans to individuals. They also offer checking and other financial services. Technically, S&Ls sell "stock" to members, rather than accept deposits from them. But, because the money is entered in the customer's account as a deposit there is little difference between making a deposit and buying stock in the S&L. People who buy stock in the S&L are its owners. Not surprisingly, most of the S&Ls' loans are then made to these stockholders. Today, S&Ls are carefully monitored by the federal government's Office of Thrift Supervision and by the FDIC. This is because S&Ls suffered substantial financial losses in the 1980s due to mismanagement and poor loan decisions. The SAIF offers $100,000 in federal deposit insurance for depositor's accounts in the nation's S&Ls.

Credit Unions

Credit unions are depository institutions that make consumer loans and provide financial services to their members—including "share draft accounts" (checking accounts). Like S&Ls, credit unions obtain their funds through the sale of stock. To purchase stock, a person must be a member of the group that established the credit union. Typical groups that form credit unions are labor unions and larger companies. Unlike other depository institutions, credit unions focus on smaller, short-term consumer loans—loans for the purchase of consumer durables, home repairs, and so on. It is rare for a credit union to extend a home mortgage loan. The National Credit Union Administration (NCUA) supervises most credit unions. Federal deposit insurance up to $100,000 for "share accounts" (savings accounts) in the nation's credit unions is provided by the National Credit Union Share Insurance Fund.

Technology and Depository Institutions

Technology has had an impact on the way business is done in many depository institutions across the United States. Much of this technology is connected to electronic funds transfer (EFT)—the use of computers to conduct specific banking tasks. For example, it has become commonplace for people to use the automatic teller machines (ATMs) at banks. ATMs usually give bank customers 24-hour access to their money—to transfer money between accounts, to make withdrawals, or perform other routine banking functions. In fact, in 1997 alone about 11 billion ATM transactions were made throughout the United States. Automatic clearing house (ACH) services permit the banks to automatically pay depositors' bills on a regular schedule. And the rising use of "home banking"—linking a depositor's personal computer directly to her checking or savings accounts at the bank—has already increased the ease with which depositors can attend to their banking needs (see chapter 8).

SAVINGS OPTIONS

Savings is often viewed as a fixed expense in a personal budget (see chapter 4). The U.S. Census Bureau reported that in 1995, 87% of all U.S. households had some kind of "transaction account"—checking, savings, or money market account. If you were opening a savings account, you would want to consider five criteria: interest rate on the deposit, ease of access to the deposit, checking privileges, required minimum deposit, and the security of deposit.

Passbook or Statement Savings Account

Sometimes called a regular savings account, passbook or statement accounts are the most common type of savings account. The only difference between the two accounts is that a record of deposits and withdrawals is made on a passbook—which must be presented at the time of the transaction at the bank—with the passbook account. Transactions with a statement account are all recorded on a monthly statement that is mailed to your home. In most cases the interest rate for a regular savings account is the lowest of any type of account. In early 2000 most banks offered less than 2% interest on depositors' regular savings accounts. Savers have immediate access to their deposits as withdrawals can be made in person, or by ATM, but regular savings accounts do not offer checking privileges. That is, checks cannot be written against a balance in your savings account. Usually, banks require that a minimum balance be held in a regular savings account, ranging from $100 to several hundred dollars. Some banks offer exceptions to this minimum balance requirement for savers under 18 years old. Virtually all deposits in these accounts are federally insured up to $100,000 by the FDIC, SAIF, or by the National Credit Union Share Insurance Fund.

Money Market Deposit Account (MMDA)

An MMDA is a type of savings account that links its interest rate to interest rates banks receive on their own investments—mainly safe government securities. Thus, the interest rate is variable. Usually, the interest rate for an MMDA is higher than that offered by a regular savings account. While it is fairly easy to withdraw money from this type of account, banks may limit the number of withdrawals and may require some advanced warning of the withdrawal. Some MMDAs also offer limited checking privileges. Again depending on the bank's policies, a minimum balance of $1,000 to $2,500 must be maintained at all times. Like deposits in regular savings accounts, deposits in MMDAs are federally insured up to $100,000.

Certificates of Deposit (CD)

A CD is a type of saving account that requires a deposit to remain in an account for a specified period of time, usually ranging from a few weeks to a couple of years. Interest rates for CDs are higher than those offered on regular savings accounts. In 1999, for example, interest rates for CDs ranged from about 4.25% to 5.25%, depending on the length of time the CD was taken out for. Access to money deposited in a CD is restricted by its "maturity date"—the final day that the depositor agreed to keep his money in the account. If the depositor needs to withdraw the money from a CD earlier than its maturity date, a financial penalty results—usually the loss of some or all of the interest that had been earned up to the premature withdrawal. There are no checking privileges with CDs, but there are often minimum deposits that range from a couple hundred dollars to $100,000. CDs, like other savings deposits, are federally insured up to $100,000.

Comparison Shop for a Bank

Comparison shopping for a bank and banking services is as important as comparison shopping for an automobile. Different banks sometimes have different requirements, penalties, or conditions connected with their savings accounts. In addition, savings options and banking services have been expanding in recent years. A thorough understanding of these services may help you decide which bank, as well as which type of savings account, best satisfies your needs.

USING CREDIT: ANOTHER KIND OF BORROWING

Credit is the use of someone else's money to buy goods or services today with the promise to repay the money at a later date. The person or institution that extends the credit is called the "creditor," while the person or institution that receives the credit is called the "debtor." In most cases, the repayment of borrowed money involves the return of the original sum that was borrowed—the principal—plus interest. In some cases, particularly with credit cards and charge cards, interest payments can be eliminated by paying off the entire balance each month.

The use of "credit" is often distinguished from "borrowing" money, despite the similarities between the two terms. Borrowing occurs when the debtor immediately receives a payment from the creditor to make the purchase. For example, to purchase a house a person may "borrow" $150,000 from a bank to complete the deal with the current owner of the house. This $150,000 sum is received by the borrower, and used immediately to pay for the house. Thus, money has changed hands—from creditor (the bank), to borrower (the buyer of the home), to seller (current owner of the home). Credit purchases, on the other hand, do not require money to change hands at the time of the transaction. For example, when a person uses a credit card to make a purchase he is merely promising to repay that sum of money to the issuer of the credit card at a later date. He did not need to apply for a loan with a bank, nor did he need a bank's cash to complete the transaction.

Reasons for Borrowing Money and Using Credit

One reason for borrowing money or using credit is that buyers can spread the payments for an expensive item over a longer period of time. In effect, the expensive good becomes more affordable in this manner. People who take out a 30-year mortgage, for example, make monthly payments on the principal and interest over a 30-year period to repay their debt to the lending bank. In 1998 the mortgage debt for 1- to 4-family houses in the United States was over $4 trillion! For smaller items, such as consumer durables, people might use credit or apply for installment loans to make the purchase. An **installment loan** is a type of borrowing where the buyer promises to repay the principal plus interest on a monthly schedule that could range from a few months to several years.

Secondly, the good can be enjoyed immediately. Imagine if you had to wait to buy a house, or a car until you could pay the full price in cash! We could predict that fewer houses and cars would be sold—and that production in many key U.S. industries would slow to a crawl! Of course, consumers don't purchase houses or cars every day. But consumers do make millions of purchases daily with credit cards and charge cards. Let's examine the use of so-called plastic money by consumers in the economy today.

Credit Cards

Credit cards are plastic cards that permit a consumer to buy goods or services at a variety of businesses. Traditionally, they were used to buy goods in department stores, restaurants, and other businesses that specialized in consumer goods. During the 1990s the use of credit cards spread into many other types of transactions including pay-at-the-pump gas stations, supermarkets, and the U.S. Post Offices! The Federal Reserve reported that by the mid-1990s the head of family in two-thirds of all U.S. households had a credit card. Some of the major credit cards are MasterCard, Visa, American Express, and the Discover Card. Credit cards are usually issued by banks or other financial institutions. In 1999, for example, the two largest issuers of credit cards were Citibank and First USA. But private corporations such as Sears, Roebuck & Co. have entered this competitive market also (Discover Card).

Comparison shopping for credit cards involves asking the right questions of the firm issuing the card. First, what interest rate will you pay on the unpaid balance? The issuing company insists on a monthly "minimum payment," but does not require full payment because it can charge you interest on the unpaid balance. In 1997 about one-half of the credit card holders in the United States carried an unpaid balance into the next month. Secondly, does the issuer charge an "annual fee"? This fee could be $25, $50, or more! But there are many credit cards that have no annual fee at all. Third, what types of "finance charges" might be applied to the monthly statement? Finance charges could take many forms, and might be added to a monthly bill simply to record an unpaid balance. Finally, is there is a fee for consistently paying the entire balance each month? Recall that interest and finance charges are linked to unpaid balances. Cardholders who regularly pay their entire balance each month do not pay these fees, hence receive the convenience of credit without paying for this service. Thus, from the card issuer's perspective, charging a fee for the use of a credit card is fair.

Charge Cards and Accounts

"Charge cards" and "charge accounts" are credit arrangements made between an individual and a specific store or other place of business. Purchases made with charge cards or accounts do not involve loans or cash transfers at the time of the purchase. Many retail businesses issue charge cards or have charge accounts for the convenience of their customers. Today, millions of people have charge cards at retailers such as Sears, Macys, JC Penney, Filenes, and others.

The most common types of credit offered by these businesses are a regular charge account, a revolving charge account, and an installment charge account. The regular charge account allows the customer to charge purchases each month up to a certain dollar limit—called the "credit limit." On regular charge accounts the customer is expected to pay the entire bill at the end of each month. An interest payment is added to the next billing if the customer fails to pay the entire bill. In contrast, the revolving charge account requires the customer to pay only a portion of the monthly bill, and then pay interest on the unpaid balance. This type of account also carries a credit limit. Stores issue a plastic card, similar in appearance to a credit card, to customers who have regular or revolving charge accounts. The installment charge account permits the customer to buy expensive items, and to repay the principal—and interest—in a series of monthly installments.

USING CREDIT RESPONSIBLY

The use of credit has made many types of transactions more convenient. But with credit use comes certain consumer responsibilities. How do the issuers of credit determine whether a person can handle this financial responsibility? And what happens when people cannot pay their bills?

Creditworthiness

Creditworthiness is a term used to evaluate whether a person should be granted credit. Major firms that issue credit cards or charge cards often look to "credit bureaus"—businesses designed to collect financial data on people—to help businesses decide whether a person is worthy of receiving the firm's "plastic."

So how do credit bureaus decide? Typically, credit bureaus use four criteria to evaluate the creditworthiness of people who apply for credit cards or charge cards. One criterion is the applicant's income. Naturally, having a steady income is a plus, while having no income is a minus. A second criterion is the applicant's wealth. Wealth refers to the applicant's personal assets. Does the applicant own a house, a car, or other valuable assets? The greater the wealth, the greater the chance the card issuer will be repaid in case the card holder tries to default on his debt. A third criterion is the applicant's past use of credit, or credit history. Has the applicant ever declared bankruptcy? Bankruptcies remain on a person's credit record for seven to ten years. Having declared bankruptcy in the past is a major minus for the applicant. Finally, credit bureaus attempt to assess the applicant's character. What kind of education or training does he have? Has he lived in the same location for a period of time? Has his employment been steady? After considering the applicant's record on each criterion, the credit bureau sends a "credit report" to the firm that requested the credit check. In this report, a recommendation about the creditworthiness is made.

Credit Abuse

Credit abuse occurs when people use credit to live beyond their means, and then discover that they cannot pay their bills. "Living beyond one's means" refers to the amount of debt a household accumulates relative to its income. According to the Federal Reserve System, in 1998 total consumer credit topped $1.3 trillion. This figure was nearly double the 1988 total of $719 billion. Note that this $1.3 trillion figure is credit debt, and does not include other categories of borrowing such as home mortgages. Further, record numbers of Americans have thrown in the towel by declaring bankruptcy—over 1.4 million people in 1998 alone, as shown in Figure 9.3. In 1999 personal bankruptcies accounted for over 97% of all bankruptcies declared in the United States, while business bankruptcies comprised the remainder.

How can people dig their way out of debt? One possible answer is through debt consolidation. To consolidate their debts, debtors sometimes contact a finance company. This finance company then pays off the accumulated bills of the debtor, and replaces them with a single

Figure 9.3
U.S. Bankruptcy Cases, 1993–1999* (in thousands)

	1993	1994	1995	1996	1997	1998	1999
Number of Bankruptcies	919	845	858	1,042	1,317	1,437	1,354

*Bankruptcies filed during a 12-month period from October 1 to September 30.

Sources: Administrative Office of the U.S. Courts, and Statistical Abstract of the United States: 1998.

monthly bill. Hence, many bills have been consolidated into a single bill. While the debtor still must pay the bill, plus interest, the repayment schedule is adjusted so that the debtor can make smaller monthly payments over a longer period of time.

Another possible solution is to seek help from your state's Consumer Credit Counseling Service. While these counseling services vary from state to state, most will help you "reschedule" debts. That is, the service will contact your creditors to reduce your monthly payments by spreading them over a longer repayment period. Credit counselors might also suggest that you increase your income by working longer hours or by taking a second job. And there is just one additional requirement—many ask you to destroy all of your credit cards and charge cards!

Credit Laws

During the 1960s and 1970s many consumer credit laws were passed by Congress to protect people's credit rights. The following list features some major pieces of legislation that protect consumers.

- Truth-in-Lending Act (1968). Lenders must inform people of all costs associated with loans or credit. Cardholders are liable only for a maximum of $50 in unauthorized purchases if a credit card is stolen, providing the cardholder reports the theft in a timely manner to the issuing firm. A three day "cooling off" period allows most credit contracts to be voided by the cardholder.

- Fair Credit Reporting Act (1970). Applicants for credit can challenge the findings of a credit bureau. Disputed items must be reinvestigated. Outdated credit information must be removed from a consumer's file. The consumer can insert a statement of disagreement with the credit report.

- Equal Credit Opportunity Act (1974). Equal access to credit is guaranteed regardless of race, gender, marital status, religion, national origin, age, or whether the applicant receives public assistance.

• Fair Debt Collection Practices Act (1977). Creditors and debt collectors cannot harass debtors through threatening behaviors, phoning them at inconvenient hours, and so on.

MAKING ECONOMIC DECISIONS: BANKRUPTCY

Bankruptcy is a legal recognition that an individual or a business cannot pay its debts. There are many sections, or "Chapters," of the bankruptcy code. These different Chapters try to deal with the different situations debtors find themselves in. The most commonly used Chapters of the bankruptcy code are Chapters 7, 11, and 13. Debtors, assisted by the courts, must decide which Chapter best addresses their situation.

Chapter 7

Chapter 7 bankruptcies apply to individuals. In 1999, 69% of all bankruptcy cases were filed under Chapter 7. Under Chapter 7, all of the individual's assets are "liquidated"—sold off—by the courts to pay creditors. To determine what assets the debtor owns, a complete list must be supplied to the federal bankruptcy court. In addition, a full accounting of all liabilities must be presented to the court. Once the assets have been liquidated, creditors start getting paid. First in line is the government! Payment of taxes gets the highest priority. Some financial obligations must be paid even after a Chapter 7 bankruptcy is finalized, including alimony and student loans. Naturally, few creditors will ever see their money because of the sad condition of the debtor's finances. And the debtor now has the bankruptcy recorded in his credit file, which means that the likelihood of receiving additional credit is slight—at least for the next ten years.

Chapter 11

Chapter 11 bankruptcies apply to businesses. In 1999, less than 1% of bankruptcy cases were filed under Chapter 11. By filing under Chapter 11, a business is allowed time to reorganize the firm, and is shielded from persistent creditors. The hope is that through reorganization, the firm can return to profitability and thereby repay some of its debts. While the firm continues with its day-to-day operations, the bankruptcy court reviews the firm's financial condition, and hears from the firm's creditors—who may ask the court to investigate the firm for mismanagement or other wrongdoing. The Chapter 11 court proceedings may take years to complete and, even if the firm's reorganization efforts are successful, there is a distinct possibility that the firm will pay its creditors only a fraction of what is owed to them.

Chapter 13

Chapter 13 bankruptcies apply to individuals who are not in the hopeless financial situation that individuals filing under Chapter 7 find themselves in. In 1999, 28% of bankruptcy cases were filed under Chapter 13. Under Chapter 13, debtors turn their finances over to the bankruptcy court. After examining the financial documents, the court decides how to deal with the situation. Often, the debtor's debts are rescheduled so that a portion of the debt can be repaid over time. In addition, a bankruptcy trustee may be appointed to oversee the case for the next few years. It is also common for the debtor's wages to be tapped by the court to help repay creditors. The benefit to the debtor is that most of his assets are protected under Chapter 13. But the bankruptcy is recorded, and the prospect of receiving future credit is slim for a decade or so.

SAVINGS, CREDIT, AND ECONOMIC GROWTH

Savings and credit promote economic growth in the economy. Savings provide a pool of money that depository institutions can loan to individuals, businesses, or the government. The availability of a large pool of loanable funds then starts a chain reaction in the economy—a reaction that ultimately leads to economic growth. **Economic growth** occurs when an economy is able to produce more goods and services over time.

First, consider the positive impact of savings and credit on the demand side of the market. Savings are a source of consumer borrowing. Credit permits people to buy more goods and services today, and pay for these goods tomorrow. In each case, the result is the same. That is, the total demand for products in the economy increases. Economists call the total demand **aggregate demand**.

Next, on the supply side of the market, producers respond to an increase in aggregate demand by increasing their rate of output. Businesses might borrow money or use credit to expand their business operations—to buy sophisticated capital goods, retrain workers, expand their research and development (R&D), or invest in innovative ideas of entrepreneurs. The result of these activities is greater output for their firms. When enough firms increase their rates of output the total supply of goods and services in the economy rises. Economists call this an increase in **aggregate supply**. When the economy can sustain higher rates of production over a period of time, economic growth is achieved!

Finally, the government can also tap into the supply of loanable funds to improve the business climate in the nation. Government borrowing takes the form of selling government securities to individuals, depository institutions, and others. The money the government receives can then be used to improve the nation's infrastructure and to provide other essential public goods—activities that tend to create jobs, improve the business climate, and encourage production.

10

WHY DO PEOPLE INVEST MONEY?

Chapter 10 examines why people invest their money. Investing money differs from saving money in that there is more risk in investments. Investments can take many forms, including government securities, corporate bonds, mutual funds, corporate stock, and "commodities." When choosing which investment options are most appropriate, individuals usually consider the anticipated return, security, and liquidity of each option. Many Americans combine different kinds of securities in their investment portfolios. The chapter also examines the structure and operation of the New York Stock Exchange, the world's largest stock market. Investing in stocks or other securities can be profitable for individuals. These investments also promote economic growth by supplying needed money for business expansion in the economy.

TYPES OF INVESTMENTS

Investment is the use of money to make more money, to increase the amount of capital goods, or both. Note from this definition that investments can be designed to accomplish two goals. The first is to make money. The second is to increase the amount of capital goods in the business community. Let's take a look at the two types of investments—financial investment and real investment—that are designed to meet these goals.

Financial investments occur when an investor uses money to purchase existing assets or wealth in order to make money. In effect, the ownership of these assets simply changes hands. For example, if you buy 100 shares of IBM the ownership of these 100 shares is transferred from the previous owner to you. Nothing new has been created from this transaction. You purchased these shares hoping to profit from your new investment sometime in the future. Other examples of financial investment include the purchase of government securities, corporate bonds, stock mutual funds, and commodities—sometimes called "futures." Each of these investment options is examined in the next section of the chapter.

Real investments occur when an investor uses money to purchase new capital goods. Capital goods are items that can be used to produce other goods. Examples include factory equipment, tractors, business computers, and so on. Real investments are often made by businesses that are expanding their facilities, upgrading their machinery, building a new plant, or the like. Real investments are crucial to economic growth.

INVESTMENT OPTIONS

People make financial investments by purchasing government securities, corporate bonds, stock mutual funds, corporate stock, and commodities. To distinguish these types of securities each option will be compared based on its potential return, its security (degree of risk), and its liquidity (convertibility into cash).

Government Securities

Government securities represent a broad range of investments in government bills, notes, and bonds. Government securities are issued by the Treasury Department. In effect, by selling these securities to investors, the investor becomes a creditor to the government and the government becomes a debtor. All federal government securities offer fixed interest rates and are fully backed by the federal government. Government securities mature from three months to 30 years. At maturity, these securities can be redeemed for cash. The interest earned on all government securities is exempt from state and local taxes—but not from the federal income tax.

Treasury bills (T-bills) typically offer the lowest interest rate of any government security. Yet, they offer the greatest liquidity because T-bills mature in just 3 to 12 months. In 1998 the average interest rate for a newly issued 3 month T-bill was 4.81%, according to the Treasury Department. T-bills are issued in one denomination of $1,000. To purchase T-bills an investor must buy at least ten—a $10,000 investment. Like all federal securities, the government guarantees the security of T-bills.

Treasury notes offer slightly higher interest rates than T-bills, but the liquidity of the Treasury note is far more restricted because it takes from one to 10 years for these notes to mature. In 1998 the average interest rate for a newly issued three-year note was 5.14%. Like T-bills, notes are issued in one denomination of $1,000 and there is a minimum purchase of $1,000 to $5,000—depending on how long the investor is willing to commit his money.

Treasury bonds also have a fixed interest rate slightly higher than that of the Treasury note. In 1998 the average interest rate for newly issued 30-year bond was 5.58%. These bonds are issued in one denomination ($1,000) and the minimum order of bonds is $5,000. Liquidity is severely limited as bonds take 10 to 30 years to mature.

Corporate Bonds

A **corporate bond** is a type of I.O.U. that a corporation sells to investors. By issuing these I.O.U.s, the corporation borrows money from investors. The corporation becomes the debtor and the investor becomes the creditor. The owner of a bond—the bondholder—does not become a part owner of the firm. Corporations sell bonds to collect a pool of money that can be used to finance any number of projects—the purchase of new equipment, the construction of a new plant, and so on. But what does the investor gain from the purchase of a corporate bond?

The most important benefit of owning a corporate bond is the return on the investment—the fixed interest payments offered by the bond. Corporations usually issue bonds in denominations of $1,000 or $5,000. Investors buy these bonds at face value. That is, a $5,000 bond's purchase price is $5,000. The fixed interest rate is clearly stated on the bond, as is the maturity date. Investors receive interest payments annually or semiannually until the bond matures. Suppose that you purchased a $5,000 bond, at 10% interest, that matured in 10 years. How would your investment pay off? Your annual interest payment would be $500 (.10 × $5,000 = $500) for a period of ten years. If a firm chose to make interest payments to its bondholders semiannually, the bondholder would receive $250 every six months. Thus, over the 10-year period you would earn interest payments totaling $5,000 (10 years × $500). In addition, at the end the tenth year, the corporation would repay to you the original $5,000 it borrowed. Typically, the interest rates for corporate bonds are higher than the interest rates for government securities.

The relatively high interest rates paid on corporate bonds are mainly due to the additional risks involved in the purchase of bonds. In 1998 bonds that were considered lower risk were paying about 6.5% interest, according to the *Economic Report of the President*. To attract investors, higher risk bonds were paying about 7.2% on average. Risk is an important feature that separates "saving" from "investing." Thus, your investment in a corporate bond is less secure than an investment in government securities. Corporations, like any business, can fail. If a corporation makes the shutdown decision what happens to the investor's bonds? Most likely the bankruptcy court will oversee the liquidation (selling off) of the firm's assets, and will disperse the money from the liquidation to the firm's creditors—you included! As a bondholder, you are one of many creditors, however. It is likely that you will receive only a portion of your original $5,000 back.

Under normal circumstances, corporate bonds are somewhat liquid. That is, you can sell a bond prior to its maturity date. Bonds, once they are issued, can be exchanged like any other security. To sell a bond the bondholder contacts a securities broker—a professional who specializes in the buying and selling of securities. The broker might use one of the major bond exchanges to find a buyer, such as the New York Stock Exchange Bond Market or the American Exchange Bond Market. The broker might also use the less formal contacts on the over-the-counter (OTC) market. The OTC market is a network of brokers who communicate by computers to buy or sell stocks or bonds. When a buyer is located there is no guarantee that the buyer will be willing to pay the entire $5,000. In the marketplace for securities, like other marketplaces, the price of bonds can fluctuate with consumer demand!

Mutual Funds

A **mutual fund** is a firm that purchases a pool of securities—stocks, bonds, government securities—and then sells shares of the mutual fund itself to investors. Buying shares in a mutual fund is like buying a tiny piece of many different securities. By 1998 there were about 6,800 mutual funds in the United States to choose from, including a variety of funds created by firms such as Vanguard and Scudder. The minimum investment varies from fund to fund, but the usual range is between $100 and $2,500.

There are several benefits to investing in a mutual fund. First, professional investors "manage" the mutual fund. These expert managers follow stock and bond markets carefully, and adjust the securities in the fund to keep investors' money safe and earning a healthy return. Another advantage is that the investor has a choice about the degree of risk he is willing to accept. The potential return on your investment will vary with the degree of risk. For example, some mutual funds are viewed as "aggressive" because the pool of stocks selected by the fund's manager is more risky—but potentially very profitable. More risky mutual funds might include stocks from newer, promising companies in high tech fields. There are also lower risk mutual funds that specialize in government securities, stocks or bonds in established companies—sometimes called "blue chip companies"—and other low-risk investments. Naturally, the return is usually lower on the low-risk mutual funds. A third benefit to investing in a mutual fund is that the pool of securities in the fund buffers the investor from the few "bad apples" in the pool. That is, several of the securities in the fund may incur losses, but as long as the rest of the securities increase in value the mutual fund is profitable.

Corporate Stocks

A **corporate stock** is a certificate of ownership in a corporation. This is different from the corporate bond that you read about earlier in that a corporate bond represents debt, not ownership in the corporation. Thus, the owner of stock in a corporation—a stockholder—is an owner of the firm. Corporations sell stock to investors to finance the start-up costs of a new firm, or to finance new building projects or other expenses of existing firms. According to the NYSE, more than 60 million Americans own stock directly. There are two types of stock that corporations issue, each with its own set of advantages and disadvantages.

The most widely issued type of stock is common stock. **Common stock** entitles the stockholder to voting rights at the annual stockholders' meeting. Holders of common stock are also entitled to "variable dividends" as their return for investing in the firm. A variable dividend is a payment by the firm to stockholders based on how profitable the firm is. When the corporation's profits are strong, variable dividends tend to rise. When profits fall, variable dividends also fall, and can even be canceled completely by the firm's Board of Directors. This is part of the risk that owners of common stock must accept. Another risk for owners of common stock is the prospect of losing their entire investment if the corporation fails. These stockholders are among the last to be paid off if bankruptcy is declared—behind the government, behind bondholders, and behind owners of preferred stock.

A lesser used type of stock is preferred stock. **Preferred stock** usually does not entitle the owner to voting rights at the stockholders' meetings. But investors in preferred stock are entitled to a "fixed dividend" as a return on their investment. Fixed dividends remain constant, regardless of the firm's profitability. Even when profits fall, the corporation is obliged to pay preferred stockholders their fixed dividends. In extreme cases, if the corporation suffers staggering losses even fixed dividends can be canceled by the Board of Directors. Like the owners of common stock, preferred stockholders stand to lose their entire investment if the corporation goes bankrupt. But in this situation, after all of the firm's debts with creditors are settled, it is the preferred stockholder who is paid off ahead of the common stockholder. The owners of common and preferred stock enjoy some liquidity in their investments. The process of buying and selling stocks will be discussed later in the chapter.

Another type of financial reward that the owners of both common and preferred stock enjoy is capital gains. Capital gains refers to the difference between the buying price of a stock and the selling price. For example, if you purchased 1,000 shares of Microsoft at $100 per share in 1999, and then sold the same 1,000 shares a year later for $125 per share, your capital gains would total $25,000. This is because you were able to sell the Microsoft stock for $25 per share more than you originally purchased it for. Your capital gains of $25,000 ($25 × 1,000 shares) is your reward for investing in a profitable company. Suppose, on the other hand, that the value of Microsoft stock dipped from $100 to just $80 per share. Then, you would incur a loss of $20 per share. Thus, your "capital losses" would total $20,000 ($20 × 1,000 shares). Did you know that the initial purchase price for Microsoft stock was $.50 per share in 1990? By February of 2000, the going price per share was $110. Is it any wonder that Bill Gates, the founder of Microsoft, is the richest person in the world?

Commodities

Commodities, also called "futures," are contracts that investors buy for many types of goods. Some typical commodities that investors buy are agricultural products such as wheat, corn or livestock; industrial goods such as coal or steel; and precious metals such as gold or silver. The terms of the contract are simple. The seller of the contract (who owns the commodity) agrees to sell a certain quantity of the commodity to a buyer (the investor) for a certain price. In this arrangement, the seller knows exactly how much money he will receive for the commodity. This brings a certain amount of security to the seller. But how does the investor earn a profit on the deal?

The investor earns a profit when he can resell the same contract— sometimes called a "futures contract"—to someone else in the future. To illustrate the process, suppose an investor purchased a contract for 10,000 bushels of wheat in May of 2000, and agreed to pay $3 per bushel for the wheat. Thus, the contract cost the investor $30,000 ($3 × 10,000 bushels). Neither the investor nor the seller of the wheat know how much a bushel of wheat will sell for in the fall. This is where the risk in futures contracts comes into view. If in the fall of 2000 the market price for wheat is $4 per bushel, the investor will sell the contract to a firm that needs wheat—perhaps to produce bread or pizza crusts. At the $4 selling price, the investor receives $40,000 ($4 × 10,000 bushels). Hence, the investor's profit is $10,000 ($40,000 − $30,000). This sounds almost too easy! But consider what happens if the price of wheat falls to just $2 per bushel by the fall. The investor stands to lose $10,000 because the cost of the contract ($30,000) is greater than his earnings from the sale of the wheat ($20,000). With futures contracts, there is great potential for profits and for losses—and little security to comfort you as you wait for the sale of your contract in the fall.

MAKING ECONOMIC DECISIONS: BUILDING AN INVESTMENT PORTFOLIO

An **investment portfolio** is a collection of the financial holdings of an individual or a household. An investment portfolio usually contains some of the investment options you just read about—government securities, corporate bonds, and so on. Portfolios might also include a number of savings options such as regular savings accounts, CDs, retirement accounts, and the like (see chapter 9). There are several principles of investing that a person should consider before jumping into the investment world. These include figuring a household budget, setting financial goals, gathering information, and diversifying savings and investment holdings.

Figuring a Household Budget

A household budget lists your monthly income and expenses (see chapter 4). Before you can even consider investing, you have to be sure that your present income can cover your monthly expenses for housing, food, medical care, transportation, and other basic expenses. From your present income you should also have money set aside in a liquid savings account for emergencies such as a prolonged sickness, an accident, or the loss of your job. Once these conditions are satisfied, the money "left over" can be invested. As a general rule of thumb, experts recommend that people should invest no more than 10% to 15% of their income.

Setting Financial Goals

Your financial goals are the short-term and long-term financial objectives that you hope to achieve. Your goals will be influenced by many personal factors. For example, you must realize that money you invest today cannot be spent on consumer goods tomorrow. Are you ready to forego present consumption of goods and services by tying up your money in securities? Next, your family situation is an important consideration. Will you need money for your children's college education, for a new house, for your retirement, or to care for elderly parents? Third, you must determine whether you want your investments to grow in value over time, or to provide a steady income to you. Investments in the stocks of "blue chip" companies tend to grow in value over time. This is because these established companies—such as Coca-Cola, IBM, Intel, and General Electric—reinvest much of their profits back into the firm. The result is that the value of these stocks typically increases over time. Years later when these stocks are sold, the investor stands to make substantial capital gains. Investments in "income stocks," on the other hand, usually pay high dividends to investors. Stocks of many utility companies are considered income stocks.

Gathering Information

Investors consult a variety of sources for investment information. Often, people start this process by contacting a securities broker. Brokers specialize in following the trends in the stock, bond, or futures markets, and are also knowledgeable about the financial conditions of many specific companies. "Full service" brokers offer advise about which securities best meet your financial needs, but charge a higher fee—called a commission—for this service. "Discount brokers," on the other hand, will buy the securities that you have selected for a lesser fee. But discount brokers do not offer investment advice. Information gathering also involves reading investment newsletters, newspapers such as *The Wall Street Journal* and *Barrons*, and magazines such as *Forbes, Money, Business Week*, and others. You may even wish to join an "investment club." Investment clubs are groups of people who pool their money—and their information—to buy stocks, usually on a monthly basis. Profits from these investments are used to buy additional stocks.

Diversify the Portfolio

Diversification is one of the most basic rules of investing. It involves buying a variety of securities, usually balancing high-risk with lower-risk investments. Of the investment options listed earlier, high-risk investments would include the purchase of futures contracts and the purchase of common stocks in newer firms that are still not firmly established in their industries. Lower-risk investments would include all types of government securities, and the securities issued by "blue chip" companies. Perhaps the most important piece of investment advice is, "don't put all of your eggs into one basket."

THE NEW YORK STOCK EXCHANGE

The New York Stock Exchange (NYSE) is the world's largest stock market. A **stock market** is a place where investors come together to "trade" stocks. "Trading" is the term used to describe the buying and selling of stocks. Stock markets serve a couple important functions. First, they provide a location for firms to raise funds needed to start or expand a company. Secondly, they assist investors in buying or selling their stock. By the late 1990s there were 3,047 companies "listed" on the NYSE. To become a "listed" company on the NYSE, there are requirements in terms of the firm's earnings, value of assets, number of shareholders, trading volume, and national interest. Today an average trading volume on the NYSE is 500–600 million shares per day, but the computerized systems have easily handled over 1 billion shares traded on a single business day.

Suppose Jared, who lives in Memphis, wants to sell 100 shares of Apple Computer, and that Wanda in Los Angeles wants to buy 100 shares of Apple. Without a stock market it is highly unlikely that Jared and Wanda would ever meet to make this trade. But using the NYSE a simple transaction like this would take a few minutes to complete. Let's trace the steps in the process of trading these 100 shares of Apple.

Trading Stocks

Most of the steps in a stock trade are invisible to the seller (Jared) and the buyer (Wanda).

- Step 1—Call your stock broker. Jared calls his broker in Memphis and instructs his broker to sell 100 shares of Apple "at the market"—the current market price. Wanda calls her broker in Los Angeles, and instructs her broker to buy 100 shares of Apple "at the market."

- Step 2—Both brokers contact the NYSE. The brokers for Jared and Wanda contact the "trading floor" of the NYSE. The trading floor is where the trading of stocks takes place. On the trading floor, different stocks are traded at different "trading posts"—17 workstations that are fully equipped with computers and people called "specialists" who assist with the trade. Over 150 stocks are bought and sold at each of the 17 trading posts. Today, technological advances permit the orders from Jared's broker and Wanda's broker to travel to the trading post in two ways. One way is through the Broker Booth Support System (BBSS). Under the BBSS, a buy or sell order is received at the NYSE by a clerk—an employee of the brokerage firm. The clerk, in turn, passes the order to a "floor broker." The floor broker then takes the order to the trading post for the trade. The second, more common way to get the order to the trading post is through the NYSE's SuperDot system, whereby the order is sent by the clerk directly to the trading post.

- Step 3—The negotiation. The floor brokers, representing Jared and Wanda, want to make the best possible deal for their clients.

That is, the broker representing Jared wants to sell the Apple stock at the highest possible price, while the broker representing Wanda wants to buy the Apple stock at the lowest possible price. The "specialist" assists in the negotiations, which may become lively if other brokers enter the negotiation—a normal occurrence. Negotiations are intense and quick. The brokers representing Jared and Wanda agree on a price.

- Step 4—Recording the trade. Immediately after the two brokers agree on the price, the specialist informs the two brokerage firms (the firms that employ Jared's and Wanda's brokers) that the deal has been completed. Jared and Wanda are contacted immediately by their brokers to tell them that the trade has been concluded. The entire process probably took a few minutes. The specialist also records the trade—the quantity and the price—to the "consolidated tape." The Consolidated Tape System (CTS) records the transaction and instantaneously transmits it to every stock exchange in the world.

- Step 5—Paying up. So how does Jared, in Memphis, receive his money for the 100 shares of Apple? And how does Wanda, in Los Angeles, actually pay for them? Jared will receive his payment from his broker within three days after the trade is recorded. He may want the money in cash, or he may want the money placed in his account with the broker. In either case, the broker's commission will already be deducted from the money Jared receives. Wanda, on the other hand, will have to pay her broker for the 100 Apple shares either out of her pocket or from an account that she may already have with the broker. The broker's commission will be added into Wanda's payment. The transfer of funds between the two brokerage firms is done electronically.

Measuring the Performance of the NYSE

There are a number of ways to measure how well stocks on the NYSE are performing. The most widely publicized measure is the Dow Jones Industrial Average (the Dow). The Dow measures the ups and downs of just 30 major U.S. companies that are listed on the NYSE. The Dow is measured in index points, not dollars, using a complex formula. For our purposes, when the Dow increases over time, this generally signals that the NYSE is healthy and investor confidence is high. When prolonged increases in the Dow occur, we say that a "bull market" exists. When the Dow declines over an extended period of time, this is a signal that the stock market is in a downturn called a "bear market." While there have been some downturns in the Dow over the past twenty years, the overall trend has been upward as shown in Figure 10.1. By 1999 the Dow had crept past the 11,000 barrier and on January 14, 2000 had reached an all-time high of 11,723. There are other measures of the NYSE's performance, including the broader New York Stock Exchange Composite Index and the Standard and Poor's Indexes.

Companies Comprising the Dow Jones Industrial Average: 2000

AlliedSignal	IBM
Aluminum Co. of America (Alcoa)	Intel
American Express	International Paper
AT&T	Johnson & Johnson
Boeing	McDonald's
Caterpillar	Merck
Citigroup	Microsoft
Coca-Cola	Minnesota Mining & Manufacturing
Dupont	Morgan (J.P.)
Eastman Kodak	Philip Morris
Exxon	Procter & Gamble
General Electric	SBC Communications
General Motors	United Technologies
Hewlett-Packard	Wal-Mart
Home Depot	Walt Disney

On November 1, 1999, four companies were added to the DJIA and four were removed. Added were Home Depot, Intel, Microsoft, and SBC Communications. Removed were Chevron, Goodyear, Sears and Roebuck, and Union Carbide.

Monitoring the Securities Industry

The U.S. securities industry is monitored at several levels. Monitoring ensures that the securities markets are free from fraud or unethical behavior by any of the participants—brokers, brokerage firms, and so on. Securities exchanges are watched over by federal regulators and by the self-policing efforts of brokerage firms and the NYSE itself.

The federal agency most directly concerned with protecting the integrity of the U.S. securities industry is the Securities and Exchange Com-

Figure 10.1
Performance of the Dow, 1980–1997

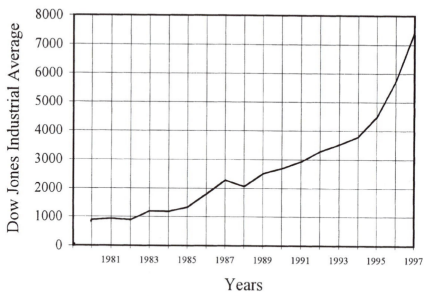

Sources: Statistical Abstract of the United States, 1998 and *Economic Report of the President, 1999.*

mission (SEC). This agency was created by the Securities and Exchange Act of 1934. Since the 1930s, SEC regulators have ensured that investors have accurate, timely information about firms that are listed on the NYSE and other stock markets. The U.S. Congress is also involved in the protection of investors' rights at the federal level. In 1970, for example, Congress created the Securities Investor Protection Corporation (SIPC). The SIPC was designed to protect investors who had money in accounts of brokerage firms that failed. The SIPC insures investors' accounts up to $500,000 per customer. In another move to ensure that trading is conducted fairly on the NYSE, Congress—with the support of the SEC—passed the Insider Trading Sanctions Act (ITSA) in 1984. This act clarified what constituted the illegal practice of "insider trading." Insider trading is the purchase or sale of a corporation's securities by "insiders"—the corporation's directors, officers, or others—based on information that has not yet been released to the public. Members of a corporation's board of directors, for example, would know about the firm's strong profits or disastrous losses before the general public. This would give them an unfair advantage in buying or selling the company's stocks. Insider trading is prohibited by the ITSA, and those found guilty of breaking the law are subject to heavy criminal and financial penalties.

Monitoring of the securities industry is also done by brokerage firms and by the stock exchanges themselves. There are 500 brokerage firms that are "members" of the NYSE, for example. That is, certain large brokerage firms are directly represented at the NYSE. Member firms self-police to ensure that trading is done fairly. The NYSE has also been active in establishing rules and regulations for all participants in the buying or selling securities. Regulators employed by the NYSE use sophisticated surveillance equipment to discover violations of the rules or codes of conduct.

INVESTMENT AND ECONOMIC GROWTH

Investments, both financial and real, promote economic growth in the U.S. economy. **Economic growth** occurs when more goods and services are produced in a nation over time. During the 1990s savings (see chapter 9) and investments by the private and public sectors have contributed to the longest period of uninterrupted economic growth since World War II by supplying vast pools of money for businesses to use.

The purchase of newly issued stocks is one type of investment that stimulates economic growth. The purchase of stocks can help a corporation to get off the ground. The first issue of stock by a newly formed corporation is called an initial public offering (IPO). Thus, IPOs can reward entrepreneurs by getting promising ideas off the drawing board and into production. Similarly, the purchase of corporate bonds assists the corporation in raising needed funds for many types of business expenses ranging from paying off company debts, to retooling a plant, to building an entirely new production facility.

Real investments by firms are also instrumental in promoting economic growth. Real investments bring new capital goods into offices, factories, and farms. In today's rapidly changing economy those firms that use a portion of their profits to invest in sophisticated capital goods are more likely to increase the productivity of their workers (see chapter 5). Real investments in research facilities also encourage product innovation by entrepreneurs. In short, firms that make real investments in themselves expand their ability to produce goods and services. When many firms accomplish this goal the total supply—the aggregate supply—of goods and services in the economy rises.

Real investments by the government promote growth by maintaining or improving the nation's economic infrastructure, supporting public education for the youth, initiating occupational training programs for certain segments of the labor force, subsidizing specialized training in institutions of higher learning, and at times providing jobs or other assistance to people. In each of these functions, the government improves the business climate—the conditions under which businesses operate.

Economic Thinkers: J. P. Morgan and Investment Banking

John Pierpont (J. P.) Morgan (1837–1913) was among America's most influential investment bankers during the late 19th and early 20th centuries. As an investment banker, J. P. Morgan bought and sold corporate securities which helped create industrial giants such as American Telephone and Telegraph (AT&T) and the world's first billion dollar corporation—the U.S. Steel Corporation.

The son of a successful banker, J. P. Morgan gained valuable experience in the world of finance from his father, Junius Spencer Morgan. By 1870 J. P. Morgan helped found Drexel, Morgan & Company. Even at this early date, he was well on his way to becoming the most important banker in the nation. During the final quarter of the 19th century, J. P. Morgan focused his attention on consolidating rival firms into "trusts." A "trust" was a new form of business organization that brought a number of firms within an industry under the control of a single Board of Directors. In this way, Morgan brought a degree of order to the growing American economy—in the railroad industry, communications, and steel. He also created enormous wealth for himself and for the other "captains of industry" in the process!

11

HOW DOES GOVERNMENT RAISE AND SPEND MONEY?

Chapter 11 deals with how all levels of government—national, state, and local—raise revenues through taxation and spend money on public goods and services. Taxes are the mandatory payments that individuals and firms make to government. At the national level, the bulk of the government's tax revenues are generated through the personal income tax and social insurance payroll taxes—especially the Social Security and Medicare taxes. At the state and local levels other taxes dominate, including the sales tax, property taxes, and state income taxes. Government collects taxes, in part, to finance public goods. Defense spending, for example, is financed at the national level. State and local governments spend much of their tax receipts on education, health care, highways, and so on. Naturally there has been a great deal of debate about how the tax dollars should be raised and spent. At the national level Congress and the President consider these questions when they form the federal budget each year. Over the past few years a new issue has surfaced—what to do with the growing federal budget surpluses.

PURPOSES AND TYPES OF TAXES

A **tax** is a mandatory payment by an individual or a firm to any level of government—national, state, or local. All societies rely on tax revenues to support their governments and the services these governments provide. Let's begin our discussion of taxes by looking at the purposes and types of taxes.

Purposes of Taxation

There are two main reasons why governments tax people. The more apparent of these reasons is that the government needs to raise revenues to pay its bills. A second purpose of taxes is to influence people's behaviors.

Taxes are the largest source of revenue for government. According to the Bureau of Economic Analysis, the federal government collected about $1.7 trillion in tax revenues in fiscal year (FY) 1997. A fiscal year at the national level runs from October 1 to September 30 of the following year. Hence FY 1997 spanned the period of time between October 1, 1996 to September 30, 1997. In 1997 revenues for state and local governments totaled $1.1 trillion. Governments at all levels use revenues from taxes and other sources to provide public goods for people. **Public goods** are goods supplied by the government that are available to all members of your society. Highways, lighthouses, schools, and nuclear submarines are all considered public goods because the benefits of each are available to all people. Government also uses tax revenues to pay off past debts and to offer a variety of transfer payments to people (see chapter 13).

Taxes are also used by government to influence the behaviors of individuals and firms. An **excise tax**, for example, is a tax on a specific product. Excise taxes make these products, such as gasoline and cigarettes, more expensive. In this way excise taxes discourage their use. That is, the tax influences the behavior of consumers. Taxes can also encourage certain behaviors or actions. For example, since 1993 the federal Empowerment Zones and Enterprise Communities Act has provided billions of dollars in tax incentives and grants to attract firms into "economically distressed" communities. Thus, tax advantages are used to influence firms' decisions about where to locate their operations.

Types of Taxes

There are three main types of taxes. To distinguish one type of tax from another, you must look at which income group bears the heaviest burden from the tax. The three categories of taxes include progressive taxes, proportional taxes, and regressive taxes.

A **progressive tax** takes a larger percentage of income from an upper-income household than from a lower-income household. For example, the federal personal income tax is a progressive tax. Lower-income persons pay as little as 15% on their taxable income, while upper-income persons could pay as much as 39.6% on a portion of their income. You will read more about the personal income tax later in the chapter.

A **proportional tax** is a tax that affects all income groups equally. That is, proportional taxes take the same percentage of income from a lower-income household as it does from an upper-income household. Some state income taxes are considered proportional taxes because they take a fixed percentage of income from all income groups.

A **regressive tax** is a tax that takes a larger portion of the income from a lower-income household than from an upper-income household. The sales tax is a good example of a regressive tax. The sales tax may seem to be a proportional tax at first glance because all people pay the same percentage on their purchases. But consider how much of a lower-income person's money must be spent on taxable items compared to an upper-income person's spending. Upper-income households tend to put some of their money into savings, investments, retirement plans, college tuition payments, mortgage payments, and other uses that are not subject to the sales tax. Many of these options are not practical for lower-income households that must spend virtually all of their incomes for basic needs. States that have a sales tax tend to soften the regressive nature of the tax by exempting certain types of goods from the tax, including food, medicines, and sometimes inexpensive clothing purchases.

TAXATION

Government at the national, state, and local levels impose taxes to raise the funds. Different levels of government rely on different taxes to finance public goods and services, transfer payments, and so on. Let's take a look at some of the major taxes at the different levels of government.

Taxation at the National Level

The most important taxes at the national level are the personal income tax, social insurance payroll taxes, and the corporate income tax, as shown in Figure 11.1. Combined, these taxes account for over 90% of the tax revenues received by the federal government. In FY 2000 the federal government collected nearly $2 trillion in taxes.

The **personal income tax** is a federal tax on a person's taxable income. In the FY 2000 budget, the government will collect $900 billion in personal income taxes. Income derived from wages or salaries, and interest and dividend payments, and other forms of income are subject to the personal income tax. Taxable income is the income that remains once all deductions are made—including deductions for dependent children, local property taxes, and so on. Because the personal income tax is a progressive tax, a higher percentage is taken by the government as a person's income rises, as shown in Figure 11.2. The term "tax rate" is used to describe the different percentages of income taken by the federal government. The lowest tax rate on taxable income in 1999 was 15%, while the highest was 39.6%. Suppose Hunter was single and had a taxable income of $65,000 in 1999. How much would Hunter owe to the

Figure 11.1
Federal Tax Receipts, FY 2000

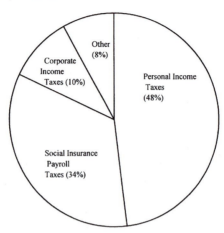

Source: Office of Management and Budget.

government in personal income taxes? Using the IRS data in Figure 11.2 for single people, the first $25,750 would be taxed at the lowest rate of 15%. Thus he would owe $3,862.50 on this portion of his taxable income (.15 × $25,750). All of Hunter's taxable income between $25,750 and $62,450—a total of $36,700—would be taxed at the next rate of 28%. Thus, on this middle portion of his taxable income he would owe $10,276 (.28 × $36,700). Finally, the remaining portion of Hunter's taxable income of $2,550 ($65,000–$62,450) would be taxed at 31%. Thus, he would owe an additional $790.50 (.31 × $2,550). To calculate Hunter's total personal income tax for 1999, he would add the amounts owed at each tax rate, a sum that totals $14,929 ($3,862.50 + $10,276 + $790.50). Each year over 100 million people file their income tax returns with the Internal Revenue Service (IRS), a branch of the Department of the Treasury. Hunter's filing status was "single." Other filing status options include "married filing jointly," "married filing separately," and "head of household."

   Social insurance payroll taxes include the FICA taxes—Social Security tax and Medicare tax—and a couple smaller insurance and retirement taxes. In FY 2000 the government anticipated collecting $637 billion from these payroll taxes. The FICA tax is withheld from workers' paychecks under the authority of the Federal Insurance Contributions Act (FICA). FICA automatically takes 7.65% of an employee's wage each pay period—a sum that the employer must match. Of the 7.65%, Social Security receives 6.2% and Medicare receives 1.45%. The FICA tax is both proportional and regressive, depending on the amount of money a person earns. This is because there is a "cap" on the Social Security portion of the FICA tax. In 2000 the cap was $76,200. As a result, on incomes up to $76,200, 7.65% was

Figure 11.2
1999 Tax Rate Schedule: "Single" Filing Status

Taxable Income	Tax Rate
$0–$25,750	15%
$25,750–$62,450	28%
$62,450–$130,250	31%
$130,250–$283,150	36%
$283,150 and above	39.6%

Source: Internal Revenue Service.

withheld in the form of a payroll tax. Because the same percentage is withheld from all workers' wages up to $76,200, the FICA tax is considered proportional. After a wage surpasses $76,200, however, it is not subject to the Social Security portion of the FICA tax. Thus, a person who earned $200,000 in income in 2000 would pay no Social Security taxes on the final $123,800 ($200,000 − $76,200) that he earned. To put the situation another way, a person who earns more than $76,200 ends up paying a lower percentage of his income on the Social Security tax than a person who earns less than $76,200. Thus, the Social Security portion of the FICA tax is a regressive tax at any income above $76,200. All wage earners continue to pay the Medicare portion of the FICA tax beyond the $76,200 cap. The FICA tax for the self-employed is 15.3% of their income, of which 12.4% goes to Social Security and 2.9% goes to Medicare.

The **corporate income tax** is a tax on corporate profits. In the FY 2000 budget, $189 billion will be collected in corporate income taxes. In many respects the corporate income tax is similar to the personal income tax. Like the personal income tax, corporations are allowed to make certain deductions before paying their income taxes to the government. These deductions usually take the form of business expenses and amounts deducted to cover the wear and tear on the corporation's capital goods. The federal revenues gained from corporate income taxes rank third, behind personal income taxes and the FICA tax.

Taxation at the State and Local Levels

State and local governments collect taxes for much the same reason as the federal government does—to finance essential public goods and services to citizens. At the state and local levels significant amounts of government revenue come from sales taxes, property taxes, and state income taxes. Another major source of revenue for state and local governments is grants from the federal government, which totaled $224 billion in 1997. The sources of state and local revenues are shown in Figure 11.3.

A **sales tax** is a tax on many of the goods and services that we pur-

Figure 11.3
State and Local Revenues, 1997

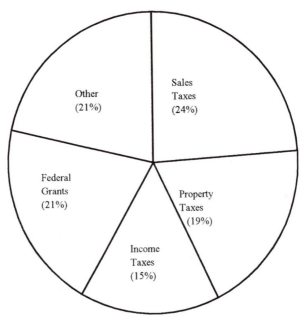

Source: U.S. Bureau of Economic Analysis.

chase. In 1997, $257 billion in sales taxes were collected at the state level.
The sales tax is considered a regressive tax because it tends to burden
lower-income households more than upper-income households (see earlier discussion of regressive taxes). By the mid-1990s, 45 states had sales
taxes that ranged from 3% to 7% on purchases. To reduce the burden on
lower-income households, most state sales taxes include exemptions for
food, medicine, and clothing up to a certain dollar limit.

A **state income tax**, like the federal personal income tax, is a tax on
people's income. In 1997, $160 billion was collected in state income taxes.
There is tremendous variety in the structure of state income taxes across
the United States, however. Many states have a form of progressive income tax, which requires higher income groups to pay a larger percentage of their incomes in taxes to the state. Others have a proportional
state income tax, which requires all people to pay a flat rate regardless
of their income. In 1999, 43 states had some form of state income tax.

A **property tax** is a tax on personal property, such as a house, buildings, undeveloped property, or a car. In 1997, $209 billion was collected
in property taxes, mainly by local governments. To tax property, a local
government first assesses the value of the property. The local government also determines what percentage of the property's value the owner

should pay in taxes. In many locations around the country, property taxes are determined by a "mill rate." A mill rate tells the property owner how many dollars is owed for each $1,000 in property—a house, a car, and so on—the taxpayer owns. Suppose Christopher owns an automobile that has an assessed value of $10,000. If the mill rate in his town is 25, Christopher would owe $250 in property taxes for the year ($25 for each $1,000 in the car's value, or $25 $\times$ 10 = $250). Property taxes are a main source of revenue for local governments.

An **excise tax** is a tax on a specific item. Excise taxes are levied by the federal government and by state governments. Excise taxes are typically higher than the more general sales taxes that are imposed by states. Items targeted for excise taxes include gasoline, liquor, and tobacco products. Excise taxes are designed to raise revenues and to influence the buying behaviors of people. By adding to the price of selected items, excise taxes discourage the purchase of these items.

MAKING ECONOMIC DECISIONS: WHAT IS A "FAIR" TAX?

You have just read about the different taxes that are used by the national, state, and local governments to raise revenues. But how do governments determine which taxes are the "fairest"? The fairness of taxes is one important element in the larger goal of economic equity (see chapter 2). While everyone can agree that government needs to raise revenues through taxation, there is considerable debate about what each person's "fair share" of the tax burden should be. To help societies decide which taxes are most fair, two principles of taxation are considered—the benefits-received principle and the ability-to-pay principle.

The **benefits-received principle** of taxation states that people who directly benefit from the use of certain public goods or services should be the ones who pay for them. For example, the tax receipts from the excise tax on gasoline and from toll plazas typically are used to build and repair the highways. Thus, people who directly benefit from the highways are paying for them. Supporters of the benefits-received principle argue that this is a fair arrangement because it resembles the way free markets work. That is, people are free to choose which public goods they wish to use, and then pay for these goods. Critics of the benefits-received principle counter that it is impossible to determine each person's "benefits" from many public goods and services. For instance, how would you calculate each person's benefit from national defense, or police or fire protection at the local level?

The **ability-to-pay principle** of taxation states that people with more income or wealth should pay more taxes. Note that the ability-to-pay principle can be based on income or wealth. The personal income tax is a good example of a tax based on the ability-to-pay based on income.

As a progressive tax, the personal income tax takes a higher percentage of income from upper-income households than lower-income households. This is because the upper-income people could pay as much as 39.6% in taxes on a portion of their taxable income, while lower-income households would pay at a far lower rate. Similarly, the local property tax is a good example of a tax based on the ability-to-pay based on wealth. Recall that property taxes are assessed on the value of property such as houses, buildings, automobiles, and undeveloped property. The higher the value of these properties, the higher the amount the owner must pay. Because upper-income households tend to own more property, they are obliged to pay higher taxes under the ability to pay based on wealth.

There are supporters and critics of the ability-to-pay principle of taxation. Supporters of ability-to-pay generally argue that people with larger incomes or wealth are in a better position to pay taxes than those with lower incomes. Critics argue that people who have earned higher incomes, or acquired more wealth, shouldn't be penalized for their success. Further, critics note that some people who have acquired wealth such as a house or property—especially the elderly who may live on fixed incomes—are not able to pay large property taxes.

So, what is the "fairest" tax? Should the national, state, or local governments use the benefits-received or the ability-to-pay principle to judge tax fairness? These are the normative questions that individuals must answer for themselves. And, in a democratic society, citizens can express their viewpoints in the voting booth to elect representatives that share their views.

GOVERNMENTS SPEND MONEY ON PUBLIC GOODS

Public goods, as you read earlier, are goods that are provided by government for use by all members of society. The government provides public goods when the private sector is unable, or unwilling to do so. One of the most important arguments that supports governments's role as the provider of public goods is the "free-rider dilemma."

Free-rider Dilemma

The **free-rider dilemma** is a problem that results when a private firm cannot prevent others—the "free-riders"—from using a good or service that it owns.

Consider one kind of good, a lighthouse, as an example. A private shipping company could build a lighthouse to safely guide its ships into a harbor. But what if other ships also used the light provided by this lighthouse to enter the harbor? These other ships would, in effect, be getting a free service—at the expense of the shipping company that originally built the lighthouse! In economics, the ships that used the service without paying for it are called "free-riders." The "free-rider dilemma" refers to the problem that firms—like the builder of the lighthouse—have in keeping others from using a good or service they did not pay for.

There are many essential goods that people need, but that would suffer from the free-rider dilemma if left to private firms to produce. The dilemma of the lighthouse owner could easily be applied to the building of highways, national parks, schools, libraries, and so on. In each case, why would a private firm produce these goods if free-riders could enjoy the benefits without incurring any costs? The answer is that private firms have no incentive to be this charitable! And that is why the government has stepped in to provide essential public goods and services to the people. The government spreads the costs of essential public goods among the citizens of the nation, state, town, or city by paying for public goods with tax dollars. You just read about the variety of taxes that are used to create the pool of funds needed for this kind of public spending.

Growth in Federal Spending

Predictably, government spending at all levels has increased throughout the 20th century. Many factors accounted for this increase in spending. Three key reasons included:

- Population growth: A larger population increases the need for public goods and services, and for social programs. According to the U.S. Bureau of the Census, the U.S. population more than tripled during the 20th century. Further, the Census Bureau expects the population to grow by about 25 million people per decade during the first half of the 21st century—a climb from 275 million in 2000 to 394 million by 2050. It is reasonable to assume that this population increase will require higher government spending in the future.

- Rising expectations: Americans have come to expect more services from their government—at all levels. Programs that were begun during the Great Depression, and expanded thereafter, have increased people's expectations that the government will provide many kinds of assistance in times of need. Some examples include health care (Medicare, Medicaid), income assistance for the poor (Temporary Assistance for Needy Families, food stamps), social insurance for the elderly (Social Security), and so on.

- International responsibilities: During the 20th century the United States emerged as a superpower and played decisive roles in World War I and World War II. These world wars, and the regional conflicts in Korea (1950s), Vietnam (1960–early 1970s), and more recently in the Persian Gulf (1991) and Yugoslavia

Figure 11.4
Federal Spending, FY 2000

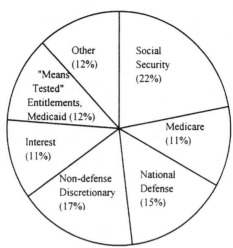

Source: Office of Management and Budget.

(1999), serve to illustrate how additional responsibilities have resulted in enormous costs to the government.

Government Spending in FY 2000

In FY 2000 budget, the federal government outlined a plan to spend over $1.7 trillion, mainly on public goods and services, social programs, and interest on the national debt, as shown in Figure 11.4.

Several of the most important components in this spending package included:

- Social Security and Medicare: The largest category of spending in the FY 2000 budget is Social Security. This $405 billion expenditure brings income and other benefits to the nation's 45 million retirees, plus disabled workers and their dependents. Coupled with the $217 billion in spending for Medicare—a federal health insurance program for 40 million elderly citizens—nearly one-third of the federal budget directly services the needs of the elderly. These portions of the federal budget will increase in the future as the life expectancy for Americans continues to rise, health care costs continue to increase, and the "baby boom" generation begins to retire.

- National defense: About $275 billion is budgeted for national defense in the FY 2000 budget. Expenditures for national defense, as a percentage of the entire federal budget, have declined since the end of the cold war in the early 1990s.

- Non-defense discretionary: About $330 billion is earmarked for "non-defense discretionary" spending. Major programs in this category include education and training, science, technology, housing, transportation, and foreign aid. In recent years this category of spending also has declined as a percentage of the budget.

- Net interest: Net interest payments of $215 billion will be paid to holders of U.S. debt—T-bills, notes, and bonds (see chapter 10). The government makes interest payments to these investors—foreigners and U.S. citizens—to repay them for purchasing U.S. securities in the past. According to the Office of Management and Budget (OMB), by 1998 the **national debt**, or sum total of all government outstanding debts—was about $5.5 trillion. Because the government's tax revenues have been greater than its spending over the past couple of years, experts believe that some of this debt may be paid off, or "retired," in the coming years. This will reduce the portion of the budget devoted to interest payments.

- Entitlements and Medicaid: "Means-tested" entitlements are the programs available to low-income groups. Eligibility for such assistance is determined by the household's income. Temporary Assistance for Needy Families, food stamps, and other public assistance programs are included. Also included is Medicaid, the federal health insurance program for America's poor on public assistance (see chapter 13).

Spending by State and Local Governments

Spending by state and local governments tends to focus on local concerns. According to the U.S. Bureau of the Census, the major categories of state and local spending in 1996 included education (36%), public welfare (27%), health care and hospitals (8.5%), and highways (8%). Other categories of spending by state and local governments included police protection, the courts and prisons, housing and community development, and other programs. These other programs accounted for the remaining 20.5% of state and local spending.

THE FEDERAL BUDGET

The **federal budget** is the government's plan to raise and spend money during a fiscal year. In the FY 2000 budget, which runs from October 1, 1999 to September 30, 2000, the government planned to raise $1.88 trillion, and spend $1.76 trillion. Who creates this massive federal budget each year? The process is a combined effort of the executive and legislative branches of government. Let's examine the budget-making process in some detail.

The Budget-making Process

The annual budget-making process is initiated by the executive branch. The President begins by directing the Office of Management and Budget (OMB) to devise a proposed budget for the coming year. In this proposed budget, the OMB lists the anticipated government revenues and expenditures. Because the OMB is an agency within the executive branch of government, the President's views on raising and spending federal funds is reflected in the OMB's budget proposal.

The President and the OMB present the proposed budget to Congress early in the calendar year—usually in February. Congress debates the merits of the proposed budget through the spring and summer months. Congressional debates focus on items listed on both sides of the budget—raising revenues through taxation, and spending money on public goods, social programs, and so on. Many compromises must be made along the way, including compromises between Republicans and Democrats, between Senators and Representatives, and between Congress and the President. These compromises inevitably result in changes in the proposed budget.

The deadline for final approval of the annual federal budget is September 30 of each year. This is because the federal government's fiscal year (FY)—the period of time covered by the budget—begins on October 1. In most cases the budget process keeps to this timetable. If the budget is not approved by September 30, however, Congress can authorize temporary funding to keep the government running until the budget is approved. In the fall of 1995, for example, Congress authorized temporary funding a few times after debate on the budget proposal became deadlocked. In response, President Clinton ordered a partial government shutdown in November of 1995 as a way to "jump start" further discussions and compromises on the budget. The partial shutdown was aimed at closing nonessential services such as national parks and national museums. Partial shutdowns do not have any impact on essential services such as national defense.

Budget Deficits and Surpluses

In some respects, the federal budget is similar to a household budget (see chapter 4). That is, each type of budget must anticipate its future

Figure 11.5
Federal Budget Deficits and Surpluses, 1970–2004* (in billions)

Year	Surplus or Deficit	Year	Surplus or Deficit
1970	−$2.8	1988	−$155.2
1971	−$23.0	1989	−$152.5
1972	−$23.4	1990	−$221.2
1973	−$14.9	1991	−$269.4
1974	−$6.1	1992	−$290.4
1975	−$53.2	1993	−$255.0
1976	−$73.7	1994	−$203.1
1977	−$53.7	1995	−$163.9
1978	−$59.2	1996	−$107.5
1979	−$40.7	1997	−$21.9
1980	−$73.8	1998	+$69.2
1981	−$79.0	*1999	+$79.3
1982	−$128.0	*2000	+$117.3
1983	−$207.8	*2001	+$134.0
1984	−$185.4	*2002	+$187.0
1985	−$212.3	*2003	+$182.0
1986	−$221.2	*2004	+$208.0
1987	−$149.8		

*Estimates by the OMB.

Sources: *The Economic Report of the President, 1999* and the Office of Management and Budget (OMB).

revenues and expenditures. There is a major difference between the two kinds of budgets, however. Unlike a household budget, the federal budget does not have to be "balanced." A **balanced budget** occurs when the federal government plans to spend as much as it collects in revenues. The federal budget is rarely "balanced." Instead, there is usually a deficit or a surplus built into the budget.

A **budget deficit** results when the government's spending is greater than its revenues. There was a continuous string of budget deficits between 1970 and 1997, as shown in Figure 11.5. These budget deficits, which topped $200 billion in some years during the 1980s and early 1990s, added to the growing national debt—the sum total of the past deficits. Naturally, when the government spends more money than it collects in taxes and fees, it must borrow to make up the difference. The government borrows by selling government securities such as Treasury notes, bonds, and bills to investors (see chapter 10). And the government must eventually repay investors the principle (original amount invested in the security) plus interest.

A **budget surplus** results when federal spending is less than its revenues. In FY 1998 the United States had its first budget surplus in a generation, as shown in Figure 11.5. This surplus was due to some belt-tightening by Congress in the 1990s, and by high tax revenues collected during the robust expansion of the period. As might be expected, the prospects for continued budget surpluses into the foreseeable future has stimulated a national debate over how the surpluses should be used. Many people, including President Clinton, favor using the bulk of the surplus money to strengthen the Social Security system. Other proposes for its use range from paying off a portion of the national debt to giving tax breaks to American taxpayers. Until policymakers can agree on the most desirable use for the budget surplus, it will be held in a reserve.

12

HOW DOES GOVERNMENT STABILIZE
THE ECONOMY?

Chapter 12 deals with the government's role in stabilizing the American economy. The government's stabilization policies are mainly devised to smooth the ups and downs in the business cycle—a recurring cycle of increases and decreases in the nation's real Gross Domestic Product (GDP). The two most important actions that the government can take to stabilize the economy are monetary policy and fiscal policy. Monetary policy is controlled by the Federal Reserve System (the Fed)—the nation's central bank. Fiscal policy is controlled by Congress and by the President. These stabilization policies are designed to stimulate a sluggish economy by increasing aggregate (total) demand, or to slow down an overheated economy by decreasing aggregate demand. Another approach to promoting economic stability is supply-side economics. Supply-siders support policies that increase aggregate (total) supply in the economy.

THE BUSINESS CYCLE

The **business cycle** shows the increases and decreases in the real GDP—the GDP adjusted for inflation—in the U.S. economy over time. That is, it illustrates the fluctuations in business activity in the overall economy. A business cycle has two main phases, as shown in Figure 12.1. One phase is called the expansion. During expansions the real GDP in the nation rises steadily until it hits a peak. Figure 12.1 illustrates an expansion from 1983 to 1990. Also shown in Figure 12.1 is an expansion that began in March of 1991. It was still going strong in February of 2000, which made it the longest expansion in the post-World War II period (107 months). When the expansion reaches its peak, a second phase in the business cycle begins—the contraction. Note in Figure 12.1 that the U.S. economy peaked in 1990, and that a brief contraction followed. Contractions occur when the real GDP declines. The lowest point in a contraction is called the trough. A **recession** is a contraction that lasts at least six months. A **depression** is a prolonged, severe recession. There have been a number of short-lived recessions in the United States since World War II—in 1949, 1954, 1961, 1970, 1974, 1982, and 1991. The most recent depression in the United States occurred during the 1930s. So, why does economic activity fluctuate?

Causes of the Business Cycle

A number of factors help account for the ups and downs in the business cycle. One important factor is consumer confidence. That is, when people are generally optimistic about the economy, and about the security of their own jobs, they tend to spend freely. High consumer spending, in turn, results in increased production of goods and services by firms. Higher rates of production lead to high employment rates and, thus, still higher demand. While the economy is riding this upward cycle, consumer optimism fuels the expansion. But consumer confidence can be shaken by many factors. News about declining business profits, hints of renewed inflation (higher prices for goods and services), declining stock values, or forecasts of an impending economic downturn could erode public confidence and reverse the cycle.

A second factor that influences the business cycle is business investment (see chapter 10). When businesses invest in new capital, more advanced technology, training for workers, and the new ideas of entrepreneurs, the result is usually higher rates of production and higher productivity. Part of the money that firms invest comes from their own profits, called "retained earnings." Firms can also raise money for investments from the sale of bonds or by issuing stock. When firms anticipate high demand for their output, they tend to increase their investments and their rates of production. Naturally, this higher output adds to the growing real GDP, and the expansion in the business cycle continues. When businesses fear that demand will slow down in the future, they tend to reduce their investments as well as their rates of production. This causes sluggish business activity and results in a contraction.

Finally, unpredictable national or international events can cause business activity to fluctuate. For example, when the OPEC oil cartel (see chapter 7) flexed its muscles in the early 1970s by imposing an oil embargo on the United States, business activity slowed dramatically. Limited supplies of oil caused oil prices—and the prices of related products

Figure 12.1
U.S. Business Cycle, 1981–1998*

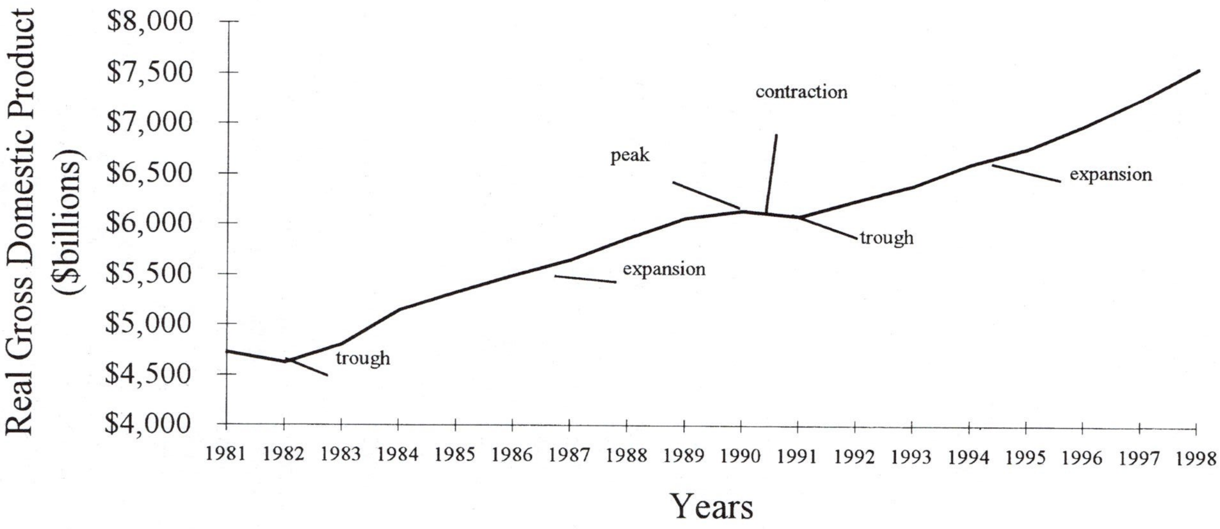

Real Gross Domestic Product
($billions)

Years

*1998 data based on the first three quarters of 1998.
Source: Economic Report of the President, 1999.

such as gasoline—to rise. Facing higher costs of production, firms reduced their rates of production and laid off workers. The oil "price shock" was a major cause of the recession of 1974. Conversely, the relatively low oil prices of the 1990s—culminating in the decline of oil prices to about $11 per barrel in early 1999—stimulated business activity in the United States and helped prolong the economic expansion of the period.

Predicting the Business Cycle

Economists have a good track record in predicting when and how serious these shifts in the business cycle can be. They do this by considering a variety of "economic indicators," the most important of which are the "leading economic indicators." The leading indicators provide useful hints to economists about the direction of the economy. One leading indicator is building permits. Building contractors take out building permits when they anticipate building new homes or businesses in the future. When the number of building permits increases, this signals a healthy construction industry—and a healthy economy—over the next few quarters (six months to a year). On the other hand, if the number of applications for building permits falls, this signals that new construction will slow and, perhaps, drag related industries down with it. Other leading economic indicators include the number of orders for consumer durables (major appliances), orders for new capital goods, and the performance of stocks on the NYSE and other stock markets. In February of 2000 the leading economic indicators remained positive, signaling that the record-breaking expansion of the 1990s would continue well into 2000.

STABILIZATION THROUGH MONETARY POLICY

Monetary policy is the plan of action by the Federal Reserve System (the Fed) to promote economic stability. That is, monetary policy attempts to moderate some of the economic problems connected with contractions, and overheated expansions of the business cycle. The three major monetary policy tools are the discount rate, open market operations, and the reserve requirement.

Monetary policy focuses on changing the nation's money supply (see chapter 8) and, thus aggregate demand in the economy. **Aggregate demand** is the total demand for goods and services in an economy at any point in time. By increasing the money supply, the Fed fights recessions. This is because a larger money supply enables people to buy more goods and services. Higher demand for products, in turn, stimulates business activity—opening new businesses, expanding existing businesses, hiring additional workers, and so on. By decreasing the money supply, the Fed fights inflation. **Inflation** occurs when the general price level in the economy rises. When the Fed decreases the supply of money, people buy fewer goods and services, and aggregate demand falls. Businesses respond to falling aggregate demand in predictable ways—by slowing the rate of production and laying off workers. The Fed's anti-inflation policies aim directly at the main cause of inflation—"too much money chasing too few goods."

Structure of the Federal Reserve System (the Fed)

The Fed has served as America's central bank since it was founded in 1913 by the Federal Reserve Act. At the national level the most important decision making body in the Fed is its Board of Governors—a seven-member body appointed by the President. The Board of Governors supervises all of the Fed's activities and determines how to stabilize the economy. Members of the Board of Governors are appointed for 14-year terms of office. These terms are staggered so that one new member is added every two years. The chairman of the Fed serves a 4-year term. Alan Greenspan has served as chairman of the Fed since 1987 and, in February of 2000, was overwhelmingly confirmed by the Senate to serve a fourth four-year term (2000–2004). Also at the national level is the Federal Open Market Committee (FOMC). The FOMC determines how to implement "open market operations," one of the Fed's most important stabilization tools. The FOMC is comprised of twelve members, including the seven members of the Board of Governors, the president of the New York Federal Reserve Bank, and four other Fed Bank presidents— who serve one-year terms of office on a rotating basis.

At the district level there are 12 district Federal Reserve banks and 25 branch banks. These 12 Fed banks each serve a geographic region in the United States. The regions include: (1) Boston, (2) New York City, (3) Philadelphia, (4) Cleveland, (5) Richmond, (6) Atlanta, (7) Chicago, (8) St. Louis, (9) Minneapolis, (10) Kansas City, (11) Dallas, and (12) San Francisco. The 12 district Fed banks stabilize the banking system and provide financial services to the federal government. For example, Fed banks help commercial banks clear checks electronically. This service applies to checks written anywhere in the United States. Secondly, Fed banks extend loans—mainly short-term loans—to commercial banks. This ensures "an elastic currency." That is, it ensures that commercial banks have sufficient funds to handle day-to-day transactions even if there is an unusually high demand for money by depositors. Third, Fed banks supervise the types of loans and investments made by commercial banks, and monitor banks to make sure that sound banking practices are followed. The Fed banks also assist the federal government by serving as the "government's bank." As the government's bank the 12 Fed banks accept deposits from the federal government and hold the federal government's "checking account." Checks issued by the federal government, such as income tax refunds and transfer payments, are written against the government's checking account with the Fed. The Fed also issues currency and holds the cash reserves of the Fed's "member banks."

At the local level are the thousands of "member banks" in the Federal Reserve System. A unique feature of the Fed is that the "member banks" own the Fed. Commercial banks that are chartered by the federal government are required to join the Fed, while state-chartered banks are free to choose whether they will become part of the system. When a bank is "chartered" by the federal government, this simply means that the bank applied to the federal government for permission to form and do business in the United States. State-chartered banks make similar applications to their own state governments. Virtually all depository institutions—member banks and non-member institutions—are required to hold cash reserves with their district Fed bank and accept the supervision of Fed bank examiners. These cash reserves can be held at the district Fed bank itself, or in the vaults of the commercial bank or other depository institution. Cash reserves create a large pool of money for the Fed banks, which enables them to respond quickly to financial crises in the banking system.

Monetary Policy Tools

The most important function of the Fed is to stabilize the economy. This it does by regulating the nation's money supply. While there is some dispute about which measure of the money supply is most important to regulate, the Fed's primary concern is with the growth of M2. The M2 is comprised of the M1 (the currency that people have in their possession, travelers checks, demand deposits, and other checkable deposits), plus a number of "near moneys" such as people's regular savings deposits, time deposits, money market deposit accounts, and mutual funds (see chapter 8). The Fed uses three major tools to regulate the money supply—the discount rate, open market operations, and the reserve requirement.

- Discount rate: The **discount rate** is the interest rate charged by the Fed to member banks, other depository institutions, and the government for loans. The Fed is a bank for banks and for the government, not for individuals or firms. When the Fed increases the discount rate, borrowing from the Fed becomes more expensive. The Fed's higher discount rate then ripples through the banking system. Banks tend to match any increases in the Fed's discount rate with interest rate increases of their own. Higher interest rates charged by banks discourage the use of credit and borrowing in the economy. The effect is that there is less spending—and a lower aggregate demand. Conversely, when the Fed decreases the discount rate, borrowing from the Fed becomes cheaper. Banks can then reduce their interest rates to consumers and firms. This stimulates buying and increases aggregate demand in the economy.

- Open market operations: **Open market operations** is the buying and selling of government securities by the government. This monetary tool is used to decrease or increase the amount of money in circulation. When the Fed sells additional government securities it is, in effect, withdrawing money from the economy. What is the result? People have less money to spend and, therefore, aggregate demand falls. Conversely, the government might choose to increase the amount of money in circulation by purchasing government securities back from investors—consumers, firms, banks, and so on. By repurchasing its securities, the government is pumping money back into the economy, thereby increasing aggregate demand.

- Reserve requirement: The **reserve requirement** is the amount of money that banks must hold as vault cash or keep on deposit with their Fed banks. The reserve requirement is expressed as a percentage of a bank's deposits. To reduce the amount of money flowing through the economy, the Fed can increase the reserve requirement. This leaves banks less money to loan to consumers or to firms. Less borrowing means less spending, and the result is a fall in aggregate demand. On the flip side, the Fed might also decrease the reserve requirement and thereby increase the amount of money that banks can loan to their customers. As the pool of loanable funds increases, borrowing increases, and aggregate demand rises.

Tight and Easy Monetary Policies

So how does the Fed use these tools to combat contractions (declining GDP and rising unemployment) and overheated expansions (rising inflation)? The answer is by using either an "easy money policy" (to combat the contraction) or a "tight money policy" (to combat inflation).

An **easy money policy** is designed to increase the money supply in order to increase aggregate demand in the economy. An easy money policy is used to fight recessions by stimulating business activity—such as increased production, more jobs, more investment, and so on. The two monetary tools most commonly used to stimulate business activity are the discount rate and open market operations. To implement its easy money policy, the Fed lowers its discount rate. This encourages other banks to do the same and, thus, create additional borrowing and spending. For example, the relatively low discount rates over the past decade, which ranged from a low of 3% in 1992 to 5.75% in February of 2000, helped fuel the business expansion of the period. Secondly, through its open market operations, the Fed buys back government securities to increase the flow of money back into the economy. In extreme situations, the third major monetary policy tool might be used—the reserve requirement. This tool is not used much because of the enormous disruption it causes within the banking system. In an extreme case, to support an easy money policy the Fed could lower the reserve requirement and, thus, increase the pool of funds that banks could loan to people.

A **tight money policy** is designed to reduce the money supply and thereby decrease aggregate demand in the economy. A tight money policy is used to fight inflation, which often occurs during the expansionary phase of the business cycle when high demand for goods and services causes prices to rise. How can the Fed implement a tight monetary policy to reduce aggregate demand? First, the Fed increases the discount rate. This makes it more expensive for banks to borrow from the Fed. Banks, in turn, raise their own interest rates. This discourages borrowing by individuals and firms, and reduces aggregate demand. For example, the relatively high discount rates in the early 1980s, which peaked at 14% in May of 1981, were used to combat severe inflation during the period. Next, the Fed sells government securities to investors. In effect, by selling Treasury bills, notes, or bonds, the government "soaks up" excess cash in the economy and reduces aggregate demand. The third, infrequently used monetary tool—the reserve requirement—could also be increased to force banks to limit the amount of money they can loan to consumers or businesses.

STABILIZATION THROUGH FISCAL POLICY

Fiscal policy is the plan of action by Congress and by the President to promote economic stability. Like monetary policy, fiscal policy attempts to smooth the ups and downs of the business cycle and deal with the related problems of unemployment and inflation by regulating aggregate demand. The most important fiscal policy tools used by the government are taxation, government spending, and tax incentives.

Fiscal Policy Tools

The government's fiscal policy tools—taxes, spending, and incentives—are designed to change aggregate demand and business activity in the economy.

- Taxation: Taxes are the mandatory payments by individuals and firms to the government (see chapter 11). But taxes are also used to regulate aggregate demand in the economy. By increasing taxes on individuals or firms, the government is able to withdraw money from the economy. This is because people's disposable incomes fall as additional taxes are deducted from their paychecks. The effect of higher taxes, therefore, is a decline in aggregate demand and a decline in business activity. Conversely, by reducing taxes the government permits people to hold onto a greater portion of their disposable incomes. This increases aggregate demand and stimulates business activity because people have more money to spend.

- Government spending: Government spending is another way for the government to change the amount of money in circulation. When the government decreases its spending, less money is pumped into the economy. The result is that people have less money in their pockets, and aggregate demand and business activity decline. When the government increases its spending, more money is pumped into the economy. This increases aggregate demand and business activity.

- Tax incentives: Taxes can also be used as an incentive or a disincentive for businesses to invest in new capital. The "investment tax credit," for example, permits firms to deduct a percentage of the money they spend on new equipment from their income taxes. If the investment tax credit is 10%, and a firm purchases $1,000,000 in new equipment, the firm is then able to deduct $100,000 (.10 × $1,000,000) from the taxes it owes the government. The government increases the investment tax credit to encourage firms to invest. This stimulates business activity in the economy by increasing the demand for new capital goods, and by encouraging firms to increase their rate of output. The government decreases the investment tax credit to discourage further investment by firms. This tends to slow an overheated economy down by reducing spending by firms and by reducing the demand for many goods.

Expansionary and Restrictive Fiscal Policies

Congress and the President use an expansionary fiscal policy to fight contractions, and a restrictive fiscal policy to fight inflation. An **expansionary fiscal policy** is designed to increase spending by individuals and firms and, thus, increase aggregate demand in the economy. Congress and the President use expansionary fiscal policy to combat recession. To pull a sluggish economy out of recession, the government decreases taxes, increases government spending, and increases the investment tax credit. By decreasing taxes, people are able to keep—and to spend—a larger portion of their disposable incomes. By increasing government spending—more defense contracts, expanding the nation's infrastructure, building schools, and so on—the government is pumping money directly into the economy. By increasing the investment tax credit, the government encourages firms to invest in new capital goods and hire additional workers.

A **restrictive fiscal policy** is designed to slow the pace of business activity and thereby decrease aggregate demand in the economy. Thus, a restrictive fiscal policy is used to fight inflation. To slow the pace of economic growth and the excessive demand fueling this growth, Congress and the President can increase taxes, decrease government spending, and lower the investment tax credit. By increasing taxes people's disposable incomes are reduced—as is their ability to spend money. Reduced spending translates into lower aggregate demand. Similarly, when the government reduces its spending programs less money circulates in the economy, and individuals and firms tend to cut back on their purchases. Finally, by lowering the investment tax credit the government reduces the willingness and ability of firms to invest in new capital.

MONETARY AND FISCAL POLICIES IN ACTION: A CASE STUDY

From May of 1960 to February of 1961 the U.S. economy slipped into a recession. The unemployment rate rose from about 5% of the labor force to 6.9%, and the GDP stagnated. An "easy money policy" by the Fed, and an "expansionary fiscal policy" by Congress and the President, were used to address this contraction in the business cycle.

The Fed's "easy money policy" employed all of its major tools to increase aggregate demand and business activity. First, the Fed reduced its reserve requirements to allow banks to loan more money to individuals and to firms. Next, through open market operations, the Fed purchased billions of dollars worth of government securities. This pumped money into the sluggish economy. Third, the Fed lowered the discount rate twice in 1960—from 4% to 3.5% and finally to 3%. This encouraged commercial banks and other depository institutions to likewise lower their interest rates.

Congress and the President (Kennedy) initiated an "expansionary fiscal policy" to strengthen the actions of the Fed. For example, by the early 1960s the investment tax credit was raised to encourage new investment in capital goods. Government spending was increased, and tax cuts in the personal income tax and the corporate income tax soon followed.

These tax policies, along with higher government spending, increased aggregate demand in the economy, and gave businesses an incentive to increase production. As the GDP steadily rose, unemployment fell. Across the nation there was a feeling that we finally understood how to "fine tune" the economy to promote stability. Periods of economic instability over the next couple of decades, including more severe and prolonged recessions in 1973–1975 (16 months) and 1981–1982 (16 months), proved that we still had much to learn.

LIMITATIONS OF MONETARY AND FISCAL POLICIES

The complexities of the U.S. economy limit the effectiveness of monetary and fiscal policies. A number of limitations are listed below.

- Political considerations: In a democracy, policies are often influenced by political pressures—by citizens, by lobbyists who represent "special interest groups," and by elected officials. Political pressure is felt most keenly by elected officials who create fiscal policy—Congresspersons and the President. But policies that are popular with voters may not be in the best interests of the nation.
- Forecasting considerations: Economic forecasting, which tries to predict future directions in the economy, is not a precise science. This is because forecasting cannot account for all of the economic factors that will influence future business activity. Thus, the nation's monetary and fiscal policies are based on the experts' "best guess" about what the economic future of the nation will be.
- Coordination considerations: There is sometimes disagreement between the Fed and the nation's highest elected officials about the appropriate stabilization policy. For example, in the early 1980s the Fed, under Chairman Paul Volcker, maintained a "tight money policy" to battle against inflation, while President Reagan and a majority of Congress were busy cutting taxes to stimulate investment and business activity. These conflicting policies sent mixed messages to the economy.
- Timing considerations: "Time lags" occur between the time the government recognizes a problem and the time it takes to form and implement an appropriate stabilization policy. Time lags are most troublesome with fiscal policy because Congress and the President must come to an agreement on specific policies that are economically sound and that will be acceptable to voting public.

Economic Thinkers: John Maynard Keynes and Demand-Side Economics

John Maynard Keynes (1883–1946) was an influential British economist. In his most famous book, *The General Theory of Employment, Interest, and Money* (1936),

Keynes supported a larger role for the government in regulating aggregate demand as a way to speed the recovery from the Great Depression.

In *The General Theory,* Keynes argued that some of the unemployment that resulted from the Great Depression was due to economic forces beyond the control of workers. Instead of the personal failings of unemployed workers, Keynes believed that much of the unemployment problem stemmed from insufficient aggregate demand. During a depression, lower aggregate demand resulted in a downward cycle of business activity—of lower production, still further loss of jobs, and still lower aggregate demand.

To reverse this downward cycle, Keynes argued that the government should develop policies to increase aggregate demand in the nation. **Demand-side economics** stresses the need to increase aggregate demand as a way to motivate producers to expand production, to invest in new capital goods, and to hire more workers. To accomplish these goals, Keynes supported an expansionary fiscal policy that included lower taxes, higher government spending, and budget deficits. **Budget deficits** occur when the government's tax revenues are less than government's expenditures.

The views of John Maynard Keynes were widely accepted during and after the Great Depression, and became the foundation for "demand-side" economics in the United States. Followers of Keynes and his ideas eventually became known as the "Keynesians."

MAKING ECONOMIC DECISIONS: THE SUPPLY-SIDE APPROACH TO STABILIZATION

Since the Great Depression economists have debated how to bring about long-term economic growth and stability. From the mid-1930s to the late 1970s, "demand-side" economics was the most widely accepted approach to keeping the economy on an even keel. Then, in the presidential election of 1980, Republican candidate Ronald Reagan brought the "supply-side" approach to stabilization to the nation's attention. The landslide electoral victory for Ronald Reagan over incumbent Jimmy Carter in 1980 was, in part, a vote of confidence for the supply-side approach to stabilizing the economy.

Supply-side Economics

Supply-side economics refers to government policies designed to provide incentives for firms to increase aggregate supply. **Aggregate supply** is the total supply of goods and services produced in an economy. Supporters of supply-side economics, called "supply-siders," look to the work of French economist Jean Baptiste Say (1767–1832) for the basic ideas behind supply-side theory. According to Say, government intervention in the economy almost always hurt the economy. Say formalized his ideas into "Say's Law." Say's Law stressed that supply created its own demand. He argued that market forces, not the government, should be the driving force behind economic growth.

In the late 1970s some economists, including Arthur B. Laffer (1941–   ), argued that supply-side economics was the best way to deal with two economic problems—inflation and unemployment—simultaneously. That is, by increasing aggregate supply, the economy could rid itself of the major cause of inflation—"too much money chasing too few goods." In addition, to increase aggregate supply, firms would have to expand production and, thus, hire additional workers. This would stimulate economic growth and move the economy closer to full employment. The supply-side approach to stabilization was put into practice when President Reagan became President in 1981.

The Supply-side Stabilization Program of the 1980s

President Reagan's (1981–1989) supply-side stabilization program rested on three main policies—cut taxes, government regulations, and social programs. Thus, at the heart of his program—called "Reaganomics" by some people—was to reduce the role of government in the economy.

The tax cuts were designed to restore incentives for people to save and invest money, to work longer hours, and to produce more goods and services. Under the Economic Recovery Act of 1981, tax cuts of 25% were made in the personal income tax and corporate income tax over a three-year period (1982 to 1984).

The plan to reduce government regulations was intended to remove costly bureaucratic obstacles to economic growth. Not surprisingly, funding was reduced for some federal regulatory agencies during the 1980s, including the Consumer Product Safety Commission and the Environmental Protection Agency.

Reduced spending on some "social programs" had two objectives—to save taxpayers money and to provide an incentive for those without work to find productive jobs. During the 1980s funding for a number of social programs was reduced.

Impact of Reaganomics

It is difficult to assess the impact of the supply-side stabilization program on the U.S. economy during the 1980s. By 1982, the economy had slumped into a serious recession and the unemployment rate had jumped to about 10%. In addition, massive federal budget deficits plagued the economy throughout the 1980s, despite the administration's pledge to balance the budget. By the mid-1980s, however, inflation was under control, and the nation was once again in an expansionary phase of the business cycle.

Was supply-side economics solely "to blame" for the recession of 1982 and for the massive federal budget deficits of the 1980s? Can the supply-siders "take credit" for the lengthy expansion that followed or the taming of inflation by the mid-1980s? Economists still disagree on the answers to these questions. What can be said is that by the late 1980s, few politicians and few economists were willing to jump onto the supply-side bandwagon.

13

HOW IS INCOME DISTRIBUTED IN THE UNITED STATES?

Chapter 13 discusses the distribution of income in the American economy. Household income comes from a variety of sources, such as wages and salaries, rents, interest, dividends, profits, and transfer payments. Wages and salaries represent the largest source of household income. Wages and salaries are influenced by market forces and by government legislation—including the minimum wage. To earn a salary or wage, a person must be employed. Thus, one's employment has a major impact on household income. To illustrate the actual distribution of income in the U.S. economy, economists use the Lorenz Curve. This curve reveals that there is a wide income gap between the rich and the poor. Thus, the problem of poverty is an important feature in our study of income distribution.

SOURCES OF INCOME

Income is the amount of money received by individuals. Income can be either "earned" or "unearned." According to the Bureau of the Census, the real median household income in the United States in 1998 was $38,885—the highest median income in U.S. history.

Earned Income

Earned income is the income people receive in the form of wages and salaries, rents, interest, dividends, or profits (see chapter 4). Wages and salaries are payments in exchange for a worker's labor. Rents are payments in exchange for the use of a person's property such as land, buildings, or equipment. Interest is the return on capital. Firms, for example, pay interest to investors such as banks or individuals in exchange for the money firms borrow from them. Dividends are the regular payments made by corporations to their stockholders. Profits are the financial rewards paid to entrepreneurs who take extra risks to establish a firm, develop a new product, or create a new way to produce a product. Profits are also the return earned by proprietors and partners in their businesses.

Note that all the sources are offered in exchange for the factors of production that people sell to businesses or to the government. The President of the United States, for example, exchanges his labor for a $200,000 salary and a mountain of other benefits—not least of which is room and board at the White House.

Unearned Income

Unearned income takes the form of transfer payments. **Transfer payments** are payments of money, goods, or services, financed by one group of citizens and distributed to another group of citizens. Governments at the national, state, and local levels are the largest distributors of transfer payments. Examples include income assistance payments made to the poor through Temporary Assistance for Needy Families, medical benefits to the poor through Medicaid, and retirement income to the elderly through Social Security. Private transfer payments most often come from company pension plans.

WAGE DETERMINATION AND INCOME

Wages and salaries account for over one-half of all income that comes into U.S. households. Thus, wages and salaries are an important determinant in how income is distributed in the economy. But how are the wages for different jobs determined? Most often, wage rates are set by a combination of market forces and by government rules or regulations.

Market Forces

Market forces are the most important factor in determining wages for U.S. workers. The "market" for labor is very similar to the "markets" for goods (see chapter 3 for more on how the market determines prices for most goods and services). That is, when the demand is high for certain workers, the wage tends to increase. Conversely, when the demand is low for certain workers, the wage drops. On the supply side of the market, when there is a scarcity of certain workers, the wage tends to increase, but when there is an abundance of certain workers the wage tends to fall. So, what factors influence the supply of and demand for workers?

The supply of workers is influenced by many factors. For example, the supply of workers in specialized fields that require extensive education, training, or natural talents is often limited. Thus, the wages for such workers—doctors, engineers, and professional athletes—is usually high. In occupations that do not require such specialized training, the wage tends to be lower. Working conditions is a second factor affecting the supply of labor. This is because fewer workers are attracted to workplaces or occupations that have uncomfortable or dangerous work environments. Towns and cities often offer attractive wage and benefit packages to the police and fire fighters to compensate them for the stress and dangers connected with their jobs. A third factor is the location of the job. If the job is inconveniently located, the number of workers willing to take the job will be smaller. American engineers recruited to rebuild Kuwait's infrastructure after the tragic Gulf War of 1991, for example, received enormous wages to travel to this distant, war-torn nation to help in its reconstruction.

The demand for workers is determined by the employer's specific needs for labor and by the demand for the good that is produced by the firm. In your school, for example, the Board of Education typically offers a decent wage to teachers and administrators to attract talented professionals to the school. Other jobs at the school, such as custodial positions, command a lesser wage. This is because the skills needed to perform some of the more routine maintenance tasks in the building are less specialized. In addition, all demand for labor is what economists call a derived demand. **Derived demand** means that the demand for laborers stems from the demand for the product that the worker makes or the service that the worker performs. For example, today there is no demand for workers who are skilled at making typewriters because the demand for typewriters has dried up. Conversely, the demand for computer service people has exploded in recent years because the demand for such repair services has increased.

Legislation

Since the Great Depression of the 1930s government legislation has also influenced wages in the United States. This legislation was designed to promote equal employment opportunities, equal pay for equal work, and fair compensation for all laborers. A summary of key legislation is shown below.

- Minimum wage (1937): The minimum wage sets a "price floor" for wages. This means that an employer cannot offer a wage below this minimum dollar amount. Today, the national minimum wage is $5.15 per hour, but a number of states have established a minimum wage higher than $5.15. The current debate about raising the minimum wage is examined later in this chapter.

- Equal Pay Act (1963): The Equal Pay Act guarantees that employers pay the same wage for the same job. This act specifically targeted wage discrimination based on gender. Employers can pay a different wage to employees based on their seniority—the number of years they have worked at a particular job—or based on a specific job category (Secretary Level 1, Secretary Level 2, and so on).

- Civil Rights Act of 1964: The Civil Rights Act of 1964 guarantees equal employment opportunities regardless of race, gender, religion, or national origin. It also created the Equal Employment Opportunity Commission (EEOC) to ensure compliance with this goal.

- Affirmative action (1965): Affirmative action refers to a series of policies and programs designed to increase job and educational opportunities for minorities and women. It was created by an executive order of President Lyndon B. Johnson in 1965 to help minorities and women overcome centuries of discrimination in the workplace and in educational opportunities. Opponents view the preferential treatment of minorities and women as a form of "reverse discrimination"—a bias against white males. During the mid-1990s affirmative action policies were being vigorously challenged in the courts throughout the United States. For example, California's Proposition 209 ended virtually all state-sponsored programs that offered preferences based on race or gender.

- Comparable worth: Comparable worth legislation is designed to increase wages in occupations traditionally held by women. The goal is to promote fairness in the distribution of income by reducing wage differentials among jobs that require similar training or skills. Supporters of comparable worth laws point to the fact that the wages of women are only about 70% of those of men. Opponents of comparable worth laws note that women's rights to equal employment opportunities, and to a fair wage, are already protected by the Civil Rights Act of 1964 and by the Equal Pay Act.

MAKING ECONOMIC DECISIONS: THE MINIMUM WAGE

A **minimum wage** sets a "price floor" on wages (see chapter 3). This means that employers cannot offer a wage below this minimum standard. The nation's first minimum wage was created by the Fair Labor Standards Act of 1937. Since 1938, when the minimum wage was set at $.25, the national minimum wage has been increased 19 times, as shown in Figure 13.1. In early 2000, it stood at $5.15 per hour—but there was considerable discussion in Congress about whether or not to raise the minimum wage once again.

Supporters of a higher minimum wage argue that the current $5.15 hourly wage does not provide a worker with a living wage, especially if the worker is supporting a family. Consider Billy's financial situation. Billy supports his family by working at his full-time job, and receives the national minimum wage as his compensation. Hence, Billy's weekly income is $206 ($5.15 × 40 hours). If Billy works every week of the year his annual income is $10,712 ($206 × 52 weeks). If Billy earned this annual income in 1998, his "family of four" would be far below the poverty line of $16,660 (you will read more about the poverty line later in the chapter). Supporters of a higher minimum wage also note that the purchasing power of the dollar declines each year due to inflation. This means that if the minimum wage is held constant, people are able to purchase fewer goods and services as the years roll by. Supporters conclude that in order to achieve the economic goals of economic security (security from the declining value of their dollars) and economic equity (a fair wage for workers) the minimum wage must be raised.

Opponents argue that a higher minimum wage would disrupt the efficient functioning of "the market"—the labor market in this case. That is, a price floor on wages overrides the true market wage that would ordinarily be set by the forces of supply and demand. And the consequences of a government-imposed minimum wage are severe. Opponents argue that a higher minimum wage would force firms to either raise their prices or lay off employees. This is because the firm incurs higher costs of production—higher wages for workers. These consequences run contrary to the economic goals of price stability (higher prices for many products could lead to inflation) and full employment (workers may lose their jobs because their labor is too expensive for employers to hire). A higher minimum wage also limits the employer's economic freedom to employ resources—in this case labor—at a price set by the market.

UNEMPLOYMENT AND INCOME DISTRIBUTION

Unemployment refers to the number of people who are without jobs, but who are willing and able to work at current wages. When speaking of unemployment, people most often refer to the **unemployment rate**, or percentage of the labor force that is without work. During the 1990s, for example, the unemployment rate has fluctuated between 4.2% in 1999

Figure 13.1
History of the U.S. Minimum Wage

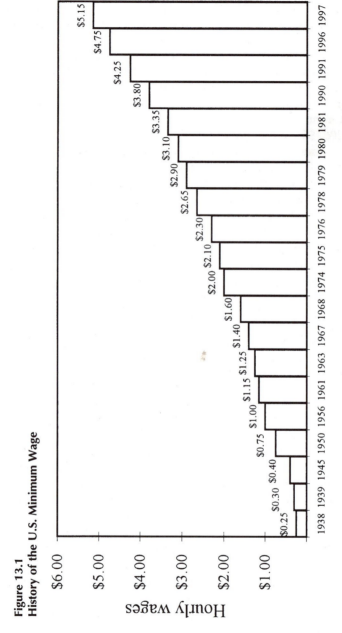

Hourly wages / Year of change

Source: U.S. Department of Labor.

and 7.5% in 1992. These fluctuations are shown in Figure 13.2. By February of 2000 the unemployment rate had dipped to just 4.0%, the lowest rate since 1970. The American labor force is comprised of about 139 million laborers who are 16 years old or older, and who are either currently working or looking for a job. Unemployment has a major impact on the distribution of income in the United States.

Types of Unemployment

There are four types of unemployment: structural, cyclical, seasonal, and frictional.

- Structural unemployment: **Structural unemployment** occurs when there is a "mismatch" between the supply of labor and the demand for labor with particular skills. For example, a booming demand for computer programmers in California will not necessarily create jobs for unskilled laborers recently laid off in Michigan. This is because the unskilled labor lacks the training and experience to step into high-tech jobs. Further, people do not easily pack up and move to far-away places. Often, technological advances in the nation's workplaces, and foreign competition, contribute to structural unemployment.

- Cyclical unemployment: **Cyclical unemployment** occurs when there is a downturn—or contraction—in the nation's business cycle (see chapter 12 for more on the business cycle). The unemployment rate rises during contractions because firms cut back on their rate of production. Less production means lay-offs for some workers. Note from Figure 13.2 that the U.S. unemployment rate increased during the recession of the early 1990s, and declined steadily during the expansion since that time.

- Seasonal unemployment: **Seasonal unemployment** occurs when people are out of work for a portion of the year because of changes in seasons. For example, in many parts of the nation the construction industry slows during the winter months. As a result, some construction workers lose their jobs. This contributes to seasonal unemployment. Seasonal unemployment is common during the "off seasons" at summer beach resorts, ski lodges, and so on.

- Frictional unemployment: **Frictional unemployment** occurs when workers are "in-between" jobs, or are "new entrants" into the labor force and are seeking their first jobs. This type of unemployment is a normal occurrence in a dynamic, changing economy such as the U.S. economy. This is because the types of jobs

Figure 13.2
U.S. Unemployment Rates, 1990–1999

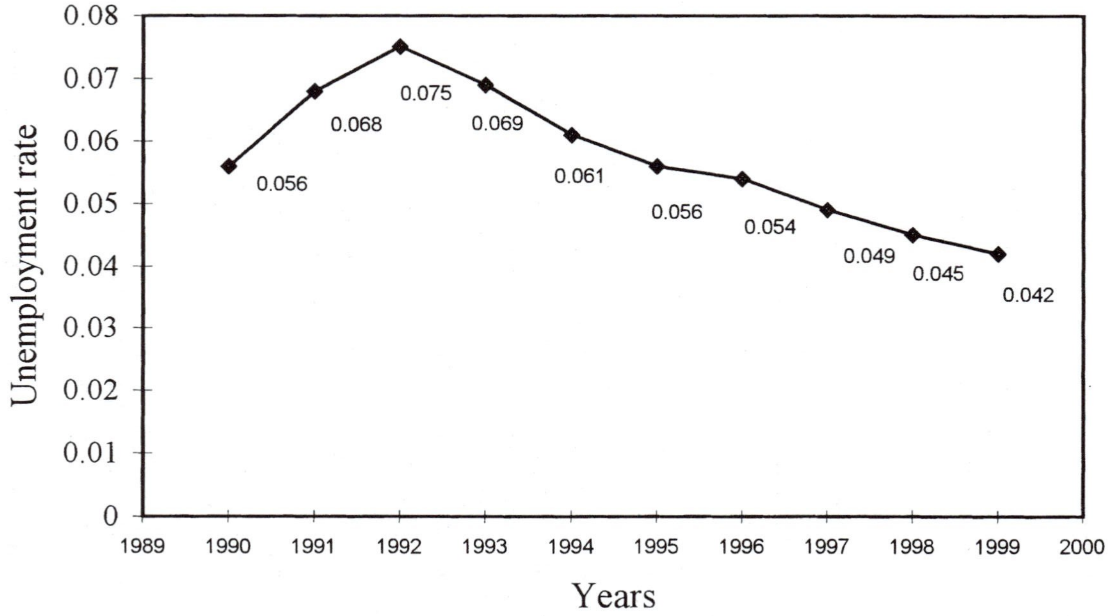

Unemployment rate

0.08
0.07
0.06
0.05
0.04
0.03
0.02
0.01
0

1989 1990 1991 1992 1993 1994 1995 1996 1997 1998 1999 2000

Years

0.056   0.068   0.075   0.069   0.061   0.056   0.054   0.049   0.045   0.042

Source: Bureau of Labor Statistics (August 1999).

demanded in the U.S. labor market change as consumer demand for new products alter the "what to produce" question. Often, the frictionally unemployed are job seekers or are people in education or job training programs designed to improve their occupational skills.

DISTRIBUTION OF INCOME

The distribution of income refers to how the nation's total income—earned and unearned—is spread among its people. This distribution of income in the United States is illustrated by the Lorenz Curve, as shown in Figure 13.3.

The Lorenz Curve

The Lorenz Curve divides the nation's population into five segments, called quintiles. Each quintile represents one-fifth (20%) of the U.S. population. Therefore, if every household received an equal amount of income, then each of the five quintiles would receive one-fifth (20%) of the income. The first quintile would receive 20% of the income, the first two quintiles combined would receive 40%, the first three quintiles combined would receive 60%, and so on. Thus, an equal distribution of income would form a straight line, as shown in Figure 13.3.

The Lorenz Curve shows the actual distribution of income in the United States. Note that the lowest quintile, which represents the 20% of the American population with the lowest incomes, accounts for just 4.4% of all earned and unearned income in the nation. At the opposite extreme the highest quintile, which represents 20% of the population with the highest incomes, accounts for 46.5% of the nation's income. The Lorenz Curve is useful in showing the actual distribution of income among different segments of the population. For example, using the Lorenz Curve you can see that on average the richest 20% of the population receives about 10 times more income than the poorest segment of the population.

Changes in Income Distribution

There have been some modest changes in the distribution of income in the United States over the past 25 years, as shown in Figure 13.4. For example, over the past quarter century, the lowest four quintiles—the 80% of the population with the lowest incomes—have received a lesser percentage of the nation's income. In 1970 the lower four quintiles received about 59% of the nation's income, while the highest quintile received 41%. By 1995 the gap between the richest quintile and the four

Figure 13.3
Lorenz Curve for the United States (in percentage)

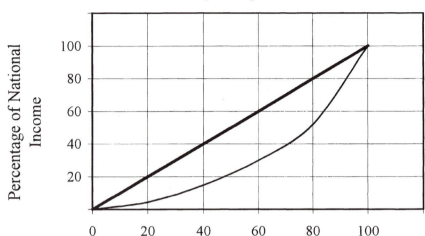

Source: *Statistical Abstract of the United States, 1998.*

lower ones had widened—the first four quintiles receiving 53.5% of the income compared to 46.5% for the wealthiest quintile.

There are some limitations in the data presented in the Lorenz Curve, however. One limitation is that fringe benefits, such as health and dental coverage, employer contributions to employees' retirement plans, low-cost day care, extended maternity leave, and so on are not counted as income. The absence of these non-income benefits distorts the analysis some. This is because these benefits improve the household's standard of living, but do not "show up" in the data. Another limitation in the data is that business transactions in the informal economy, sometimes called the underground economy are not considered. The "underground economy" represents the unreported business activity in the economy. For example, a worker may work for an employer, in exchange for an "under the table" cash payment. In this way, the employee avoids paying federal and state income taxes, and the FICA taxes. The employer also avoids the FICA taxes. While this type of exchange is illegal, it does exist in the United States, and in other nations of the world. It is assumed that a substantial amount of unreported income changes hands in the underground economy.

The gap between the rich and the poor in the United States has sparked debate throughout the 20th century. At the center of this debate has been the question of what role the government should have in redistributing some of the nation's income from the wealthier segments of the population to the poorer segments. Let's explore this aspect of income distribution in the United States.

Figure 13.4
Distribution of Income by Quintile, 1970–1995

Income Quintiles	1970	1975	1980	1985	1990	1995
Lowest Income Quintile	5.4	5.6	5.3	4.8	4.6	4.4
Second Quintile	12.2	11.9	11.6	11.0	10.8	10.1
Third Quintile	17.6	17.7	17.6	16.9	16.6	15.8
Fourth Quintile	23.8	24.2	24.4	24.3	23.8	23.2
Highest Quintile	40.9	40.7	41.1	43.1	44.3	46.5

Source: *Statistical Abstract of the United States, 1998.*

Economic Thinkers: Herbert Spencer and Social Darwinism

Herbert Spencer (1820–1903) began adult life as a railway engineer, then drifted into a successful career as a journalist. By the mid-1850s, Spencer gained national attention for his philosophy about the "survival of the fittest" in America's competitive economy—a philosophy that soon become known as "Social Darwinism."

Social Darwinism focused on people's struggle for survival. According to Spencer, societies evolve just as living organisms do. That is, the "most fit" survive while the weak do not. It followed, then, that to create a stronger society the government should not disrupt this process of "natural selection" by providing relief for the poor, the infirm, or other "less fit" groups. Social Darwinism gained much support during the late 19th and early 20th centuries especially, as you might imagine, among the rich— who believed they had demonstrated their superiority by rising above the common man.

Since the Great Depression of the 1930s support for Social Darwinism has faded, mainly due to people's recognition that unemployment, poverty, or other economic problems can strike individuals or families through no fault of their own. And, while the nation has rejected Social Darwinism, the debate over the proper role for government in assisting the needy continues.

POVERTY IN THE UNITED STATES

The study of income distribution is the United States includes an examination of poverty and the poor. Who are the poor? What causes poverty? How has the government addressed the problem of poverty? These questions provide the focus for our study.

The Poverty Line

People are considered poor if their household income falls below the official poverty line. The "poverty line" is a dollar figure equal to three times the cost of a family's minimum food budget for a year. The Department of Agriculture sets the poverty line each year after calculating this minimum food budget.

In 1998 a "family of four" was "poor" if its household income fell below $16,660. Naturally, the poverty line was set at a higher dollar figure for larger households and a lower dollar figure for smaller households. According to the Bureau of the Census, the total number of Americans living in poverty in 1998 was 34.5 million people—about 12.7% of the total population. A more detailed profile of America's poor is shown in Figure 13.5.

Causes of Poverty

There are multiple causes for poverty in the United States. Some people fall into poverty because of a lack of opportunities. For example, opportunities are limited by substandard schools, or by the lack of job training programs. Combined, these factors restrict people's freedom of choice in the labor market because they have few marketable skills. Opportunities might also be limited by discrimination or by racism. A second cause of poverty stems from assorted personal problems of individuals. Such problems include teenage pregnancies, out-of-wedlock births, desertion by parents, or other personal traumas. A third cause of poverty is health problems, including those associated with drug dependence, alcoholism, mental illness, or other disabilities. A fourth cause of poverty is unemployment—at least some of which occurs because low-skilled workers have been displaced by technological changes in the workplace or have lost their jobs due to foreign competition. Finally, ineffective government programs have, at times, created a "cycle of dependency" by encouraging people to stay on the public dole rather than to find productive jobs.

Most likely, many of the nation's poor find themselves in poverty for several of these reasons. The fact that 34.5 million Americans are poor has necessitated a response by the government. Many government programs have been created, especially since the 1930s, to address the needs of the poor through a redistribution of income in America.

The Redistribution of Income by Government

To redistribute income in the United States the government must first tax individuals and firms. These tax revenues provide the funds needed to finance programs for the needy (see chapter 11 for more on raising revenues through taxation). The government's traditional response to income redistribution has been to provide public transfer payments to the needy. **Public transfer payments** are government payments to individuals who do not provide a good or service in return. Public transfer

Figure 13.5
A Profile of America's Poor, 1998

Total U.S. population: 271,059,000

Poverty line (family of 4): $16,660

Total number of poor: 34,476,000

Percent of total population living in poverty: 12.7%

Race: White (23,454,000), Black (9,091)

Percent of population living in poverty by race: White (10.5%)
                                                    Black (26.1%)

Hispanic poor: 25.6% of total Hispanic population*

Number of children living in poverty: 12,845,000 (37% of the nation's poor)

Age: Highest poverty rate: Children under 18 years (18.9%)
       Lowest poverty rate: Adults 45–64 years (8.0%)
       Under-represented group: 65+ years (10.5%)

Poverty by region of the U.S.:   Northeast: 12.3%
                                 Midwest: 10.3%
                                 South: 13.7%
                                 West: 14.0%

Education of householder: No high school diploma (42%)**
(25 years old or older)   High school diploma, no college (33%)
                             Some college, no diploma (19%)
                             Bachelor's degree or more (6%)

Work experience of householder: Worked during the year (55%)**
(16 years old or older)   Did not work (45%)

Poverty line for 1999: $17,028 (preliminary)

*Persons of Hispanic origins may be of any race.
**1996 data.

Sources: U.S. Bureau of the Census and Statistical Abstract of the United States, 1998.

payments are classified as either "public assistance" programs or "social insurance" programs.

A **public assistance program** is any government program that offers transfer payments to people, for which they do not pay. Examples include Temporary Assistance for Needy Families, which provides income payments to the poor; Supplemental Security Income (SSI), which provides income payments to the elderly who live in poverty; food stamps, which provide food coupons to stretch the food dollars of the poor; and Medicaid, which provides health care and hospitalization benefits to the welfare poor. In recent years, less money has been spent on Temporary Assistance for Needy Families mainly because the number of recipients as declined by nearly 50% since the mid-1990s, according to the Department of Health and Human Services. At least some of this decline in the welfare rolls can be attributed to 1996 welfare reform legislation, which has stressed work over welfare, and has given individual states the authority to spend federal "block grants" to run their own welfare programs. Expenditures for Medicaid, on the other hand, continue to climb reaching about $100 billion in 1998 according to the Office of Management and Budget (OMB).

A **social insurance program** is any government program that offers people transfer payments, for which they have made some monetary contribution. The largest social insurance program in the United States is Social Security, which provides income payments to retirees, their spouses, or dependents. Another important social insurance program is Medicare, which provides health insurance to the elderly. Unemployment compensation is a third social insurance program, which provides temporary income payments to the unemployed who have lost their jobs through no fault of their own. Workers and employers are expected to pay a FICA payroll tax to fund the Social Security and Medicare programs. Many employers pay into the unemployment compensation fund. Social Security and Medicare benefits comprise the largest portion of the federal budget. By 1998 federal spending on these two programs totaled $572 billion—approximately one-third of the entire federal budget for the year, according to the OMB (see chapter 11 for more on government taxes, spending, and transfer payments).

The Redistribution Debate

Since the Great Depression there has been heated debate over the merits of redistributing people's income.

Supporters of the government's role in the redistribution of income argue that a nation as wealthy as the United States can afford to supply the needy with the necessities of life including food, housing, clothing, medical care, and so on. Further, they note that many of the nation's poor find themselves in poverty through no fault of their own. Children, for example, represent 37% of the nation's poor, according to the Bureau of the Census. But how can the children be blamed for being poor? Supporters of a redistribution of income also argue that some public assistance and social insurance programs support the efforts of the poor to work their way out of poverty. One recent program, the Welfare to Work Partnership, has successfully found private sector jobs for hundreds of thousands of former welfare recipients.

Opponents of government redistribution efforts argue that transferring income from the productive sector of the economy to the nonproductive sector is unfair. That is, they question why the more affluent should be penalized for their economic success. Further, opponents argue that the existence of a comprehensive "safety net" of government programs reduces the incentive for the poor to find work, and places a burden on ordinary taxpayers—costs that not only include the transfer payments but also the costs connected with administering these programs.

Economic Thinkers: Michael Harrington and the Other America

Michael Harrington (1928–1989) was a well-known American political activist and writer. In his famous book, *The Other America: Poverty in the United States* (1962), Harrington wrote about the plight of the poor in a land of plenty.

Harrington's *The Other America* brought the problem of poverty into the national spotlight during the presidencies of John F. Kennedy and Lyndon B. Johnson. Harrington argued that the poor had become "invisible" in the United States, hidden in pockets of poverty in urban and rural areas. To deal with the problem of poverty, and a poverty rate topping 22% in 1960, he advocated a concerted government response to relieve the suffering of the poor. So influential was *The Other America* that Harrington was invited to help draft an antipoverty program for the government in 1964.

Harrington's views provided some of the inspiration for President Johnson's "war on poverty" during the 1960s. This "war on poverty" was comprised of a series of programs designed to reduce poverty and the suffering of the poor in the United States. These programs included the founding of the Medicare and Medicaid programs, and the expansion of Aid to Families with Dependent Children (AFDC).

14

HOW DO LABOR AND MANAGEMENT COME TO TERMS?

Chapter 14 discusses the relationship between laborers and management in the business setting. Laborers, either individually or in labor unions, have traditionally worked to improve their wages, fringe benefits, working conditions, and job security. Management, on the other hand, is responsible for holding production costs—including labor costs—to a minimum. By holding production costs down, management can improve the firm's competitiveness. Labor unions were formed to increase the power of laborers in their negotiations with management. Today, while the worker's right to unionize is protected by law, many workers choose not to join unions. Still, both organized labor and management have significant power in contract negotiations.

THE LABOR FORCE

The **labor force** is comprised of people who are 16 years old or older, and who are either employed or actively seeking employment. According to the Bureau of Labor Statistics, there were 139.4 million workers in the American labor force in 1999. Of this total, 133.4 million were employed. This means that the "employment rate," or the percentage of the labor force that was employed, was 95.8%. The remaining 5.9 million workers were unemployed. Thus, the "unemployment rate," or the percentage of the labor force that was not employed in 1999, stood at 4.2%. About two-thirds of all Americans 16 years old or older are in the labor force.

Figure 14.1
Level of Education of the U.S. Labor Force, 1996*

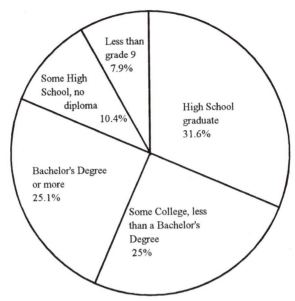

*Measures educational level of householders of at least 25 years of age.
Source: U.S. Bureau of the Census, *Current Population Reports*.

Characteristics of the Labor Force

By the late 1990s there were nearly as many women in the labor force as there were men. In 1997 the Bureau of Labor Statistics reported that 52.4% of the U.S. labor force was male, and the remaining 47.6% was female. Over the past century, the participation of women in the labor force has grown from less than 20% in 1900 to its present level (47.6%).

The American labor force is highly educated. Over 80% of the labor force earned at least a high school diploma, as shown in Figure 14.1. In addition, nearly one-quarter of these workers had earned a bachelor's degree or more. So why is an education important to a worker? Generally speaking, the more education a person receives the more "sellable" his skills will be in the labor market. In 1999 the Bureau of Labor Statistics reported that a worker with less than a high school diploma was three times as likely to be unemployed as a worker with a college degree. Further, according to the Bureau of the Census, the median income in 1996 for a college graduate ($59,978) was three times that of a person who started high school but dropped out before graduation ($19,652). This data presents a compelling case for students to remain in school, and improve their skills, as they prepare for the world of work.

The U.S. labor force is largely service-oriented. The U.S. Department of Labor reported that in 1998 the great majority of workers were employed in service occupations (72.4%) rather than in manufacturing (24.9%) or agriculture (2.7%). Services include occupations such as doctors, sales clerks, insurance agents, bankers, real estate agents, taxicab drivers, plumbers, and teachers. Manufacturing occupations are concentrated in the industrial production, such as machine operators, and in construction. Agricultural occupations center on the farms, producing grains, dairy products, meat, fruits, and vegetables, and in forestry and fishing. According to the Bureau of Labor Statistic's *Strategic Plan* for the years 1997–2002, the trend toward a continued growth of service jobs, and a decline in jobs in the manufacturing sector, will continue into the 21st century.

Labor Issues

Throughout American history, laborers in the United States have concentrated on "bread and butter" issues. That is, they have sought better wages, benefits, working conditions, and job security when they negotiated with management for a contract. A **contract** is a binding agreement between two parties—in this case between the workers and management of a firm.

Wages are often the most important labor issue in contract discussions. From the laborer's perspective, the size of the wage directly affects his standard of living. Many factors influence the wage rates of workers, including how much demand there is for a worker's skills, the available supply of certain workers, and even government regulations on wages (see chapter 13 for more on wage determination). It is common for workers to seek a wage increase at least equal to the prevailing inflation rate. This is because inflation—the general increase in the price level of goods and services in the economy—reduces the purchasing power of the worker's dollar. If workers accept an increase in their wage rate that is less than the inflation rate, their "real wage" (the wage adjusted for inflation) will actually decline.

Fringe benefits are another important labor issue. Fringe benefits are the non-wage benefits that are included in a labor contract. Traditionally, fringe benefits have focused on vacation time, medical insurances, dental plans, paid sick days and holidays, the option to purchase company stock at reduced prices, and so on. During the 1990s many additional types of fringe benefits have been added to the list to cater to the changing needs of workers. Included are company financed day-care facilities for employees' children, college courses for employees, transportation to and from work, and other benefits that assist workers to meet their personal and professional responsibilities.

A third labor issue is working conditions. During the early stages of the Industrial Revolution in America, the horrors of the industrial workplace—often called sweatshops—made life miserable for many industrial laborers. Over the years negotiations between labor and management, along with government laws and regulations, have resolved some of the problems related to working conditions. Issues involving working conditions include the worker's safety, the number of hours in the work week (the work week today is defined as 40 hours), the worker's job description, the power of management, and others. In most contracts a grievance procedure is in place to allow employees to contest substandard working conditions.

Finally, job security is an important labor issue. Job security refers to the ability of a worker to protect her job at a firm. For example, workers often negotiate to include a "seniority" system into their contracts. Seniority means that those who have worked at the firm the longest have the most security in case the firm lays off workers. In your school, teachers usually have a "tenure" system to protect the more experienced—and higher paid—professionals from being arbitrarily replaced by younger and less expensive teachers.

LABOR UNIONS AND LABOR POWER

A **labor union** is an organization of workers designed to increase the power of laborers in their negotiations with management. Labor unions can form to represent workers in a single firm, to represent workers in an entire industry, or to represent workers employed by any level of government. In 1999, 16.5 million workers in the United States belonged to a union—or 13.9% of the labor force.

Sources of Labor Union Power

The most important source of union power is its ability to bargain collectively with management. **Collective bargaining** occurs when union leaders speak with a single voice for all employees in a firm or industry. The goal of collective bargaining is to equalize labor's power with that of management, and to negotiate a contract that is fair to both sides. In most cases collective bargaining results in a contract. At other times, negotiations break down. If this occurs, labor unions have a number of ways to pressure management to make additional concessions, including:

- Strikes: A strike is a work stoppage initiated by laborers. Strikes seek to stop production at a firm, or in an entire industry until management makes concessions to wages, fringe benefits, or other

Figure 14.2
Work Stoppages, 1960–1998*

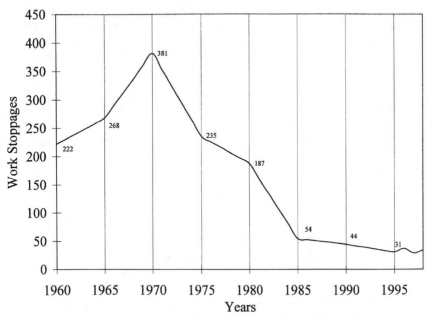

*Includes stoppages due to strikes or lockouts involving at least 1,000 workers.
Source: Bureau of Labor Statistics, 1998.

issue. When production stops, firms usually lose money. Labor strikes have been used since the early days of the labor movement. Striking workers typically "picket" the plant to discourage others from doing business with the firm, to discourage union members from "crossing the picket line" to go to work, and to draw public support for the strike. In 1998, for example, 200,000 production workers at General Motors' North American plants went on strike to protest health and safety problems at its Flint, Michigan facility, and to protest GM's decision to withhold promised investments in Flint. After an eight-week strike the United Auto Workers (UAW) and GM came to terms on some of these issues, and the UAW called an end to the strike. The strike by thousands of engineers and technical workers at Boeing in February of 2000 involved more traditional issues such as wages, bonuses, and insurance coverage. In recent years, there have been fewer major strikes and lockouts, as shown in Figure 14.2.

- Boycotts: A boycott is designed to stop consumers from purchasing the good or service that a firm produces. If a boycott is successful, the firm stands to lose money because of reduced demand for its output. One of the most successful boycotts in American history occurred during the 1960s when labor organizer Cesar Chavez organized a national boycott of California grapes. The goal of this boycott was to improve the wages and working conditions of migrant farm workers and to gain recognition for the recently formed United Farm Workers (UFW) union. After a number of years, the boycott was successful.

- Coordinated strategy: A **coordinated strategy** involves the use of a combination of union techniques to settle a dispute with management. That is, the union coordinates the strike, picketing, and boycott to pressure management to make contract concessions. For example, when negotiations between labor and management at United Parcel Service (UPS) broke down in 1997, union members—in this case the Teamsters—used a coordinated strategy. The Teamsters coordinated the strike and picketing by UPS workers to reduce the flow of packages through UPS facilities. The Teamsters mounted a major public relations campaign to increase support for the strike. They also encouraged consumers and businesses to boycott UPS, and to use other mail carriers—including the U.S. Postal Service and Federal Express—until the strike was over. After several weeks the two sides came to agreement on the use of temporary labor by UPS, and the coordinated strategy was ended.

The Rise of Labor Unions

Labor unions in the United States began to form in the mid-1800s, mainly in response to the abuses of industrial workers by big business. The factory system created an enormous gap between the wealthy industrialists and the wage laborer. In addition, the long hours, dangerous working conditions, meager wages, and other sweatshop conditions made it a struggle for many people to merely survive. Under these conditions, labor unions sprung up. At first some were organized as "secret societies." This was to protect union organizers from being fired and blacklisted—placed on a list of "labor agitators" who should not be employed by other firms.

One of the first national unions was the Knights of Labor. The Knights of Labor permitted all workers to join—skilled and unskilled, white and African-American, men and women. As an "industrial union," workers in different trades were invited to join. The Knights of Labor supported higher wages for industrial workers, a shorter workday, and improved working conditions. It opposed child labor and the exploitation of the industrial worker by powerful industrialists. Under the leadership of

Terence Powderly, the Knights' membership grew during the 1880s, especially after they organized successful strikes against powerful telegraph and railroad companies. A terrorist bombing at a Knights' rally in Chicago in 1886—at Haymarket Square—resulted in the deaths of several police and union members. Public support for the Knights declined rapidly after this incident. Many workers looked for an alternative, which some found in the newly formed American Federation of Labor (AFL).

The AFL was founded in 1886 under the leadership of Samuel Gompers (see Economic Thinkers). Unlike the Knights, the AFL was a federation of "craft unions." This meant that only skilled crafts unions were permitted to join the AFL. Therefore, for a worker to become a part of the AFL, he would first have to organize a "local" craft union which, in turn, could apply for membership in this "federation" of craft unions. The AFL also restricted membership. It excluded unskilled workers, African-Americans, and women in most cases. The AFL gained strength during the 1890s and early 1900s, preferring to use its power to bargain collectively with management—but prepared to use the strike when necessary. By the 1920s the AFL claimed millions of members. The lingering question of who should be allowed to join the AFL resulted in a bitter split in the union by 1937. Within a year, an alternative national union—the Congress of Industrial Organizations (CIO)—was formed.

The CIO was officially formed in 1938 and its first president, John L. Lewis, quickly set about to rally labor support from skilled and unskilled workers, African-Americans and whites, men and women. His goal was to organize workers on an industry-wide basis. The United Mine Workers (UMW), an industry-wide union that Lewis had been president of, served as a model. Other major industry-wide unions, including the United Auto Workers (UAW) and the United Steel Workers (USW), joined ranks with the CIO. Even before the CIO was officially formed, the UAW had staged a new type of strike, called a "sit-down strike," against the General Motors (GM) corporation. A "sit-down strike" occurs when striking workers occupy the plant so that replacements—who the union members called "scabs"—could not be hired to take the strikers' jobs. The success of this 1937 CIO strike against the powerful GM boosted support for the industry-wide concept of unionization that Lewis backed.

The AFL and CIO merged in 1955, and thus formed the AFL-CIO. Under the leadership of its first president, George Meany, the AFL-CIO expanded the voice of labor in negotiations with management. The merger also served to expand the political power of unions, which by this time had already become a political force by turning out the vote and by making significant campaign contributions to pro-labor political candidates. But the newly merged AFL-CIO had its share of problems. In 1957, for example, the 1.6 million member Teamsters union was expelled from the AFL-CIO because of union corruption. Other major unions also withdrew for a number of years, including the UMW and the UAW.

Labor Legislation

During the early years of the labor movement, the government consistently sided with big business against organized labor. Since the 1930s, however, the rights and responsibilities of unions have been more clearly spelled out by federal labor legislation, including:

- Norris-La Guardia Act (1932): This act prohibited the "yellow dog contract"—a type of contract that stipulated that a worker could not join a union. The yellow dog contract had been common prior to 1932 as a means of preventing unions from organizing.
- Wagner Act (1935): This act declared that workers had the right to form labor unions, and that management was obliged to bargain in good faith with these unions. The Wagner Act also created the National Labor Relations Board (NLRB) to monitor and regulate unfair labor practices by employers or by the labor unions.
- Fair Labor Standards Act (1938): This act created the nation's first "minimum wage" ($.25 per hour) and maximum work week (44 hours). Since 1938, the minimum wage has been raised many times and today stands at $5.15. The work week, on the other hand, has been reduced from 44 hours to 40 hours.
- Taft-Hartley Act (1947): This act restricted the power of unions by outlawing the **closed shop**—an arrangement by which a worker had to be a union member before he could work for a firm. This act also permitted the government to issue an "injunction" to block a strike for 80 days, if the strike could harm the well-being of citizens or the nation.
- Landrum-Griffin Act (1959): This act established rules for unions to follow. It insisted on democratic elections for union leaders, the reporting of union revenues with the Department of Labor, and procedures for forming unions. The act followed disclosures of union corruption by the 1.6 million member Teamsters union.

Labor Unions Today

The largest labor union in the United States today is the AFL-CIO, which represents about 13 million workers. As a "federation" of unions, the AFL-CIO is a type of umbrella organization that many local unions have chosen to join. By affiliating (joining) with the AFL-CIO, local un-

Figure 14.3
Union Membership, 1935–1999

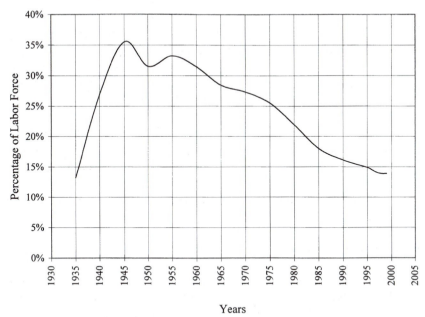

Years

Source: Bureau of Labor Statistics, *Current Population Surveys*.

ions can draw on its resources, including its legal staff, financial resources, and experts in the field of negotiations.

Under the leadership of Lane Kirkland (1979–1995) many "independent unions" which had either left the AFL-CIO voluntarily or had been
expelled from the union were brought back into the AFL-CIO. An **independent union** is a labor union that is not affiliated with the AFL-
CIO. Included in this list of unions that had reaffiliated with the
AFL-CIO were the United Auto Workers, the Teamsters, the West Coast
Longshoremen, the Chemical Workers, and the Mine Workers. Other
unions have chosen to remain independent, including the National Education Association (NEA), which has about 2 million members.

The AFL-CIO has also worked to support labor interests through political action. For example, the AFL-CIO and other unions have organized
political action committees (PACs) to support political candidates friendly
to the interests of organized labor. A **political action committee** is an organization that collects contributions from its membership—unions in this
case—and then donates these funds to political candidates. According to
the Federal Election Commission, there were 332 PACs representing labor
groups in the United States in 1996. These PACs made $48 million in cam-
paign contributions to political candidates that year. At the international

Figure 14.4
Profile of Union Membership, 1999

Gender:	Male (16.1%), female (11.4%)
Ethnicity:	Black (17.2%), white (13.5%), Hispanic (11.9%)
Gender and ethnicity:	Highest union membership rate: Black males (20.5%); lowest union membership rate: White women (10.9%), Hispanic women (10.4%)
Age:	16–24 year olds (5.3%), 25 year olds or older (15.6%)*
Sector:	Public sector (37.3%), private sector (9.4%)
High membership industries:	Government workers (37.3%), transportation/utilities (25.5%), construction (19.1%), and manufacturing (15.6%)
Low membership industries:	Agriculture (1.8%), finance, insurance, and real estate (2.1%)

*In 1998.

Source: *Current Population Surveys*, January 27, 2000.

level, the AFL-CIO also supported the activities of labor organizations in nations where governments had traditionally oppressed the rights of labor, including Poland, South Africa, China, and Chile.

Membership in labor unions has been declining since 1945, when union membership peaked at 35.5% of the total non-farm labor force. By 1999 union membership had dropped to just 13.9% of the non-farm labor force, or 16.5 million workers, as shown in Figure 14.3. The main reason for the decline in union membership over the past half century is the shift in the U.S. economy from manufacturing—a traditional stronghold for labor unions—to a service economy. Other causes for the decline of unions include negative public perceptions of some unions because of past union corruption, the unresponsiveness of some unions to the changing needs of workers, and a general feeling that workplace reforms and government regulations offer sufficient protections against worker abuse. Some federal legislation since World War II has also restricted the growth of unions. For example, the Taft-Hartley Act of 1947 outlawed the "closed shop" (see labor legislation) and allowed states to enact "right-to-work" laws. Right-to-work laws create "open shops." In an **open shop** workers can choose whether or not to join the union. Unions prefer the **union shop**, which stipulates that all workers must join the union within a certain period of time after they are hired.

In recent years labor unions have sought to reverse the downward trend in union membership. Part of the union strategy has been to expand the types of services they provide to members. For example, some unions offer members attractive savings or retirement plans, or low-interest credit cards. Secondly, unions have addressed the needs of the changing labor force by putting new issues on the table when negotiating with management—such as providing day care and permitting flexible working hours. Third, unions have stepped up their efforts to recruit union members from occupations that have shunned unions in the past, particularly in the service industries. In some of these industries, especially in the public sector—teachers, police, and firefighters—there have been significant gains. In 1998, for example, about 44% of all government employees at the local level are union members, according to *Current Population Surveys*. Finally, unions have publicized the benefits of union membership in fact sheets, brochures, and other publications. One statistic useful in the recruitment process is that the median weekly earnings for union workers was significantly more than their non-union counterparts. For example, the *Current Population Surveys* reported that union workers earned $672 per week compared to $516 per week for non-union workers in 1999. A profile of union membership is shown in Figure 14.4.

Economic Thinkers: Samuel Gompers and the AFL

Samuel Gompers (1850–1924) was born in England, and immigrated to the United States in 1863. Throughout his adult life, Gompers worked to strengthen the American labor movement and to improve the standard of living for the common laborer.

Gompers entered the labor force soon after his arrival in the United States. By 1864 he was rolling cigars—and was a willing member of the Cigar Makers' International Union (CMIU). By 1875 he was president of Local 144 of the CMIU. It soon became apparent to Gompers that unions representing different "crafts" should join together to strengthen their bargaining position with management. To this end, Gompers helped to organize the Federation of Organized Trades and Labor Unions in 1881. In 1886, after some re-organization, this federation of unions was renamed the American Federation of Labor (AFL). For most of the next 40 years Gompers served as the president of the AFL.

The AFL and its member craft unions had specific goals—to gain higher wages, to reduce working hours, and to improve working conditions for union members. To achieve these "bread and butter" goals, Gompers believed in collective bargaining, legislative lobbying, and strikes when necessary. Gompers and the AFL consistently opposed the more revolutionary beliefs and tactics of the Industrial Workers of the World (IWW), which was also gaining strength in the early 20th century. Members of the IWW—sometimes called "Wobblies"—opposed the capitalist economic system and advocated class struggle to end it. Gompers worked within the capitalist system and, in doing so, laid the foundation for the largest union in contemporary America—the AFL-CIO.

MAKING ECONOMIC DECISIONS: VOTING ON
CERTIFICATION OR DE-CERTIFICATION

Certification is the process by which a particular union is recognized by the National Labor Relations Board (NLRB) as the bargaining union for a certain group of workers. Suppose a group of forklift operators at an area warehouse wanted to organize a local union, and then join up with the American Forklift Operators (AFO)—a national labor union. How could they "certify" the AFO to represent them?

The first step is for these workers to gather the signatures of a substantial number of forklift operators on "authorization cards." When these cards are sent to the NLRB, the process for certification officially begins. This initial stage in the certification process is sometimes referred to as the "petition" to certify.

The NLRB then decides if a certification election should take place. The NLRB sends fact-finders to determine the amount of support the AFO has among the workers at the warehouse. The input of the employer can also be heard at this time. If a dispute occurs over the facts, the NLRB holds a hearing to determine the truth.

Finally, if there is evidence of significant support for the AFO, the NLRB will grant permission to hold the certification election. If the AFO receives a majority of the workers' votes, it becomes certified to bargain on behalf of the forklift operators at the plant. The NLRB supervises the election.

Suppose you were a forklift operator. What factors would you consider before voting in favor of or against certification? Four considerations might help you decide, including:

- Your view of unions: Do you think unions have benefited the working class over the years? Or, do you view unions unnecessary—even detrimental to the operation of firms?

- Reputation of the union: Has the union been successful in past labor negotiations? Has it been involved in corruption or scandals?

- Worker self-interest: Will the benefits of union membership outweigh the financial costs—especially dues payments?

- Strength of the union: Will the union be able to deliver on its promises to increase wages and fringe benefits, and to improve the working conditions and job security at your workplace?

Another decision that a worker may one day have to make is whether or not to de-certify a union. De-certification is the process of withdrawing support for an existing union and, thus, removing it as the bargaining agent for the workers in contract negotiations. De-certification occurs when the "rank and file" union members do not feel that the union is adequately representing their interest. The de-certification process can be initiated by one employee, a group of employees, or by an alternative union acting on their behalf. A petition to de-certify, signed by at least 30% of the union membership, is sent to the NLRB to start the de-certification. As was the case with union certification, the NLRB then supervises the de-certification election—also done by secret ballot. The employer is not permitted to petition to de-certify. Nor is the employer permitted to instigate or assist in the preparation of the petition to de-certify.

MANAGEMENT AND MANAGEMENT POWER

Management is the process of using resources to achieve the firm's goals. Usually, when we speak of a firm's "management," we are referring to its leadership. The management of a firm can take many forms. The management of a major corporation, for example, would likely include a chief executive officer (CEO), a president, a number of vice presidents, and department heads. The management of a sole proprietorship, on the other hand, might be just the proprietor herself (see chapter 6 for more on different types of business organizations).

Functions of Management

While there are many types of "managers"—the people within the management structure—all have similar functions. That is, managers are responsible for the planning, organizing, leading, and controlling of the factors of production used by the firm.

- Planning: Planning refers to the manager's ability to set goals and to state how these goals will be accomplished. All other functions of management are designed to meet these goals.
- Organizing: Organizing refers to the manager's ability to arrange and coordinate production to meet the firm's goals. This means that workers' jobs and responsibilities are clearly stated, and that other resources—such as capital goods and materials—are organized in an efficient manner.
- Leading: Leading refers to the manager's ability to motivate workers to work hard and to accomplish the tasks that are assigned to them.
- Controlling: Controlling refers to the manager's duty to evaluate the performance of workers. If problems are detected, it is the manager's responsibility to take action to correct them.

Sources of Management Power

The power of management to negotiate with workers stems from its leadership position in the firm—and its control of the firm's "purse strings!" The unified voice of management represents the will of the firm, and its owners—whether it is the voice of the sole proprietor in her flower shop, or the voice of a CEO in a multibillion dollar corporation. From management's perspective, the firm must earn profits to survive. To achieve this goal management sometimes comes into conflict with laborers. From laborers' perspective, better wages and fringe benefits are necessary to improving their standard of living. Compromises between management and workers are usually worked out during the negotiations between the two groups. When negotiations break down, however, management can use a number of techniques to gain concessions from its workers, including:

- Lockouts: A **lockout** occurs when management chooses to close the business until an agreeable contract is reached. The 6-month lockout of professional basketball players during the 1998–1999 season illustrates the power of lockouts. After being forced to sit out much of the season, the National Basketball Association Players' Union made major concessions in the areas of maximum salaries, and freedom of movement of players from one team to another. A shortened season followed the lockout.

- Replacement workers: **Replacement workers** are workers hired by management to replace striking employees. From management's perspective, a labor strike is no reason to stop producing goods. The hiring of replacement workers weakens the bargaining power of laborers by limiting the effectiveness of its weapon of last resort—the strike.

- Relocation: Relocation occurs when a business moves from one place to another. By threatening relocation, management holds down laborers' demands for improved wages, fringe benefits, or working conditions. In recent years there have been numerous plant relocations from the heavily unionized Northeast to the South, and from the United States to low-wage nations in Latin America and Asia.

- Injunction: An **injunction** is a court order that prohibits a strike. Under the Taft-Hartley Act of 1947, the government can issue an injunction if a strike threatens the health or safety of people, or if it threatens the operation of vital industries. In 1978 President Carter used the injunction to force striking coal miners back to work after their strike had dragged on for several months. Management can appeal to the government to take this type of action against strikers.

Management Today

During the first half of the 20th century, the most common management models favored authoritarian leadership, and a regimented production process to promote efficiency. These models did not consider the implications of these production techniques on workers however (see chapter 5 for more on "scientific management"). Today, there is a far greater emphasis on creating a workplace that promotes both efficiency and worker satisfaction. Modern management techniques tend to look at the human side of production—to the individual talents and abilities of workers and how these talents can be best used in the workplace. Modern management techniques often include:

- a recognition that management techniques can vary from firm to firm, and from industry to industry. Thus, the manager's challenge is to develop—and continually adapt—its techniques to a changing economy and a changing workforce.

- a recognition that labor is pivotal to increasing productivity. Workers that are secure in their positions, compensated fairly for their contribution to production, and offered challenging jobs are more satisfied and loyal to their companies.

- a recognition that risks are necessary in the development of new and better goods and services. Thus, the manager provides a work environment that encourages entrepreneurship and product innovation.

- a recognition that teamwork, shared goals, and a shared vision for the company benefits laborers and management alike. The manager's task, therefore, is to communicate with workers to build the necessary teamwork.

15

WHY DO NATIONS TRADE?

Chapter 15 examines international trade—why nations trade and why they sometimes place limits on trade. Trade benefits nations by allowing them to specialize in the production of goods and services that they produce most efficiently. They can then exchange these products for goods that have been efficiently produced by other nations. At times, nations restrict the free flow of goods and services across national borders by imposing barriers to trade, such as tariffs or quotas. Despite these barriers to trade, conscious efforts have been made to create freer trade in world markets since World War II. In the 1990s the rise of regional trade associations has helped reduce trade barriers among participating nations. There is still considerable debate about what type of trade policy the United States should have, however. The record-breaking U.S. trade deficits of the late 1990s intensified the debate between those who favor freer trade and those who favor protectionism.

INTERNATIONAL TRADE: IMPORTING AND EXPORTING

International trade occurs when individuals, firms, or governments import or export goods or services. **Imports** are the goods or services that are purchased from other nations. **Exports** are the goods or services that are sold to other nations.

Imports and Exports

According to the Bureau of the Census, the United States imported about $1,030 billion worth of goods in 1999. What types of goods does

Figure 15.1
U.S. Merchandise Imports, 1997

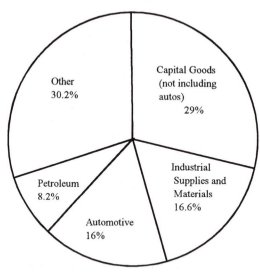

Source: Department of Commerce, Bureau of Economic Analysis.

the United States import? The largest single category of imports is capital goods, including different kinds of machinery and equipment, as shown in Figure 15.1. Other important imports include industrial supplies and materials, automobiles and auto parts, and petroleum and related petroleum products. Most of America's imports come from the industrialized nations of the world. In 1998 the United States imported more goods from Canada than from any other nation ($173 billion). The United States also imported significant amounts of merchandise from other industrialized nations including Japan ($122 billion), Germany ($50 billion), UK ($35 billion), France ($24 billion), and Italy ($21 billion). During the 1990s imports from the developing world also increased. By 1998, four of the top ten importers of goods to the United States were less developed nations including Mexico ($95 billion), China ($71 billion), Taiwan ($33 billion), and South Korea ($24 billion). These figures represent U.S. imports of goods, or merchandise, but do not include services.

The Commerce Department also reported that the United States exported about $683 billion worth of goods in 1999. The most important category of U.S. merchandise exports in the 1990s was capital goods. This is predictable because the United States is a highly industrialized nation capable of producing sophisticated machinery and equipment. Other important categories of exports included industrial supplies and materials, automobiles and parts, and agricultural products (including feed grains) as shown in Figure 15.2. In 1998 most of America's exports were sold in

Figure 15.2
U.S. Merchandise Exports, 1997

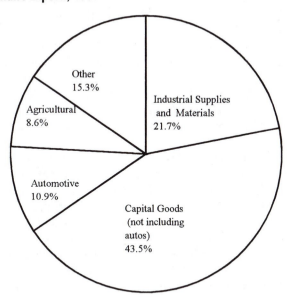

Source: Department of Commerce, Bureau of Economic Analysis.

the industrialized nations, including Canada ($157 billion), Japan ($58 billion), UK ($39 billion), Germany ($27 billion), Netherlands ($19 billion), and France ($18 billion). The largest buyer of U.S. exports in the developing world was Mexico ($79 billion).

Balance of Trade

The **balance of trade** shows the relationship between the nation's total merchandise imports and its merchandise exports in a given year. When the value of a nation's imports are greater than the value of its exports, the nation has a merchandise **trade deficit**. This is because the nation is paying more money out to other nations to buy their goods than it is receiving from these nations. When a nation has a trade deficit, economists say that it has a "negative balance of trade." According to the Department of Commerce, in 1998 the United States had its largest trade deficits with Japan (−$64 billion), China (−$57 billion), Germany (−$23 billion), Canada (−$17 billion), and Mexico (−$16 billion). When, on the other hand, the value of a nation's exports are greater in value than its imports, the nation has a merchandise **trade surplus**. This occurs because the nation is receiving more in money payments for its goods than it is paying out to other nations for their goods. Economists sometimes call a trade surplus a "positive balance of trade." The Department of Commerce also reported that in 1998 the United States recorded its largest trade surpluses with the Netherlands (+$11 billion), Australia (+$7 billion), Belgium and Luxembourg (+$6 billion), Brazil (+$5 billion), and Saudi Arabia (+$4 billion).

The United States has experienced merchandise trade deficits every year since 1975. These trade deficits have been increasing since the 1970s, and by 1999 the trade deficit hit a staggering $347 billion ($1,030 in imports and $683 billion in exports), as shown in Figure 15.3. The average merchandise trade deficit in the 1970s was about $10 billion per year, in the 1980s was $94 billion, and in the 1990s had grown to $173 billion per year.

There are many reasons for the U.S. trade deficits since the 1970s. One reason has been the soaring prices of some important imports, such as oil. During the late 1970s and early 1980s, for example, imported petroleum and related products regularly accounted for more than a quarter of all U.S. imports—close to one-third of all imported goods in 1980—compared to under 10% by the late 1990s. The strength of the OPEC oil cartel was a major reason for the dramatic increase in world oil prices (see chapter 7 for more on OPEC). Another reason for U.S. trade deficits has been the success of foreign products in key U.S. markets. Automobiles, for example, accounted for less than 5% of U.S. imports in 1965, or about $1 billion. By 1997 autos accounted for 16% of all U.S. imports, or a staggering $141 billion. Other foreign products have also made significant gains in U.S. markets including electronic equipment, textiles, and motorcycles. A third reason for U.S. trade deficits has been the overall strength of the U.S. economy compared to other economies in the world. The U.S. expansion of the 1990s—the longest since World War II—has increased the confidence of the American consumer. This confidence, in turn, has increased the demand for consumer goods, both foreign and domestic. Some other economies have not been so fortunate. Japan's recession deepened by the late 1990s, and many of the economies in Asia experienced downturns about the same time. What does this mean for American exporters? It means that fewer U.S. goods will sell abroad because both money and confidence are in short supply.

Trade in Services

In addition to trade in merchandise, nations also conduct trade in services. The United States has experienced a trade surplus in services in most years since World War II. A **trade surplus in services** occurs when the value of services exported from a nation is greater than the value of services imported by the nation. During the 1990s the United States enjoyed an average trade surplus in services of about $67 billion per year. Included are financial services such as banking and insurance, telecom-

Figure 15.3
U.S. Trade in Goods and Services, 1990–1999 (in billions)*

Year	Merchandise Trade Balance	Services Trade Balance	Trade Balance in Goods and Services
1990	−$109	+$28	−$81
1991	−$74	+$43	−$31
1992	−$96	+$59	−$37
1993	−$133	+$63	−$70
1994	−$166	+$68	−$98
1995	−$174	+$76	−$98
1996	−$191	+$87	−$104
1997	−$197	+$92	−$105
1998	−$247	+$83	−$164
1999	−$347	+$76	−$271

*Rounded to nearest billion.

Source: U.S. Department of Commerce, Bureau of Economic Analysis.

munications, tourism, and so on. U.S. trade surpluses for the 1990s are shown in Figure 15.3. This figure also shows the combined U.S. trade balance in goods and services from 1990 to 1999. The United States hasn't had a **trade deficit in services**—where the value of services imported into the nation are greater than those exported from the nation—since 1970.

Trade and Specialization

So why do nations trade? Despite the trade deficits that the United States has incurred over the past quarter century, there are several compelling reasons to trade with other nations. One reason is that trade connects us to many affordable products that would otherwise not be available. Take a look around you. Where was your television, VCR, and CD player produced? Where was your car, truck, or motorcycle produced? Do you have any clothing that was made in a different country? Did you have time to have a cup of cocoa, coffee, or tea before coming to school? Where are these crops grown? Most likely there are a number of goods that you or your family are willing to buy that are not produced in the United States. Without trade there would be fewer choices for American consumers.

From an economist's perspective there's another important reason for international trade—specialization promotes a more efficient use of resources, and thereby increases the total output of goods. **Specialization** occurs when nations produce those goods that are best suited to their available resources. For example, coffee grows well in Brazil because its resources are well suited to this crop. The warm climate, the rains, the fertile soil, and so on give Brazil an advantage over other nations with less hospitable environments. Coffee does not grow well in the United States, however, because the United States lacks the mix of resources needed to grow the crop. It makes sense, therefore, for Brazil to devote resources to the production of coffee, and then sell some of its coffee crop to the United States. The United States, in turn, can use its resources to grow crops more suited to its environment. For example, the United States produced about 40% of the world's supply of corn, and nearly one-half of the world's supply of soybeans in the mid-1990s. The United States specialized in the production of these crops because its climate and soil suited the production of these crops. Some corn and soybeans were sold within the United States, and the rest were exported to other nations.

A nation has an **absolute advantage** in the production of a good when it can produce a good more efficiently than another nation. The United States has an absolute advantage over Brazil in the production of corn and soybeans. Brazil, on the other hand, has an absolute advantage over the United States in the production of coffee. What we are really saying is that the United States can produce a greater quantity of corn and soybeans, using fewer resources, than Brazil can produce. Brazil can produce a greater quantity of coffee, using fewer resources, than the United States can. The benefits of trade are clear in this situation. Each nation would benefit from specializing in the crop or crops it produces most efficiently, and then trading its surplus to the other.

But suppose one nation has an absolute advantage over another nation in two products. Should trade occur? The answer is most likely yes. Let's say that Japan has an absolute advantage over the Philippines in the production of both televisions and VCRs. Japan can produce three times as many televisions as the Philippines, with a given amount of resources. Japan can also produce two times as many VCRs as the Philippines with a given amount of resources. Thus, Japan's greatest advantage is in the production of televisions where it is three times as efficient as the Philippines. Japan is only twice as efficient as the Philippines in the production of VCRs. Economists say that Japan not only has an absolute advantage in the production of televisions, but also a comparative advantage in the production of televisions. A **comparative advantage** in the production of a good occurs where one nation has its greatest advantage over another nation or, at least, a lesser disadvantage. Japan's comparative advantage in this hypothetical case is in the production of televisions because Japan can produce three times as many televisions as the Philippines (compared to just two times as many VCRs). The Philippines, on the other hand, has a comparative advantage in the production of VCRs and, thus, should produce VCRs. This is because the size of its "disadvantage" is smaller in the production of VCRs than it is in televisions. An important thing to remember is that the highly industrialized nations of the world—including Japan and the United States—have an absolute advantage in the production of many goods. But like all nations there are scarcities of resources. Even the rich nations must make choices about how to use their scarce resources. Producing goods in which the nation enjoys a comparative advantage is one way to increase both efficiency and total output.

This discussion of absolute and comparative advantage may seem abstract, and difficult to follow. But consider a more personal example. Suppose you have an excellent history teacher at school. And suppose that this history teacher can also cook better than the person in charge of food services at your school. In economic terms, this history teacher has an absolute advantage over the food services person in both teaching and cooking. But the history teacher's time—a resource—is scarce. He cannot cook and teach at the same time. The teacher may be twice as good a cook as the food services person, but ten times as good a teacher as the food services person. How should the teacher use his time? While you will miss some tasty lunches in the cafeteria, the teacher should specialize in that area in which he has the greatest advantage—teaching!

Trade and Exchange Rates

When nations specialize in the production of certain goods, they do so in anticipation of selling these goods to other nations. But countries have different currencies, each of which has a different value. How do you know the value of a Mexican peso, a German mark, or a Japanese yen compared to the U.S. dollar? Without a mechanism for converting one currency into an equivalent value of another, international trade would be nearly impossible.

Nations use an **exchange rate** to determine the worth of one currency against other currencies. The exchange rate is published daily in major financial newspapers. When exchange rates are published in the newspaper they usually list the name of the country, the name of the currency, the value of the foreign currency compared to the U.S. dollar (U.S. equivalent), and the value of the U.S. dollar compared to the foreign currency (currency per U.S. dollar). A typical newspaper listing is shown in Figure 15.4.

To read the exchange rates, consider the following example. Suppose you planned to travel to France for a vacation. Before leaving the United States, however, you decided to convert $100 (U.S.) at your bank for an equivalent in French francs. Based on the exchange rate shown in Figure 15.4, you would receive 660.45 francs for your $100 ($100 × 6.6045 =

Figure 15.4
Foreign Exchange Rates, February 9, 2000

Country/Currency	U.S. Equivalent	Currency per U.S. Dollar
Argentina/Peso	1.0002	.9998
Britain/Pound	1.6170	.6184
Canada/Dollar	.6921	1.448
China/Renminbi	.1208	8.2778
France/Franc	.1514	6.6045
Germany/Mark	.5078	1.9692
India/Rupee	.02294	43.585
Japan/Yen	.009169	109.06
Mexico/Peso	.1060	9.4300
Poland/Zloty	.2416	4.1390
Russia/Ruble	.03486	28.685
Taiwan/Dollar	.03259	30.685
Euro	.9932	1.0068

Source: The Wall Street Journal, February 10, 2000.

660.45 francs). Thus, when you arrived in France you would know that each franc you spent was worth about 15 cents in U.S. currency.

But suppose a friend of yours from France came to visit you in the United States. How would she use the exchange rates in the newspaper? She would want to convert her francs into U.S. dollars. Using the exchange rates in Figure 15.4, if she decided to exchange 1000 francs for U.S. dollars, she would receive $151.40 (U.S.) in return for her francs (1000 francs × .1514 = $151.40). When she spent her money, she would have to remember that each U.S. dollar in her pocket was worth almost seven francs.

On a larger scale, U.S. firms that do business in other countries can calculate very precisely the costs of resources, or the prices of goods, in other countries by converting these currencies into U.S. dollars. But there is a complication—the value of nations' currencies change over time, sometimes from day to day! This is because since 1973 the United States and the other nations of the world have operated under a combination of flexible exchange rates and managed exchange rates to determine the value of currencies.

A **flexible exchange rate** allows the forces of supply and demand to determine the value of a currency. Flexible exchange rates are often called "floating exchange rates." While it may be surprising to you, world currencies are bought and sold just like securities, commodities, or services in international markets. Currencies are traded in **foreign**

exchange markets—an international network of commercial banks and other financial institutions. If the demand for the U.S. dollar increased in the foreign exchange markets, the value of the U.S. dollar would rise in relation to other currencies. That is, it would take more Chinese renminbi, Polish zloty, and Mexican pesos to equal $1 (U.S.). If the demand for the U.S. dollar decreased in foreign exchange markets, however, the value of other currencies would rise in relation to the dollar. The demand for a currency often is determined by the strength of the nation's economy at that moment in time. If the economy is experiencing robust economic growth, full employment, price stability, and so on, the demand for its currency tends to rise. If the economy is sinking into a recession, on the other hand, the demand for the currency tends to weaken.

Managed exchange rates involve government intervention in foreign exchange markets. By purchasing large quantities of a currency, governments can stabilize the demand for a currency and, thus, stabilize its value. For example, in 1979–1980 the United States purchased billions of U.S. dollars to prevent the dollar from losing more of its value. From time to time other governments have done the same. Thus, exchange rates in the world today are determined by a combination of market forces, and government intervention. By the late 1990s, about $1.5 trillion dollars worth of currencies were handled in foreign exchange markets every day!

BARRIERS TO TRADE

Barriers to trade are government actions that are designed to reduce or even halt international trade. Calls for the government to erect barriers to trade—also called trade barriers—are common in the United States. These calls are loudest when the trade deficit rises, when foreign competition forces the closure of U.S. firms, and when other nations impose trade barriers on U.S. products (you will read more about the arguments for and against the use of trade barriers later in the chapter). Trade barriers that exist today are tariffs, quotas, embargoes, voluntary restraints, and other restrictions.

- Tariffs: A **tariff** is a federal tax on an imported good. The Constitution gives the federal government the power to levy tariffs. A tariff increases the price of an imported good. This is because the seller of the good passes at least some of the tax along to the consumer. As a result the higher priced imported good becomes less attractive to buyers, and the demand for competing domestic goods increases. In the 1980s the United States imposed tariffs on certain Japanese motorcycles. The effect of these tariffs was to reduce the quantity demanded of some Japanese motorcycles and to increase the demand for motorcycles produced by U.S. firms such as Harley-Davidson. In 1999 the United States imposed 100% tariffs on 15 categories of European luxury goods—including some Italian cheeses and British cashmere sweaters—to protest European trade restrictions that were placed on Latin American bananas that U.S. firms distribute in European markets. U.S. tariffs on Japanese and Brazilian steel were also approved by Congress in 1999.

- Quotas: A **quota** sets a specific limit on the amount of a good that can be imported during a period of time. This limit could be expressed as a number of goods, the weight of the good (pounds, tons), or other measurement. During the 1980s and into the 1990s, for example, Congress placed quotas on foreign sugar, mainly from the Caribbean. In 1999 the United States imposed quotas on lamb imported from Australia and New Zealand—a move that both Australia and New Zealand have appealed to the World Trade Organization (you will read more about the WTO later in the chapter).

- Embargoes: An **embargo** occurs when a government cuts off some or all trade with another nation. Embargoes are often placed on nations for political purposes. In the early 1960s, for example, the United States placed an embargo on virtually all trade with the nation of Cuba to protest the creation of a communist government in Cuba under Fidel Castro's leadership. In 1980 the United States placed an embargo on the sale of U.S. wheat to the Soviet Union to protest the 1979 Soviet invasion of neighboring Afghanistan. In 1985 the U.S. embargo of certain high-tech products to South Africa was an attempt to pressure the South African government to end its racist apartheid policies. More recently, in 1999 the United States was joined by many other nations in its embargo against the repressive Yugoslavian regime to halt the slaughter of ethnic Albanians in the province of Kosovo.

- Voluntary restraints: **Voluntary restraints** limit the quantity of a good that can be imported. While the limits are binding on the exporting nation, voluntary restraints are agreed to through diplomacy rather than Congressional legislation. The most important voluntary restraint used by the United States in recent years was the limit set on Japanese automobile exports to the United States during the 1980s. In 1981, for example, Japanese auto imports were limited to just 1.68 million. By the mid-1980s President Reagan lifted this voluntary restraint on Japanese autos. Other voluntary restraints have been placed on shoes from Taiwan and South Korea, clothing from the People's Republic of China, and color television sets from Japan.

• Other restrictions: There are a variety of additional ways that nations can restrict or prevent trade between nations. One way is for a nation to simply ban a certain product from its market. In 1999, for example, the European Union—a regional trade organization comprised of 15 European nations—banned hormone-treated beef produced by the United States. (You will read more about regional trade organizations later in the chapter.) By mid-1999 a series of compromises were being explored to end the ban. Another trade barrier is government limits on the number of import licenses that are issued to firms. Firms need an import license to bring goods into a nation. If the government limits the number, or creates other obstacles to obtaining import licenses, the result is fewer imports.

PROTECTIONISM: PRO AND CON

Protectionism is the government's use of trade barriers to limit foreign imports. Those who favor the use of protectionism are sometimes called protectionists. When a nation imposes protectionist policies, it might use a single trade barrier, such as a tariff, or a combination of several trade barriers. Protectionism tends to help certain groups and hurt others. Let's take a look at the main arguments in the debate between protectionism and freer trade (the absence of trade barriers).

Infant Industries Argument

Protectionists believe that newer industries, called infant industries, need government protection from more established foreign competitors. This protection could be in the form of a tariff, a quota, or other trade barrier. From the protectionist's viewpoint, trade barriers should remain in place until the young industries can stand on their own in competitive world markets. Those who favor freer trade, on the other hand, believe that protecting infant industries encourages them to remain inefficient. This is because government protections shield these industries from competition and, therefore, there is no incentive to become efficient. And it is consumers who end up paying higher prices for the output of these inefficient firms.

Employment Argument

Protectionists argue that trade barriers protect domestic jobs and the wages of domestic workers. They argue that imports are to blame for plant closures and job losses. Adding fuel to this argument is the notion that imports from low-wage countries can be produced more cheaply than American-made goods because foreign workers are exploited. In effect, protectionists argue, the purchase of foreign goods not only creates unemployment at home, but also supports the unfair treatment of low-wage laborers in other lands. Supporters of freer trade counter that millions of U.S. laborers work in export industries and, thus, rely on trade for their livelihoods. If trade barriers were imposed on foreign goods entering the United States for example, other nations would likely retaliate. This retaliation could even start a trade war between two or more nations. **Trade wars** occur when more severe trade barriers are imposed by nations to retaliate for earlier ones. The result of trade barriers would be lower production of goods, higher unemployment, and lower wages for all workers.

The Dumping Argument

Protectionists argue that trade barriers or other restrictions are necessary to prevent dumping. **Dumping** occurs when foreign firms sell their output in the United States at prices lower than prevailing prices in their own country—or even at prices below the cost of producing the product. Over the past couple of decades, protectionists say foreign countries have dumped many products in U.S. markets including steel, clothing, shoes, television sets, automobiles, and other goods. Dumping hurts domestic producers of these products, causing plant closures and unemployment. Thus, the fairest way to deal with dumping is to slap high tariffs on these goods (to raise their prices) or to ban them completely. Free traders also view dumping as a potential problem. They insist, however, that it is difficult to prove when dumping has occurred. Further, they note that domestic industries tend to accuse foreign firms of dumping whenever foreign goods compete favorably against domestic products. Free traders believe that the benefits of competition—efficiency in production and lower prices for consumers—should make us weary of "crying foul" every time a foreign good sells well in the American market.

Self-sufficiency Argument

Protectionists argue that a nation must not become too dependent on other nations for essential goods or resources. In their view, nations that overspecialize could later be victimized by hostile nations (which could withhold these goods or resources in times of war), or by sagging demand for goods that are produced in domestic industries (which could reduce the prices of these goods). Further, protectionists point out that some goods are simply too important to leave to other nations to supply—even if other nations could produce these goods more efficiently.

Included in this list are items produced by the defense industry, such as missiles, fighter aircraft, and submarines. Supporters of free trade acknowledge the need to maintain a reliable, domestic defense industry as a way to preserve the security of the nation. But supporters of freer trade argue that nations should be encouraged to produce and trade products in which they enjoy a comparative advantage. This results in an efficient use of the nation's resources, greater world output, and a higher standard of living for all people.

PROMOTING FREER TRADE

Since World War II the degree of international cooperation between nations to promote freer trade has increased. Two developments in the post-war world illustrate nations' willingness to drop some of their trade barriers—international trade agreements to promote world trade, and the creation of regional trade organizations.

International Trade Agreements

The most important post-World War II international trade agreement was the 1947 General Agreement on Tariffs and Trade (GATT). GATT's goal was to bring nations together to pursue **free trade**—international trade without trade barriers or other government restrictions. Membership in GATT grew from the original 23 nations in 1947 to about 120 nations by 1995—when GATT was absorbed into the newly formed World Trade Organization (WTO).

GATT provided a forum for members—called "contracting parties"—to discuss trade barriers and trade disputes. From 1947 to 1995 GATT was responsible for reducing or eliminating trade barriers on thousands of manufactured goods and agricultural goods around the world. One way that GATT achieved these successes was through its **most-favored-nation** (MFN) policy—a policy that required that any trade concession granted to one member nation automatically applied to all other member nations. At the final "round" (the name given to a series of negotiations over a period of years) of GATT, called the Uruguay Round (1986–1994), member nations established the World Trade Organization to replace GATT.

The WTO expanded on GATT's central mission by promoting freer trade not only in manufactured goods and agricultural goods, but also in services and intellectual property—such as books, computer software, and recordings. Today, most nations in the world belong to the WTO. One notable exception is the People's Republic of China, which, by 1999, had gained the support of the Clinton Administration for admission, and which had opened formal negotiations with the European Union (EU) in January of 2000 to solicit its support. The WTO's members must extend trade concessions given to one nation to all member nations. Member nations are also required to abide by the decisions of WTO review committees if trade disputes arise. The United States, for example, bowed to a WTO committee decision to lift its trade restrictions on imports of Costa Rican underwear after the WTO ruled the restrictions were illegal. The EU, on the other hand, rejected WTO orders to lift its restrictions on banana imports by U.S. companies, or to lift its ban on U.S. hormone-treated beef in the spring of 1999.

Regional Trade Organizations

Another major development toward freer international markets in the post-World War II era was the rise of regional trade organizations. A **regional trade organization** is an economic alliance among nations that reduces or eliminates trade barriers among member nations. The largest and most powerful regional trade organization is the EU.

The EU was founded in 1993 by the Maastricht Treaty. It replaced the 12-nation European Community (EC), and expanded on the EC's mission to create a "free-trade zone" in Europe. A free-trade zone is an economic region that does not restrict trade or investments among member nations. The 15 members of the EU include Austria, Belgium, Denmark, Finland, France, Germany, Greece, Ireland, Italy, Luxembourg, the Netherlands, Portugal, Spain, Sweden, and the United Kingdom. Membership in the EU has strengthened the position of member nations in trade relations with other parts of the world. Currently, the EU is the largest economic unit in the world, producing more goods and services than any single nation—including the United States. Adding to the unity of the EU is The European Council (the EU's highest political decision-making body), the powerful European Central Bank for the EU (which determines the organization's monetary policies), and the use of a common currency—the euro. The euro will be phased in as the currency for 11 EU nations between 1999 and 2002. Other nations currently negotiating to join the EU include Cyprus, the Czech Republic, Estonia, Hungary, Poland, and Slovenia.

Another important regional trade organization is The North American Free Trade Agreement, or NAFTA. NAFTA took effect on January 1, 1994. Its three member nations include the United States, Canada, and Mexico. NAFTA established a free-trade zone across much of North America by providing for a gradual elimination of most trade barriers among the member nations over a 15-year period. The most important goals of NAFTA are to promote free trade and economic growth in its member nations. In the first five years of NAFTA, trade between member nations has increased by about 75%, from $289 billion in 1993 to over $500 billion by 1999.

Other regional trade organizations around the world are also working to integrate their economies and increase trade. In South America, MERCOSUR went into effect in 1991. By 2000, MERCOSUR was comprised of six nations including Argentina, Bolivia, Brazil, Chile, Paraguay, and Uruguay. Formal discussions among the NAFTA and MERCOSUR nations, along with a number of other Latin American nations, began in the late 1990s to form a Free Trade Area of the Americas (FTAA) by 2005. Among the other regional trade organizations currently operating are the Association of Southeast Asian Nations (ASEAN), the Asia-Pacific Economic Cooperation group (APEC), and the European Free Trade Agreement (EFTA).

MAKING ECONOMIC DECISIONS: FAST TRACK TRADE AUTHORITY

Fast track trade authority gives the President the authority to negotiate trade agreements with foreign governments. Under the provisions of fast track trade authority, the President or his representatives can negotiate with other nations to reduce trade barriers or otherwise promote trade relations. But under fast track rules, Congress can only accept the agreement or reject it. Congress cannot amend it in any way. Fast track trade authority has been used a number of times in recent history. During the 1990s, for example, fast track negotiations resulted in the creation of NAFTA (1993) and the U.S. approval of trade policies from the Uruguay Round of GATT (1994).

Supporters of fast track trade authority argue that this process is quicker and more efficient than forming trade agreements in Congress. Fast track trade authority allows negotiators to speak on behalf of the President. Both parties in the negotiations also know that what is agreed to only can be accepted or rejected by Congress—but that no further changes can be made in the agreement. And, while the role of the President is greater under the fast track process, Congress still has the power to reject the agreement if it believes the agreement will harm the nation. Since 1995 President Clinton has worked to regain fast track authority, but Congress has refused to grant it.

Opponents of fast track trade authority argue that fast track trade authority places too much power in the hands of the President to make trade concessions and to dictate the rules of trade to the nation. They point to NAFTA to show how policies formerly in the hands of elected officials have been absorbed by NAFTA. For example, NAFTA now decides on the types of pesticides that can be used on fruits and other foods, and on the length and weight of trucks that can travel on U.S. highways. Thus, opponents have severe reservations about how much power fast track trade authority takes out of the hands of their elected officials and places in the hands of bureaucrats.

GLOSSARY OF ECONOMIC TERMS

Ability-to-pay principle (of taxation)   A principle of taxation stating that people with more income or wealth should pay more taxes.

Absolute advantage   Occurs when a region or a nation can produce a good more efficiently than another region or nation.

Advertising   A paid announcement by a firm designed to provide information about a product to consumers and to persuade consumers to buy the product.

Aggregate demand   The total demand for goods and services in an economy in a given period of time. Measured in total spending for these goods and services.

Aggregate supply   The total supply of goods and services produced in an economy in a given period of time. Measured by the real Gross Domestic Product (GDP).

Antitrust legislation   A series of federal laws to protect competitive markets in the United States. Examples are the Sherman Antitrust Act of 1890 and the Clayton Act of 1914.

Balance of trade   The relationship between the nation's total merchandise imports and its merchandise exports in a given period of time.

Balanced budget   Occurs when the federal government's spending is equal to its revenues.

Bankruptcy   A legal recognition that an individual or business cannot pay its debts. The most often used sections of the bankruptcy code are Chapters 7, 11, and 13.

Barriers to entry   Refers to factors that limit entry into an industry, including high costs for capital, expensive research and development, the need for a skilled labor force, and patented technology.

Barriers to trade   Government actions designed to reduce or halt international trade. Examples include tariffs, quotas, voluntary restraints, and embargoes.

Barter   The direct exchange of one good for another.

Basic economic questions   The questions that all economies face, including what to produce, how to produce, and for whom to produce.

Benefits-received principle (of taxation)   A principle of taxation stating that people who directly benefit from the use of a public good or service should pay for it.

Bonds (corporate bonds)   A type of I.O.U. that a corporation sells to investors. A way corporations borrow money from investors.

Boycott   Designed to stop consumers from purchasing a good or service. Boycotts are used by consumer groups, workers, or other groups to pressure firms to change a policy, or to solve a problem.

Budget deficit (federal)   Occurs when the federal government's spending is greater than its revenues.

Budget surplus (federal)   Occurs when the federal government's spending is less than its revenues.

Business cycle   Shows the increases and decreases in the real GDP in the U.S. economy over time. The two phases of the business cycle are expansion and contraction.

Capital goods (capital)   Items made for the purpose of producing other goods (one of the factors of production). Examples include office buildings, tractors, business computers, and garbage trucks.

Capitalism   A type of economic system based on private ownership and control over the factors of production—natural resources, human resources, and capital goods. Often called a free enterprise system or a market economic system. Examples include the United States, Japan, and Taiwan.

Capital stock   The total amount of capital goods that a country has to produce goods and services.

Cartel   A formal agreement or organization among firms that produce an identical product. An example is the Organization of Petroleum Exporting Countries (OPEC) which produces oil.

Cause-effect fallacies   Errors in reasoning that stem from misreading connections between one event and another. These errors often result from connecting unrelated events just because they are correlated in time (occur at the same time), or from oversimplifying a subject.

Ceteris paribus   A basic assumption in economics that permits economists to hold all variables constant, except price, when studying the impact of price on buying or production decisions.

Channel of distribution   The path that a product travels to move from the producer to the consumer.

Charge card   A plastic card that permits a consumer to purchase goods or services at a particular store, and then repay the store at a later date.

Closed shop   Refers to an arrangement by which a worker must belong to a labor union before he could work for a firm; outlawed by the Taft-Hartley Act of 1947.

Collective bargaining   Occurs when union leaders negotiate with management on behalf of all union members in a firm or an industry.

Collusion   An illegal practice where "competing" firms work together to make production and pricing decisions.

Command economy   An economy in which the government decides how to answer the basic economic questions.

Commodities   A contract to buy a certain amount or number of a product for a specific price in the future. Investors in commodities sell the contract at a later date for a profit or a loss, depending on the market price for the good at the time of the sale.

Common stock   A type of corporate stock that entitles the stockholder to voting rights at the annual stockholders' meetings; offers variable dividends.

Communism   A type of economic system in which the government owns or controls the great majority of the means of production—the factories, farms, and other firms—and dictates the answers to the basic economic questions. A type of command economy. Examples include the People's Republic of China, Cuba, and North Korea.

Comparative advantage   Occurs in the production of a good where a region or a nation has the greatest advantage, or at least, a lesser disadvantage. Resources are used most efficiently when regions or nations specialize in the production of goods in which they have a comparative advantage.

Comparison shopping   Occurs when a consumer considers the purchase of alternative goods to satisfy a want or need. Comparisons are made on the good's price, quality, warranties, and so on.

Complementary goods   Goods that are commonly used in conjunction with one another. An example is batteries and flashlights.

Consumerism   The consumer movement that combined the efforts of government, consumer groups, and individuals to protect consumer interests.

Consumers   The people who purchase goods and services.

Contract   A binding agreement between two parties. Examples include a labor contract, purchasing contract, or partnership contract.

Cooperative   A voluntary association of people that conducts a business activity to serve its members rather than to earn a profit. Examples include food cooperatives and credit unions.

Coordinated strategy   The use of a combination of union techniques such as the boycott, picketing, and the strike, to settle a dispute with management.

Corporate bond   A type of I.O.U. that a corporation sells to investors; the bond represents the corporation's debt that is owed to the investor and does not represents ownership in the corporation.

Corporate income tax   A federal tax on corporate profits.

Corporate stock   A certificate of ownership in a corporation.

Corporation   A type of business in which the ownership of the firm (stockholders) is separated from the operation of the firm (management).

Costs of production   The payments that firms make in exchange for the factors of production. Included are wages, rents, interest, and profits (to the entrepreneurs).

Credit   The use of someone else's money to buy goods or services today, with the promise to repay the money at a later date.

Credit card   A plastic card that permits a consumer to buy goods or services at a variety of businesses, and then repay this sum to the company that issued the card at a later date.

Cyclical unemployment   Occurs when there is a downturn (contraction) in the nation's business cycle.

Deflation   Occurs when the general price level for all goods and services in an economy decreases. Usually occurs when there is insufficient demand for the products produced in an economy.

Demand   The amount of a resource, good, or service that people are willing and able to buy at a series of prices in a given period of time.

Demand-side economics   Federal economic policies designed to promote stability by changing aggregate demand.

Democratic socialism   A type of economic system that combines socialist planning with free market economic activities and a democratic political system. Examples include India, Sweden, and West Germany.

Depository institutions   Institutions that accept savers' deposits and grant loans, such as banks, savings institutions (S&Ls and mutual savings banks), and credit unions.

Depression   A prolonged and severe economic recession.

Derived demand   The demand for labor results from (is derived from) the demand for the good that this labor produces.

Diminishing marginal utility   Occurs when the consumption of an additional unit of the same good offers less utility (satisfaction) than the consumption of the previous unit.

Discount rate   The interest rate charged by the Federal Reserve System to member banks and to the government for short-term loans. An important monetary policy tool.

Division of labor   Occurs when individual workers perform a narrow range of tasks in a larger production process. The division of labor is the basis for the assembly line method of production.

Downsizing   The process a firm goes through to eliminate waste and become more efficient. Also called restructuring or streamlining.

Dumping   Occurs when a foreign firm sells its output in another country at prices below those in its own country, or for prices below the cost of producing the product.

Easy money policy A type of monetary policy designed to increase the money supply in order to increase aggregate demand in the economy. It involves buying government securities, lowering the discount rate, and possibly decreasing the reserve requirement.

Economic goals The broad objectives that a nation tries to achieve in its economy. The commonly accepted goals in the U.S. economy include economic freedom, efficiency, equity, security, growth, full employment, and price stability.

Economic growth Occurs when an economy is able to produce more goods and services over time. Typically measured in terms of a rising real Gross Domestic Product (a GDP adjusted for inflation).

Economics The study of how people choose to use their resources in order to satisfy their nearly unlimited economic wants.

Economies in transition A type of economy that is moving away for its communist past and toward a market-oriented future. Examples include Russia and the former communist nations of Eastern Europe.

Economies of scale Describes how average production costs fall as additional units of a good are produced. This is the most important argument in favor of maintaining natural monopolies.

Economists People who study the economy, particularly the choices that individuals, firms, and the government make in the economy.

Economy All of the production and consumption decisions, and all activities that relate to the use of resources in a society.

Elasticity of demand Measures the impact of prices on the quantity demanded of a good or service. An elastic demand is very flexible, and changes readily with a change in price. An inelastic demand is more inflexible and does not change readily with a change in price.

Elasticity of supply Measures the impact of prices on the quantity supplied of a good or service. An elastic supply is very flexible and changes readily with a change in price. An inelastic supply is more inflexible, and does not change readily with a change in price. A perfectly inelastic supply occurs when a number or amount of a good is fixed, such as stadium seats.

Electronic commerce Refers to the many cashless ways transactions take place, such as point-of-sale (POS) and automatic clearing house (ACH) systems.

Electronic money (e-money) Describes the new "currency" made of electronically transmitted messages, rather than of paper or coin.

Embargo Occurs when a government cuts off some or all trade with another nation. Embargoes are often used to pressure nations to change a policy or behavior.

Entrepreneurship The actions of innovators in the economy, called entrepreneurs, who create new products, new ways to produce products, or new firms. Some economists consider entrepreneurship to be a factor of production.

European Union (EU) The world's largest regional trade organization. The EU has created a 15-member free-trade zone in Europe.

Evidence fallacies   Occur when there is insufficient, irrelevant, or incorrect data to support an author's conclusions.

Exchange rate   Determines the worth of one currency against other currencies.

Excise tax   A tax on a specific item, levied by the federal and state governments. Examples include excise taxes on gasoline, tobacco products, and alcohol.

Expansionary fiscal policy   A type of fiscal policy designed to increase aggregate demand in the economy to fight recession. It involves decreasing taxes, increasing government spending, and expanding tax incentives.

Exports   The goods or services that individuals, firms, or the government sell to other nations.

Factors of production   The resources that are used to produce goods or services, including natural resources, human resources, capital goods, and entrepreneurship.

Fast-track trade authority   Gives the President the authority to negotiate trade agreements with foreign governments. Congress retains the power to accept or reject the agreement, but not to amend it.

Federal budget   The federal government's plan to raise and spend money during a fiscal year (FY)—October 1 through September 30 of the following year.

Federal Reserve System (Fed)   The central bank of the United States. Coordinates the nation's monetary policy, and provides other banking services.

Financial investments   Occur when an investor uses money to purchase existing assets or wealth in order to make money; for example, the investment in stocks or bonds.

Firm   An organization that uses the factors of production to produce goods or services.

Fiscal policy   The federal plan of action by Congress and the President to promote economic stability. It involves the use of taxes, government spending, and tax incentives.

Five-year plans   Establish the goals, production targets, and plans for the use of society's resources to achieve these goals. Used by socialist and communist economies.

Fixed costs (FC)   The costs that do not change as the rate of output changes. Included are rent on property, interest on debts, local taxes, and insurance premiums.

Flexible exchange rate   Occurs when the forces of supply and demand for a currency establish its worth in relation to other currencies.

Foreign exchange markets   The international network of banks and other financial institutions that trade currencies.

Franchise   A type of business that uses a parent company's name to sell a product yet maintains a degree of independence from the parent company. The person opening the business is called the franchisee, while the parent company is called the franchisor.

Free market economy   An economic system in which individuals and firms, rather than the government, make the great majority of economic decisions. Also called a market economy.

Free-rider dilemma A problem that results when a private firm cannot prevent others (the free-riders) from using a good or service that it owns. A main reason for government to provide public goods.

Free trade International trade without trade barriers or other government restrictions.

Frictional unemployment Occurs when workers are "in-between" jobs or are new entrants into the labor force.

General Agreement on Tariffs and Trade (GATT) The world's leading trade agreement between 1947 and 1995 (when it was absorbed into the WTO). Designed to promote free trade in the world.

Geographic monopoly A type of monopoly that exists when one firm is the sole provider of a good or service in a geographic region.

Glasnost A type of political reform by the former Soviet Union to bring about an "openness" in the political arena, an end to the Communist Party's control over the government, and free elections.

Good Any physical object that satisfies a person's wants.

Government monopoly A type of monopoly that exists when the government grants itself the exclusive right to produce a good or service. An example is first class mail delivery by the U.S. Postal Service.

Government securities The broad range of investments in government bills, notes, and bonds.

Green revolution Introduced new technology to agriculture in the form of advanced capital goods, fertilizers and pesticides, irrigation techniques, and hybrid seeds. The result has been increased crop yields throughout the world.

Gross domestic product (GDP) The total dollar value of all newly produced goods and services in an economy in a given year.

Gross savings rate Includes the savings of individuals, businesses, and federal and state governments.

Human resources (labor) The human element in production (one of the factors of production). Examples include teachers, assembly line workers, doctors, and building contractors.

Imports The goods or services that individuals, firms, or the government buy from other nations.

Incentives The financial factors that motivate laborers to work, firms to produce, investors to take risks with their money, and so on. Incentives are strongest in economies that lean toward the market model.

Income Any payment received by a household. Earned income includes wages or salaries, rents, interest, dividends, or entrepreneurial profits. Unearned income comes mainly from transfer payments.

Independent union A union not affiliated with the AFL-CIO. An example is the National Education Association (NEA).

Indicative planning A type of government planning that sets economic goals and then makes recommendations about how the nation's resources should be used to achieve these goals.

Industry The entire group of firms that produce a similar product.

Inflation Occurs when the general price level for all goods and services in an economy increases. Usually results when there is "too much money chasing too few goods."

Informal economy An "underground economy" based on barter or other exchanges without the government's knowledge.

Injunction A court order that prohibits a strike.

Installment loan A type of borrowing where the buyer promises to repay the principal plus interest on a monthly schedule that could range from a few months to several years.

Interest The return that savers receive for their deposits in savings accounts or from their investments in corporate or government bonds. Also, a cost of production to firms.

International trade Occurs when individuals, firms, or governments import or export goods or services.

Investment The use of money to make money, to increase the amount of capital goods, or both. Financial investment occurs when an investor uses money to purchase existing assets such as stocks or bonds. Real investment occurs when an investor uses money to purchase new capital.

Investment portfolio The collection of financial holdings of an individual, household, or firm.

Labor force Comprised of people in a nation who are 16 years old or older and who are either employed or actively seeking employment.

Labor union An organization of workers designed to increase the power of laborers in their negotiations with management. The source of union power is collective bargaining, but union power is also increased by its power to call strikes, boycotts, or coordinated strategies. Union organization might be open shop or union shop. The closed shop has been illegal since 1947.

Laissez-faire capitalism An economy in which the government does not regulate business activity or otherwise direct the use of the nation's resources.

Law of demand States that there is an inverse relationship between the price of a good and the quantity demanded of the good. As the price increases, the quantity demanded decreases, and vice versa.

Law of supply States that there is a direct relationship between the price of a good or service and the quantity supplied of the good. As the price increases, the quantity supplied increases, and vice versa.

Lockout Occurs when management closes a business until an agreeable contract with employees has been reached.

Lorenz curve Shows the actual distribution of income in the United States.

Macroeconomics The branch of economics that deals with how the overall economy functions. Included in the study are changes in price levels, aggregate supply and aggregate demand, and unemployment.

Managed exchange rate Occurs when governments intervene in foreign exchange markets by buying or selling a currency, to stabilize the value of the currency.

Management The process of using resources to achieve the firm's goals. In common usage, the term management also refers to the firm's leadership, such as the CEO or president of a corporation. Management's power stems from its control of the purse strings of the firm and its ability to impose a lockout, hire replacement workers, relocate the plant, and appeal for an injunction.

Marginalism Refers to people's decisions to purchase an additional unit of a good, to work an additional hour, to produce an additional unit of output, and so on. Many economic decisions are made "at the margin."

Marginal utility The amount of satisfaction that a person receives from consuming an additional unit of the same good in a given period of time.

Market economy An economic model of an economy based on private ownership and control of the factors of production. In common usage the term market economy can be used interchangeably with free enterprise system, capitalism, and free market system.

Market equilibrium The compromise that must be reached so that both consumers and producers are satisfied with the price of a good and the quantity available for purchase.

Market mechanism An informal network of signals that influence consumers' demand for goods and services, and firms' use of resources to supply goods to consumers. The most important signal is price, which coordinates the millions of buying and selling decisions that occur in a free market economy every day.

Market structure Refers to the way an industry is organized, particularly with regards to the degree of competition that exists in the industry. The four types of market structure are perfect competition, monopolistic competition, oligopoly, and monopoly.

Merger Occurs when two corporations are legally joined under single ownership.

Microeconomics The branch of economics that deals with how the participants in the economy interact with one another. Participants include consumers, firms, workers, savers, investors, and others.

Minimum wage A price floor on wages. The federal minimum wage is currently $5.15, but many states have higher state minimum wages.

Ministry of International Trade and Industry (MITI) A quasi-public institution that helps guide resource use in Japan by offering incentives to firms to produce certain items and not others.

Mixed economy An economy that combines the features from the traditional, command, and market models. All of the world's economies today are mixed economies.

Monetary policy   A plan of action by the Federal Reserve System (the Fed) to promote economic stability by using open market operations, or by changing the discount rate or reserve requirement.

Money   Any item that can be used to purchase goods or services, or settle other financial obligations such as taxes. Includes commodity money, representative money, and fiat money.

Money supply   Consists of a nation's currency, financial instruments that function as money, and near moneys. The four main measures of the money supply include M1, M2, M3, and L.

Monopolistic competition   A type of market structure in which many firms produce similar, but differentiated products.

Monopoly   A type of market structure in which one firm produces virtually all of the industry's output.

Most-favored-nation (MFN)   A policy that requires that any trade concession granted to one nation, automatically applies to other MFNs. Individual nations can grant MFN status to economic allies. Major trade agreements, such as GATT and the WTO, have included MFN status as a condition of membership.

Multinational corporation   A corporation that has production facilities in more than one country.

Mutual fund   A firm that purchases a pool of securities, such as stocks, bonds, and government securities, then sells shares of the mutual fund to investors.

National debt   The sum total of all outstanding federal government debts.

Nationalization   Occurs when the government takes ownership of a firm or industry, but compensates the previous owner.

Natural monopoly   Occurs when a monopoly can produce a good or service more efficiently than a number of competing firms could.

Natural resources (land)   The gifts of nature that are used in production (one of the factors of production). Examples include sunlight, soil, minerals, trees, rivers, and so on.

Nominal Gross Domestic Product   Measures the value of all newly produced goods and services in an economy in a given year, not adjusted for inflation.

Nonprofit organization   An organization, usually organized as a corporation, that provides services to people, but not for profit. Examples include the Red Cross and many charitable organizations.

Nonrenewable resources   Resources that are used up in production, cannot be replenished, and are in fixed supply. Examples include oil, natural gas, coal, and other minerals.

Normative economics   Presents a viewpoint on an economic problem or issue, often expressed as what should or ought to occur.

North American Free Trade Agreement (NAFTA)   A regional trade organization comprised of Canada, Mexico, and the United States.

Oligopoly   A type of market structure in which a small number of firms produce most of the industry's output.

Open market operations The buying or selling of government securities by the Fed to stabilize the economy. A major monetary policy tool.

Open shop Refers to an arrangement by which a worker can choose whether to join a union at the firm where he is employed.

Opportunity cost The second best use of resources by society, by a firm, or by an individual. What is given up if resources are used one way rather than another way.

Partnership A type of business that is owned by two or more people, each of whom has a financial interest in the firm.

Patents Legal protections granted by the government to inventors, researchers, or others who develop new products or processes.

Perestroika A "restructuring" of the economy of the former Soviet Union that included policies to reduce corruption and alcoholism in the workplace, to establish incentives to boost output, and to create a "competitive atmosphere" among firms.

Perfect competition A "model" market structure in which thousands of independent firms produce an identical product to sell to consumers.

Personal decision-making The process an individual uses to make the best use of his or her resources. The process involves identifying the personal problem, listing the alternatives and the criteria, evaluating the alternatives, and then making the decision.

Personal budget A household plan to balance monthly income with monthly expenses.

Personal income tax A federal tax on a person's taxable income. A type of progressive tax.

Personal savings rate The percentage of people's disposable incomes that is saved in a depository institution in the United States.

Political Action Committee (PAC) An organization that collects contributions from its membership to donate to political candidates friendly to the interests of their organization.

Positive economics Presents factual statements of "what is." Positive statements can be tested or verified with data.

Poverty Occurs when the income of an individual or family falls below the poverty line. The poverty line is a dollar figure equal to three times the cost of a family's minimum food budget for a year.

Preferred stock A type of stock that offers a fixed dividend, but usually does not entitle the stockholder to voting rights at the annual stockholders' meetings.

Price The amount of money required to purchase a resource, intermediate good, or finished good or service.

Price ceiling A government imposed maximum price for a resource, good, or service. Rent controls are a type of price ceiling because they set an upper limit on the rents that landlords can charge their tenants.

Price floor   A government guaranteed minimum price for a resource, good, or service. The minimum wage is a type of price floor because it forbids most employers from paying a wage below this minimum standard.

Privatization   The process of transferring state properties, such as state-owned firms, to private individuals or firms.

Production   Occurs when firms transform the factors of production into goods or services.

Production possibilities curve   An economic model that illustrates the range of possible production choices that nations or firms might make and the inevitable opportunity costs that result from these choices.

Productivity   Measures the amount of output that is produced by a firm per unit of input (factor of production).

Progressive tax   A tax that takes a larger percentage of income from upper-income households than from lower-income households. An example is the federal personal income tax.

Property tax   A tax on personal property such as a house, building, undeveloped property, or a car. A major source of government revenue for towns and cities.

Proportional tax   A tax that takes the same percentage of income from all income groups. Some state income taxes are proportional taxes.

Protectionism   The government's use of trade barriers to limit foreign imports to protect domestic businesses.

Public assistance program   A type of government program that provides transfer payments to people for which no payment is made; for example, Temporary Assistance for Needy Families, Medicaid.

Public good   A good supplied by the government that is available to all members of society. Examples include highways, libraries, and schools.

Public transfer payment   A government payment to individuals who do not provide a good or service in return.

Quota   Occurs when the government sets a limit on the amount of a good that can be imported during a period of time.

Real GDP   Measures the value of all newly produced goods and services produced in an economy in a given year after the GDP has been adjusted for inflation.

Real investments   Occur when an investor uses money to purchase new capital goods; for example, factory equipment or business computers.

Recession   A contraction in the business cycle that lasts for at least two consecutive quarters (six months).

Regional trade organization   An economic alliance among nations that reduces or eliminates trade barriers among member nations. Examples include the EU and NAFTA.

Regressive tax   A tax that takes a larger portion of the income from lower-income households than from upper-income households. An example is state sales taxes.

Renewable resources Resources that can be replenished. Examples include plants, animals, sunlight, and the wind.

Replacement workers Workers hired by firms to replace striking employees.

Reserve requirement The amount of money that banks must hold as vault cash, or on deposit with their Fed bank. An infrequently used monetary policy tool.

Restrictive fiscal policy A type of fiscal policy designed to reduce aggregate demand in the economy to fight inflation. It includes increasing taxes, decreasing government spending, and reducing tax incentives.

Revenue The money a business receives from the sale of its output.

Sales tax A tax on many of the goods and services that people purchase; a type of regressive tax.

Saving The non-consumption of income.

Scarcity Exists whenever there are insufficient resources to satisfy people's nearly unlimited wants; sometimes referred to as the universal economic problem.

Scientific management A management style that calculates the time it takes to perform tasks, and then to integrate these smaller tasks into a larger production process. Sometimes called Taylorism after its founder, Frederick Winslow Taylor.

Scientific method The five-step process that enables scientists, including social scientists, to analyze topics systematically. The process includes identifying the problem, collecting relevant information, proposing a hypothesis, testing the hypothesis, and assessing the validity of the hypothesis.

Seasonal unemployment Occurs when people are out of work for a portion of the year because of changes in the seasons. An example is some contractors are out of work during the winter months.

Service Any productive activity that satisfies a person's wants.

Social cost Occurs when a neutral third party (one not connected with the production or consumption of a good) is harmed by negative side-effects of production. An example is pollution.

Social decision-making The process people use to make decisions that affect the community, state, nation, or world. The process involves identifying the social problem, listing the alternatives and the criteria, evaluating the alternatives, and then making the decision.

Social insurance payroll taxes Taxes that are deducted from an employee's paycheck, including the FICA taxes (Social Security and Medicare taxes). Employers must match the FICA taxes.

Social insurance program A type of government program that provides transfer payments to people who have made monetary contributions to the program; for example, Social Security, Medicare.

Social science The branch of science that deals with human relationships and the behaviors of individuals and groups. Economics, for example, is a social science.

Sole proprietorship A type of business that is owned by one person called a proprietor.

Specialization Occurs when individuals, firms, regions, or nations produce a narrower range of goods in which they have a natural advantage. Specialization encourages trade within nations and between nations.

State income tax A state tax on people's income; some state income taxes are progressive, while others are proportional.

Stock (corporate stock) A certificate of ownership in a corporation. The two types of stock are common stock and preferred stock.

Stock market A place where investors come together to trade (buy or sell) stocks. The New York Stock Exchange is the world's largest stock market.

Strike A work stoppage initiated by workers. A technique used by workers to gain a more favorable contract.

Structural unemployment Occurs when there is a "mismatch" between the supply of labor and the demand for labor with particular skills. Often the result of new technology or foreign competition.

Subcontractors Firms that are contracted to produce goods for another firm.

Substitute goods Goods that are similar to one another and could be used almost interchangeably. An example is different brands of cola.

Supply The amount of a good or service that producers are willing and able to sell at a series of prices in a given period of time.

Supply-side economics Federal policies designed to promote economic stability by changing aggregate supply.

Tariff A federal tax on an imported good. Tariffs can be designed to raise a revenue for the government or to discourage imports.

Tax A mandatory payment by an individual or a firm to any level of government. Taxes are designed to raise a revenue for the government, to influence people's behaviors, or both. The three types of taxes include progressive, proportional, and regressive taxes.

Taxation (principles of) The benefits-received principle states that people who benefit from the use of a public good should pay for it. The ability-to-pay principle states that people with more income or wealth should pay more in taxes.

Technological monopoly A type of monopoly that exists when a firm develops new technology (which is then patented) to produce a new product or a new way to produce a product.

Tight money policy A type of monetary policy designed to decrease aggregate demand in the U.S. economy. It involves selling government securities, increasing the discount rate, and possibly increasing the reserve requirement.

Total costs (TC) Are calculated by adding a firm's fixed costs (FC) and variable costs (VC) in the production of a good or service.

Trade The voluntary exchanges of goods or services between people, regions, or nations.

Trade deficit Occurs when the value of a nation's imports (of goods) is greater than the value of its exports (of goods); also called a merchandise trade deficit.

Trade deficit in services Occurs when the value of services imported into a nation is greater than the value of services exported from the nation.

Trade-offs Occurs when an individual, firm, or the government chooses to use its resources one way rather than another way. The specific good or service that is the "trade-off" is called the opportunity cost (the second best use of your resources).

Trade surplus Occurs when the value of a nation's exports (of goods) is greater than the value of its imports (of goods); also called a merchandise trade surplus.

Trade surplus in services Occurs when the value of services exported from a nation is greater than the value of services imported into the nation.

Trade war Occurs when two or more countries impose severe trade restrictions on one another to limit imports. Often a result of protectionist trade policies.

Traditional economy An economy that allows customs or traditions to answer the basic economic questions.

Transfer payments Payments of money, goods, or services financed by one group and distributed to another. Types of transfer payments include public assistance (Temporary Assistance for Needy Families, food stamps) and social insurance (Social Security, Medicare).

Treasury bills (T-bills) A type of government security with a relatively low interest rate, and a maturity of 3 to 12 months.

Treasury bonds A type of government security with an interest rate above T-bills or Treasury notes, and a maturity of 10 to 30 years.

Treasury notes A type of government security with an interest rate slightly higher than T-bills, and a maturity of 1 to 10 years.

Unemployment The number of people who are without jobs but are able and willing to work at current wages. The unemployment rate is the percentage of the labor force that is unemployed. Four types of unemployment include structural, cyclical, seasonal, and frictional.

Unemployment rate The percentage of the labor force that is without work.

Union shop Refers to an arrangement by which a worker must join a union at a firm within a certain period of time after he is hired.

Utility Measures how much satisfaction a person receives from the consumption of a good or service.

Variable costs (VC) The costs to a firm that change as the rate of production changes. Included are wages and materials (natural resources and intermediate goods).

Voluntary restraint Government limit on the quantity of a good that can be imported or arrived at through diplomacy rather than legislation.

World Trade Organization (WTO) Currently the world's most important trade agreement designed to create freer trade in manufactured goods, agricultural goods, services, and intellectual property. Absorbed GATT in 1995.

SELECTED BIBLIOGRAPHY

GOVERNMENT PUBLICATIONS

Budget of the United States Government: Fiscal Year 2000. Washington, DC: U.S. Government Printing Office, 1999 (annual).

Economic Report of the President: 1999. Washington, DC: U.S. Government Printing Office, 1999 (annual).

Occupational Outlook Handbook: 1998–99. Washington, DC: U.S. Department of Labor, 1998 (annual).

U.S. Bureau of the Census. *American Factfinder.* Washington, DC, 1999.

U.S. Bureau of the Census. *Historical Statistics of the United States: Colonial Times to 1970.* Parts 1 and 2. Bicentennial edition. Washington, DC, 1975.

U.S. Bureau of the Census. *Statistical Abstract of the United States: 1998.* 118th ed. Washington, DC, 1998 (annual).

OTHER PUBLICATIONS

Black, John. *Dictionary of Economics.* Oxford: Oxford University Press, 1997.

Brobeck, Stephen, ed. *Encyclopedia of the Consumer Movement.* Santa Barbara, CA: ABC-CLIO, 1997.

Brunner, Borgna, ed. *The TIME Almanac: 1999.* Boston: Information Please LLC, 1998.

Consumer Reports: Buying Guide. Yonkers, NY: Consumers Union of the United States, 1998 (annual).

Egendork, Laura K., ed. *Opposing Viewpoints: Poverty.* San Diego, CA: Greenhaven Press, 1999.

The European Union: A Guide for Americans, 2000. Washington, DC: Delegation of the European Commission in the United States, 1999 (updated periodically).

Folsom, W. Davis. *Understanding American Business Jargon: A Dictionary.* Westport, CT: Greenwood, 1997.
Geisst, Charles R. *Wall Street: A History.* Oxford: Oxford University Press, 1997.
Hallett, Anthony, and Diane Hallett. *Entrepreneur Magazine Encyclopedia of Entrepreneurs.* New York: Wiley, 1997.
Hardaway, Robert M. *Population, Law, and the Environment.* Westport, CT: Praeger, 1994.
Hazlitt, Henry. *Economics in One Lesson.* 3d ed. New York: Three Rivers Press, 1979.
Heilbroner, Robert L. *The Worldly Philosophers.* 6th ed. New York: Simon & Schuster, 1992.
Hillstrom, Kevin, and Laurie Collier Hillstrom. *Encyclopedia of Small Business.* Vols. 1 and 2. Detroit: Gale Research, 1998.
Hoover's Billion Dollar Directory: The Complete Guide to U.S. Public Companies. Austin, TX: Business Press, 1997.
Jacobs, Jane. *Cities and the Wealth of Nations.* New York: Random House, 1984.
Klein, Daniel B. *What Do Economists Contribute?* New York: New York University Press, 1999.
Krantz, Les. *Jobs Rated Almanac: The Best and Worst Jobs.* New York: St. Martin's Griffin, 1999.
Lendol, Calder. *Financing the American Dream: A Cultural History of Consumer Credit.* Princeton, NJ: Princeton University Press, 1999.
Lewis, Herschell G., and Carol Nelson. *Advertising Age Handbook of Advertising.* Lincolnwood, IL: NTC Business Books, 1999.
Longe, Jacqueline L., ed. *How Products Are Made: An Illustrated Guide to Product Manufacturing.* Vol. 4. London: Gale, 1999.
The New York Public Library Business Desk Reference. New York: Wiley, 1998.
Price, Robert W., ed. *Annual Editions: Entrepreneurship, 1999–2000.* 1st ed. Guilford, CT: Dushkin/McGraw-Hill, 1999.
Sora, Joseph, ed. *Corporate Power in the United States.* The Reference Shelf. Vol. 70, no. 3. New York: H. W. Wilson Company, 1998.
Swartz, Thomas R., and Frank J. Bonello, eds. *Taking Sides: Clashing Views on Controversial Economic Issues.* 8th ed. Guilford, CT: Dushkin Publishing Group, 1998.
Turner, Barry, ed. *The Statesman's Yearbook: 1999–2000.* 136th ed. New York: St. Martin's Press, 1999 (annual).
The World Almanac and Book of Facts: 2000. Mahwah, NJ: World Almanac Books, 1999 (annual).

UNITED STATES GOVERNMENT WEB SITES

Bureau of Economic Analysis (http://www.bea.doc.gov/)
Bureau of Labor Statistics (http://www.bls.gov/)
Bureau of the Census (http://www.census.gov/)
Consumer Product Safety Commission (http://www.cpsc.gov/)
Department of Agriculture (http://www.usda.gov/)

Department of Commerce (http://www.doc.gov/)

Department of Energy (http://apollo.osti.gov/)

Department of Health and Human Services (http://www.dhhs.gov/)

Department of Housing and Urban Development (http://www.hud.gov/)

Department of Labor (http://www.dol.gov/)

Department of the Treasury (http://www.ustreas.gov/)

Economics Statistics Briefing Room (http://www.whitehouse.gov/fsbr/prices.html)

Economy at a Glance (http://stats.bls.gov/eag.table.html/)

Environmental Protection Agency (http://www.epa.gov/)

Federal Communications Commission (http://www.fcc.gov/)

Federal Deposit Insurance Corporation (http://www.fdic.gov/)

Federal Reserve System (http://www.bog.frb.fed.us/releases/)

Federal Trade Commission (http://www.ftc.gov/)

FedStats (http://www.fedstats.gov/)

Internal Revenue Service (http://www.irs.gov/)

International Trade Commission (http://www.usitc.gov/)

Office of Management and Budget (http://www.whitehouse.gov/OMB/)

Securities and Exchange Commission (http://www.sec.gov/)

Small Business Administration (http://www.sbaonline.sba.gov/)

Social Security Administration (http://www.ssa.gov/)

INDEX

About the Authors

DAVID E. O'CONNOR is a nationally recognized economics teacher, author and consultant. He has taught economics at the Edwin O. Smith High School in Storrs, Connecticut, since 1975. He has served as a College Board Economics consultant and as president of the Connecticut Council for the Social Studies. He is the author of a number of books and teachers' guides in the fields of economics, ethnic history, and world history including *Economics: Free Enterprise in Action* (1988) and *The Global Economy: A Resource Guide for Teachers* (2000) and has contributed articles to historical and educational journals, including *Social Education*.

CHRISTOPHER FAILLE is author of *These Last Four Centuries: A Romp through Intellectual History* (1988) and *The Decline and Fall of the Supreme Court: Living Out the Nightmares of the Federalists* (Praeger, 1995).